Volleyball From A
Christian Perspective

Volleyball From A Christian Perspective

Skills, Drills, and Devotions for Building an Effective Program and a Winning Team

Donald Casey

ᓚ

Aventine Press

Acknowledgments

This book is the culmination of years of playing and coaching volleyball, but it would not have been possible without much help along the way. I am indebted to my former coaches, Val Keller, Henry Collis, Marv Veronee, Dick Caplan and Jim Coleman for their faithful training of the game. There have been many teammates and players who have contributed their love and support to me throughout the years, and I thank them with a full heart.

I appreciate so much my wife, Marcia, for her love, patience, encouragement, prayers and sacrifices she made during the many times I was away from home.

I thank typists Susan Bell, Susan Charleston, Shannon Hunter, and Cathy Trask. I also received a lot of valuable input from my son, Paul, and also from former player, Cathy Trask, who also graciously posed for the photographs in this book along with Shannon Hunter.

I would like to thank Jeri Harte for taking the photographs.

Julie Scudder Dearyan gave of her insights and worked on this book. Thanks in part to her encouragement, this book was published. She was and is a very special friend.

I am thankful that my wife, Marcia, and son, Paul, along with Nancy Schuyler, contributed their proofreading skills to this project.

I also appreciate so much all those friends who have prayed and continue to pray for me.

I would like to dedicate this book to the memory of my playground teacher and mentor, Mr. Lamon Kipp. May the Lord Jesus Christ continue to bless as we continue to do all for His glory and praise.

My Life Verse Whether therefore ye eat, or drink, or whatsoever ye do, do all to the glory of God. 1 Corinthians 10:31

Table of Contents

Part 5 Team Devotions

Part 6 Letters

Foreword

Both of us want to thank Don Casey for the many years he has spent teaching and coaching volleyball. There are many lives that he has touched and made a definite impact on, and we have watched and patterned our own coaching styles after his for many years. Now, this book is a compilation of all his learning and teaching, and it will be an invaluable aid to those who love the game.

From Vickie Grooms:

It began when I was a brand new coach out of college and coaching at Marquette Manor. Don Casey coached the rivals of Oak Forest. I knew very little about coaching volleyball and wanted to learn more. Coach Casey mentored me. Besides just teaching me about the skills of the game, he modeled how a Christian coach should conduct himself. I watched his rapport with his team and how he taught spiritual lessons through the sport.

Later, I traveled with a few of Coach's players on a sports mission trip. As I talked with his players, their love and respect for their coach was obvious. He practiced what he preached, and his players saw it and knew he was a genuine Christian coach who loved them and wanted to see God's best in their lives.

Over the years I have seen some of his players go on and play at the college level. Some have played for me and some have played for the opponents.

It wasn't until Cathy Trask came to Clearwater Christian College that I was able to coach one of Coach Casey's players for her entire college career. Cathy helped to turn our volleyball program into a national championship team; but more importantly, she had such

a sweet Christian spirit. They say players take on the personality of
their coach, and when I coached Cathy Trask, I saw Coach Casey.
Vickie Grooms Denny, Ph.D.
Department of Physical Education Chair
Women's Volleyball Coach
Clearwater Christian College
Clearwater, Florida

From Marsha Jackson:

Don Casey has been such a blessing and asset to Maranatha
Baptist Bible College's Volleyball Camp. Don has been a hero to
me both as a coaching model and as a Christian. I have learned so
much from him that I have applied to coaching and my life.

Coach Casey is a great teacher and a wonderful role model
for Christian coaches across the nation. If you take the words of
this book to heart, the skills, drills, devotions and gentle words
of wisdom, your skill level will increase. If you are a coach, your
team's level will increase not only physically but spiritually as well.

Together we highly recommend this book to athletic directors,
players, coaches and really anyone who loves the sport of volleyball
and desires to glorify God.
Marsha Jackson
Women's Volleyball Coach
Maranatha Baptist Bible College
Watertown, Wisconsin

Part 1
109 Years and Getting Better All the Time

Volleyball has a fascinating history culminating in the powerful game it is today. Throughout the years, I enjoyed this sport first as a player and later as a coach. It has given me some wonderful opportunities to serve God and try to please Him in all that I do.

Chapter 1

For the Love of the Game

Why another volleyball book? There are dozens and dozens of volleyball books on the market written by the best minds of our time. The "why" in this case is my favorite verse, First Corinthians 10:31 which states, "Whether therefore ye eat, or drink, or whatsoever ye do, do all to the glory of God." Throughout the years of learning, playing and coaching, the game of volleyball has been one of the great joys of my life; but through it all, I only did it for one purpose—to bring God the glory in whatever I do. I wish to honor our great God and His Son as it reads in John 5:23, "That all men should honor the Son, even as they honor the Father. He that honoreth not the Son honoreth not the Father which hath sent him."

My prayer is that after you read this book, you will re-examine your attitudes, desires, goals and techniques to see if they really bring glory to the Lord. I hope the words contained in the following pages will be an encouragement and blessing to you.

Three Types of Players

Three types of players will read this book. The first is the "play it" group. These are people who play the game of volleyball because their friends play. Perhaps they want some exercise or they feel it is something to do or even because they enjoy being athletic. If the season had to be cancelled, the player in this group would not be bothered or upset. They would just find something else to do. It would be no real loss to them if they couldn't play.

The next type of player is the athlete who likes the game. They really do enjoy playing it, and they do everything the coach says in practice. They enjoy learning the skills and the different factors that make the game so fascinating, but outside of practice and in the off-season, they do nothing to improve their skills and practice no conditioning on their own. The game is just that to them—a game. Nothing more. Nothing less. They are glad someone has taken the time to show them how to play it, but that is about where it ends. If the season was cancelled, the players in this group would be disappointed, but not for long. They would go on to something else without thinking too much about it.

My favorite player is the one who loves the game and enjoys it to the extent that it becomes a passion with them. This athlete enjoys it so much that he or she wants to practice and play it all the time. Years ago, I had a player that would turn on her porch light in the evening and practice setting and passing against the garage. This same competitor, after playing her last match as a senior, shed tears because she didn't want to take her jersey off for the last time.

This is the kind of player who loves the game and as a result of that love is motivated to work on skills and conditioning all the time. Remember though that the players in this third group aren't necessarily the most athletic or talented, they just love the game and that love is a motivation for them to get better every chance they get. If the season had to be cancelled, the players in this group would be devastated. They would try their hardest to get the season going again even if it took extreme sacrifice for them to do so.

Your Next Level

Remember this, whatever point you are at right now you can move on to the next level. If you are in the first group, I hope I can nudge you toward the "like" group. If you are in the second group, maybe I can nudge you toward the "love" group. If you are already in the "love" group, maybe I can help that love to grow. My own love for the game is so strong that one of my chief joys has been teaching other people to love it as well. That is my hope for you.

But remember, first things first. You need to make a commitment to play volleyball for the right reason. What is this reason? To glorify

God. Two verses that have meant a lot to me through the years are, "Whatsoever thy hand findeth to do, do it with thy might; for there is no work, nor device, nor knowledge, nor wisdom in the grave, whither thou goest." (Ecclesiastes 9:10) and "Whatsoever ye do, do it heartily, as to the Lord and not unto men." (Colossians 3:23). Volleyball is an excellent opportunity for Christians to glorify God whether it be through their commitment to athleticism, their refusal to participate in unsportsmanlike conduct or the opportunity to meet with other teams who possibly don't know Christ as Savior so as to be a witness to them.

Why don't you take a moment right now to decide to play volleyball for the right reason, the spiritual reason? I encourage you to take a moment to pray this prayer:

Lord, I want to ask you to give me wisdom as I read and study this book about Volleyball. Help me to become wiser in your ways and help me to play this sport only to glorify You in my every word and deed. In Jesus Name, Amen.

If you don't know for sure you are going to Heaven, I encourage you to go to the last chapter called "Closing Thoughts" and go over the verses that I've included there. They will help you for all eternity.

Sometimes, I wish I could just wave a magic wand that would make every reader a successful athletic director, coach, player or participant. But there is nothing magical about any of this. It just doesn't work that way. All of the wishing in the world will not make this so. While some of you might have great natural ability like some of my past players and it might be easier for you to be successful, most people are not born in that category. It is up to you to work harder than everyone else. The players that I have admired the most over the years are the ones who worked the hardest. If you work hard, you'll get better, and by getting better you'll enjoy it even more. You'll become a "love it" player.

I'm firmly convinced that success will only come when a player works diligently every time they practice. Too many times I have seen players just go through the motions and routines and get nothing from them because their minds are on other things. Some players talk about other things while they are drilling and do not focus in on what they are doing. They might as well stop practicing, because they are not benefiting from it. You must think that every ball you touch in practice is the most important play of a game or match. You must visualize these plays in a game situation. You cannot let your mind wander. The effort you give in practice must be total. Someone has said that if you do what you should do in all your practices, the games will take care of themselves. That means that if you practice correctly, you will have success in the games.

One of my colleagues in the school district where I teach is a high school volleyball coach in a public school. It is a fairly large school. I was talking to him about volleyball one day, and he said, "Do you know what I look for first in a potential player?" I thought he would say someone who is tall, or someone who jumps like a kangaroo, or someone who is very quick. Instead he said it was intelligence. I thought to myself how different his answer was from the one I thought he would say. However, as the years have gone by, I now understand. It is difficult to show and teach a player something and have them do it over again and again and again, but it doesn't really seem to stick. It makes it seem like you are not getting through. If you tell an intelligent person something, you only have to tell them once, and they have it.

I have coached "A" students in the classroom, but when you put them on the court you would think they were "C" or "D" students. Conversely, I have coached "C" students in the classroom, and they perform on the court like "A" students. This is the beauty of Christian athletics; it gives opportunities for all types of players to excel even if they don't necessarily excel in class.

The Right Attitude

As you read this book, remember what Vince Lombardi, the famous football coach who has the Super Bowl trophy named after him said, "Fatigue makes cowards out of all of us." Sometimes as you put in the necessary time and effort to play this sport, you will feel fatigued physically and even emotionally. When you are tired the attitude becomes "I can't do that. I can't reach that ball, so I won't try very hard to get it." As a player there were times that I got to a ball that I did not think I had a chance to reach, but because I gave the effort, I was able to get the ball. You must think that every ball is playable and nothing is out of reach. But as you make that extra effort for the ball, jump a little higher to cram a spike and mentally keep yourself in the game even when your brain is screaming for you to stop, you will discover much truth about yourself and what you can accomplish. You will discover that God has given you the ability to work hard, and you will give Him the glory for allowing you to serve Him.

Please remember the following keys.
1. Play to glorify God.
2. Arrive at practice and games ready to play mentally, physically, emotionally, and spiritually.
3. Play every ball in practice with total effort like it is match point in a game.
4. Do not let your mind wander.
5. Visualize making perfect plays.
6. Make it a habit of calling for the ball on every play.
7. Pray daily for your teammates and coaches.
8. Be an encourager.

Following these keys will unlock the door toward becoming a player who glorifies God and loves the game.

Chapter 2
The History of Volleyball

The true competitor never stops moving from the moment the official blows the whistle signaling the beginning of play. The ball spirals over the net where it is picked up by the libero, set expertly, then smashed back over the net all in a matter of seconds. No question about it. The power game of volleyball doesn't resemble its original recreational form officially created by William G. Morgan, a YMCA physical education director in 1895. At a YMCA facility in Holyoke, Massachusetts, the game was dubbed "Mintonette," and it was to be played preferably indoors by any number of players. Some of the characteristics of both tennis and handball were brought into this new exciting game. The first rules, which Morgan himself wrote down, called for a net six feet, six inches high, a 25 x 50 foot court and any number of players. A match was composed of nine innings with three serves for each team in each inning. There was no limit to ball contacts allowed each team before sending the ball to the opponent's court. As in tennis, a second try was allowed if the first resulted in an error. I certainly wouldn't want to bring that rule back today, but there have been times when I was anxiously watching a final match point and a player missed her serve, that I wouldn't mind reinstating it, at least for one play!

If at first you don't succeed...

In 1906, the YMCA accepted and published the rules modified by W.E. Day. Now the net height was up to seven feet, six inches. Twenty-one point match lengths were now the norm. By 1908, Hyozo Omori, a graduate of Springfield College, demonstrated the rules of the game in Tokyo. China and the Philippines started playing the game in 1910.

Innovations came as the sport was played and enjoyed by many countries around the world. By 1912, some of the main guidelines as we know them today were set with the exact circumference (26 inches) and weight (between seven and nine ounces) of the ball. Now only six players per team participated and before service, the players now rotated. But it seems the number of players was still a variable. Teams could have from two to six players per team in 1915.

As the American soldiers fought in World War I on the French beaches of Normandy and Brittany, they sometimes played volleyball in their downtime, introducing the sport to Europe where it became exceedingly popular as well as in the Eastern countries.

The Bomberino

For most of my coaching years, the score for a game was 15 points. In 1916, the score for the game dropped from 21 to 15. Also teams needed to win two out of three games to win a match, and I have been thankful for that rule through the years. The net height became eight feet and the ball weight became ten ounces. Some of the key elements of volleyball were established such as the rule that holding the ball was a foul and the player could not have a second contact with the ball unless it had been played by another teammate. Volleyball also became part of the NCAA program, the body that oversees college and university sports in the United States. In the Philippines, an offensive style of passing the ball in a high trajectory to be struck by another player (the set and spike) was introduced. The Filipinos developed the "bomba" or kill, and called the hitter a "bomberino".[1] The next time I'm at a clinic teaching the skill of spiking, I wonder how the hitter would feel being called a "bomberino".

In 1918, the number of players was again set at six. I find it interesting that this rule wavered so much in the early years.

Now you can observe volleyball teams with six players and beach volleyball teams with two players.

Volleyball increased in popularity when Dr. George J. Fisher, as secretary of the YMCA War Work Office, made volleyball a part of the program in military training camps both in America and abroad by giving over 16,000 volleyballs to be used for this purpose.[2]

By 1920, court size changed to 30 x 60 feet, and the familiar rule of three hits per side was established. In 1922, players in the back line could not spike and the "double hit" fault was added. Now at 14-14, the game had to be won by two points, changing the dynamics of the end of the game for years to come.

Entering the picture in 1923 were numbered jerseys and 12 official substitutes were added. The player in the right back corner served the ball. Volleyball then appeared with other American games during the Olympic Games in Paris.[3]

Time Out

When I stand to call my first time-out during a game, I am reminded that in 1925, two time-outs were permitted per game. Also when it came to scoring, no longer did a team have to score two consecutive points. They just had to have a two-point advantage. In 1926, net length was to be 32 feet. In 1928, the United States Volleyball Association (USVBA) began using YMCA principles as the organizing body for the sport.

When the referee's whistle blows signaling the end of a time-out, I glance at the clock and am always amazed at how fast (or how slow, depending on the momentum of the game) that one minute time-out went by. This rule, established in 1932, again sped up the game.

In 1938, the Czechs perfected blocking. For almost twenty years, blocking had been a part of the game but didn't have an official description in the rules. The Czechs and soon the Russians began to bring decisive importance to this new skill.

One year later, the USVBA published the first *Reference Guide and Official Rules of the Game of Volleyball*. In 1942, sixty-eight year old William G. Morgan died. He had followed the progress of the game with enthusiasm throughout his life. Volleyball continued to increase in popularity as matches drew crowds among the troops during the Second World War. It was believed that volleyball taught teamwork and strengthened morale among the troops. In 1948, the rules were clarified even more with better definitions given to blocking, the place of the serve and the rule that players had to be in the right places during service. The official three minute rest began that year as well, and I've often watched my players have to drink water quickly, listen to my instructions for the next game and mop perspiration from their brows in that short three minutes.

New Offensive Strategies

During the 1949 Men's World Championship in Prague, the setter began coming from the back lineup to set the ball, enabling the game to strengthen with three player attacks. The International Volleyball Federation (FIVB) decided to forbid screening the serve from view and limited the invasion at the net into the opponent's court to a foot. Also, the USVBA added a collegiate division for competitive college teams. For the first ten years, collegiate competition was sparse. Teams formed only through the efforts of interested students and instructors. Many teams disbanded when the interested players graduated.

In 1962, the World Championships were played in Moscow with the USSR men again winning and the Japanese women winning for the first time.

In 1964, a second hit was permitted to the blockers. Antennae limited court air space in 1968. In 1982, the Women's World Championship debuted in Peru where China took the title after an outstanding performance. Two years later, the United states won the men's Olympic gold while China again triumphed over the women. The Brazilians, silver medalists, showed the world a powerful skill—jump serves. The idea wasn't new; Argentina had tried it at the 1982 World Championships, but no one had ever seen it used so effectively before. In 1985, the USA men won the World

Cup. Again the USA men won the World Championship in 1986, and beach volleyball received official status by the FIVB. In 1988, the USA men won the men's gold medal in the Olympic Games while the USSR took the women's after a dramatic final match against Peru. It was this year that the World Congress approved the turning of the fifth set into a tie-break rally point system in which each serve is worth a point. Final scoring per set was limited to 17 points with a one point difference.

The USA women won the women's Grand Prix in 1995.

Today, the game continues to evolve with changes to the traditional side-out scoring of 15 points to rally scoring of 25 points until the deciding game, which is then rally scoring to 15. We now have a libero player, really a defensive specialist, who has changed the game's substitution policies, bringing the defense to a new level.

No Longer Mintonette

Volleyball is no longer mintonette or even a combination of handball and tennis. It is its own powerful sport with millions of people around the world participating in it and enjoying its athletic benefits and the strong teamwork it teaches. My goal is that as a result of reading this book, you will gain a new awareness of how this sport, when done to the best of our ability, is really a microcosm of the Christian life. Just as when a school, team, coach or individual decides to give their best to this sport, thereby gaining wonderful results, so when we give our best to the King of Kings, He gives us His blessing. It is for His glory that we continue to work to please Him.

Chapter 3

Volleyball Days

My first recollection of volleyball was as a fifth grader at Davis Elementary School on the south side of Chicago. We played in a gym class and were winning the game by just hitting the first ball back over the net as soon as it came to us. The physical education teacher told us to try to get three hits on the ball. When we attempted to do this, we began rapidly losing points. I remember thinking that this advice wasn't smart. Little did I realize that someday I would really play the game and understand fully the value of three hits.

I became more interested in the game later at the playground next to the school. The playground had an outdoor court with loose gravel on a clay base. As I played, I remember thinking how much I liked the game because of the teamwork involved between the setter and spiker. We served underhand and did a lot of lifting and catching that in today's game would have been whistled off the court. We played the low ball with open hands, palms up, and would sometimes purposely spin the ball over the net from this hand position. The spikers just stood by the net and jumped to hit the ball without an approach. But it was still challenging and a lot of fun. Of course, sliding on the loose gravel often resulted in dirty clothes and scrapes on my legs and arms.

As teenagers, we won the city playground championship and a special city tournament sponsored by the *Sun Times*, a Chicago newspaper. The success we enjoyed increased my interest in the sport.

Mr. Kipp

One of my brightest memories of that time was my playground teacher, Mr. Kipp. This Swedish gentleman used many Christian principles in his life to teach us. He stressed good sportsmanship and teamwork.

Early one summer, Mr. Kipp and I put horseshoe stakes on one of the courts. He took the long metal stake and held it near the top with his hand while I had the sledge hammer in mine. He said, "Hit the stake!" I looked at him surprised, "Aren't you afraid I'll hit your hand?" He replied loudly, "You're a ball player; hit the stake!"

I see now that he was trying to instill confidence in me, and the fact that he trusted me has helped me throughout my entire life.

One spring our softball team was practicing and I was playing third base. We played with a 12 inch softball without gloves. One of my teammates hit a line drive, a scorcher right at me, and I instinctively reached out and grabbed it. I was feeling pretty good about my catch when Mr. Kipp said to the hitter, "Way to go! That's hitting the ball on the nose." I said, "What about the catch?" He said something like, "That's your job; I expect you to catch it."

He paid me the ultimate compliment by telling my mom that if he had a son, he would want him to be like me. I've used this with some of the girls I've coached when I've said that if I had a daughter, I would want her to be just like them.

He taught me about working hard to achieve a goal and how to win and lose with dignity. He was very special in my life. Like many young people, I'm sure I took him for granted. I owe a lot to him. I'm very thankful he helped shape my character.

I didn't play much volleyball in high school because the sport was limited to gym class and intramurals. My most memorable happening was the boy's and girl's all-star game. It was memorable because the girls (really one girl named Rhoda Hellmer) beat us. They played what was called "Two Tap Girls" in those days. It was legal for a girl to hit the ball two consecutive times. Rhoda would get the ball and set it to herself and then spike it.

College Play

In June of 1955, I graduated from Kelly High School in Chicago, Illinois. I enrolled at the University of Illinois at Chicago, located then at Navy Pier. My major was physical education. While there, I participated in intramurals and enjoyed the opportunity to officiate volleyball matches. The intramural director, Peter Berrafato, was another positive influence in my life. Pete was a 1946 graduate of George Williams College. At that time, the University of Illinois at Chicago was a two-year school. As I approached the completion of my second year, I didn't have a clue what to do next. I took a trip with some students down to the University of Illinois in Champaign. The school was so huge that I knew I didn't want to go there.

I visited George Williams College at 53rd and Drexel in Chicago, which specialized in training people for physical education teaching, Boys Clubs, YMCA and camp work. The college required many swimming courses and because I was weak in this area, I decided this wasn't the school for me. I finished my second year at the University of Illinois but still didn't know what to do. I was thinking of staying at the University and taking a few extra courses, but Mr. Berrafato suggested George Williams College. As a result of our conversation, I decided to enroll at George Williams rather reluctantly in the fall of 1957.

Power Volleyball

George Williams had sponsored a varsity men's volleyball team for many years. Interested, I decided to go to some of the practices. It took only a short time to realize that this was a different kind of volleyball than I had ever experienced. In "power volleyball", everybody served overhand, played balls below the waist with hands clasped together, set balls consistently with a soft touch and spiked consistently with power. At first when I attempted to play the ball below the waist, I closed both hands into fists, put them close together, and tried not to make double contact. Now looking back on it, I can't believe I was as green as grass. I worked hard at learning the proper way to play the game and my skills started to improve. I remember one of our setters, Russ Hoff, giving me a tip. He said to try to contact the ball on the sides of it rather than close to the back of it. That simple suggestion helped me a lot.

Our coach that year was Val Keller, an excellent spiker. Val eventually moved to California where he coached some top YMCA teams and got to coach one of our USA teams. He wrote a book, *Point, Game and Match! Championship Volleyball Techniques for Players and Coaches* in 1968. In 1973, he became the first technical director for USA Volleyball which was the first year they implemented year round national team programs.

During the first year at least three or four setters had better technique and ability than I had at the time. One dropped out of school, another became ineligible, and so I did get some opportunities to play that first year. I can still remember, after all these years, going to my first tournament at the Terra Haute, Indiana YMCA and putting up the first set of my career. Dave Tweedly, hitting on the strong side (called that at the time) buried my set and it was a great feeling.

During the season, I was about the number three setter on the team. We went to Scranton, Pennsylvania for the National Collegiate and Open Tournaments and finished fourth in the collegiate division. Florida State won the championship, beating Kansas University in the finals. I sat on the bench during the whole collegiate tournament and didn't play a single point.

Playing in the US Open Division

After the collegiate tournament was finished, we played in the US Open Division with the best teams in the country. Coach Keller put me in, and all I remember is diving everywhere saving balls. It was really fun making those saves when the other teams thought the ball was down. I had a great time. After we were eliminated from the Open Division, Coach Keller came up to me and said that if he knew I could play that well he would have played me in the collegiate division. I still wonder if I had just started to play well at that time and had not shown enough talent before that, or if he had misjudged what I could do. It was probably the first premise because he was a good coach.

On the way back from Scranton our car blew a rod on the Indiana Toll Road, and we had to catch a bus back to Chicago. That first year was a real learning experience and I developed a love of the game of volleyball that has not diminished over these many years.

The second season started with a new coach, Henry Collis, who had an excellent career as a setter in California. Our team was loaded with talent that year. I believe we had more depth than any of the four years that I played in college. Our top five spikers were very good with two additional good backups, and we had three good setters. Two of our new spikers, Roger Seehafer and Joe Tobolik, were very tall and could hit with a lot of power. One of the high spots for me that season was being chosen Most Valuable Player in the Eastern Collegiate in Meadville, Pennsylvania.

We won the National Collegiate Championship at Des Moines, Iowa, beating Kansas University in the finals. We lost only one individual game in the collegiate division. We bombed out in the US Open Division, losing our first two matches. I felt that our coach made some questionable substitutions that really hurt us. The team should have finished much higher in the Open Division. It was a real disappointment. Four of our players did make the Collegiate All-American Team.

The Arf Set

The next season was our best and the most fun. We had only four players return from the previous year but we picked up two spikers—Art Brown and Gayle Hunt. Art developed into a really good spiker, and Gayle was already a great spiker. He had the best cut shot I ever saw. The rules at that time did not allow the blockers to go over the net to block which helped Gayle's cut shot. He also was unstoppable with a called play of a low set just above the setter's head. He called it an "arf" or a "baby." Watching him jump and spike was a real treat. He was just like a quick cat. Roger Seehafer, our other spiker, developed into a great offensive threat. He loved to hit the high outside set. He too was proficient with the "arf" or "baby" set. His nickname was "the Crane", and so our pet saying was "Unchain the Crane." Our fourth hitter, Darrel Sumner, was not blessed with a great jump or powerful hit, but he used his head and was proficient at hitting off the blockers. Bob Hansen, who was All-American the year before, was the other setter along with me. Bob was a steady setter who was also a good blocker and server. Our coach that year was a man from Chicago, Marv Veronee, a former setter and defensive player. He had traveled as part of a USA team to Europe at a time when the USA was the top team in the world. He was a terrific guy and a very good coach. We had a great season leading up to the national tournament by winning the Midwest Collegiate, the Ball State Invitational and the Great Lakes Collegiate Championships.

The National Tournament

The National Tournament was held in early May of 1960 at Southern Methodist University in Dallas, Texas. We drove down in two cars with Coach Veronee driving his old Plymouth and me with my 1954 Dodge. The National Collegiate Division started first. In an early round we defeated a team from Mexico called Polytechnical Institute 16-14, 15-17, 15-8. They were a very strong team. I remember one incident in the tournament when one of our best spikers caught a live, in-play ball because he heard a whistle. He didn't realize that the whistle was from an adjoining court. Needless to say, he was embarrassed. Polytechnical came through the loser's bracket and we had to face them again for the National Championship. We split the first two games winning 15-5 and losing 6-15. In the third game of the match, we quickly jumped out to an 8-0 lead and it looked like we were home free. But it quickly turned, and the next thing we knew we were down 10-14. There were only about two minutes left to play. In those days we played to 15 points or 8 minutes of ball in-play time. It looked like we really blew it but the momentum shifted again. With some exciting play we rallied to win 17-15. I can still remember diving all over the floor to make saves. I think it was the best I ever played. At the end of the game Coach Veronee congratulated the team and he told me that I had played great. He said that he hoped others had seen it as well, meaning the All-American selection people. I was selected to the Collegiate All-American Team.

The United States Open Division

After the Collegiate Tournament, we played in the United States Open Division which included the best teams in the country. Here we were, some green college kids, playing against the older, more experienced and more talented players. We lost our opening match against Honolulu, Hawaii 7-15, 12-15. In the loser's bracket we defeated Tulsa, Oklahoma YMCA. 15-7, 16-14. Our next opponent was Raadom of San Francisco, California. At the time we were winning the National Collegiate they were winning the National Armed Forces Championship. I'm sure you couldn't have found anyone who thought we had a chance to defeat them. To everyone's surprise we beat them 16-14, 15-4. Our next opponent was the fifth ranked team of the tournament from Nashville, Tennessee. Again we surprised everyone by winning 15-8, 18-16.

One specific play from the match still brings chills. The opponent put up a four-man block on one of our best hitters. In those days, you could bring up a player from the back row for blocking purposes. The four-man block still couldn't stop Gayle Hunt from putting the ball down. We finally lost in the next round to the Ukrainian Volleyball Club of New York, who eventually finished in fifth place with scores of 7-15, 8-15. The Ukrainian team was led by Gabe Budishin who had played on the Yugoslavian National Team. He had the best jump serve. His hand didn't come directly over the top of the ball, but slightly to the right side. The ball would come to you with topspin, but then it would tail off from his right to his left or for the receivers, his left to his right. It was common for him to go back and score ace after ace after ace. As a receiver, his serve drove me crazy, along with anyone else who had to receive it. Just as you had your body lined up with arms ready, the ball would tail off, hit your arms and go out of bounds. He was a fantastic server. We did finish tied for ninth in the US Open which was our best finish ever. We drove back to Chicago, arriving in the evening to a special surprise. The students and staff welcomed us back with congratulatory banners and a party in our honor. As I reminisce on that season, it was everything for which I could have hoped or dreamed.

Last Year of College Competition

Marv Veronee was again our coach for my last year of collegiate competition. I think the thing that prevented us from winning three national collegiate championships in a row happened even before the season began. We lost one of our best spikers, an All-American from last year, Roger Seehafer, who went to Germany as an exchange student. This really destroyed our chances of a three-in-a-row. We lost two other starters from the previous year, but Roger's loss was the killer. We did win the Midwest Collegiate Championship at Michigan State University, winning 16 straight games, and the Detroit Institute of Technology Collegiate Tournament, winning 13 out of 14 games.

The 1961 Nationals were held in Duluth, Minnesota. We beat the University of Kansas to get to the championship match. Santa Monica City College defeated us in two straight games to win the tournament. To this day I still wonder if Roger had not gone to Germany if we could have won that three-in-a-row. The next year Santa Monica won again, but Roger was back and he was unstoppable. He hit over their block, time after time after time. They couldn't block him or dig him, but his efforts were in vain because the supporting players on his team were not as strong as in previous years.

The Ravenswood YMCA

After graduation I joined the Ravenswood YMCA team which featured Al Kuhn, an All-American spiker as coach, and Dick Caplan, a former All-American setter as manager. I spent some time on the bench but did get some opportunity to play. Al paid me a compliment when he said "You're not that great a player, but when you're in there, we seem to play better."

That season we had Gabe Budishin on our team and at the National Tournament in Philadelphia, he started to spike some second balls from the back row. The coach wanted those balls set so he pulled him out and put me in his place. He was so hurt. I remember him saying, "My teammates—they don't understand me. They think that Casey is a better player than me." That, of course, wasn't true. He was a great player. After that match (we lost but it was a double elimination tournament), he went up in the stands and refused to play with us. He relented after we won a few matches and got further along in the loser's bracket. We tied for seventh place in the country in 1962. Here are some of the match results: defeated Norristown YMCA 15-7, 15-8; defeated Woonsocket 15-10, 15-9; lost to Hollywood, California 3-15, 12-15; defeated St. Joe Lead Co. from Pennsylvania 15-7, 15-6.

USVBA Men's Volleyball Team

I had been talking with some of my teammates at George Williams College while we were still together about the possibility of forming our own Open team. As the 1962 season got close to the end we decided to go for it. We put together a team of twelve: Chris Ziola, Division Street YMCA; Jim Wolf, Dick Caplan, Don Ferguson, Rick Riccardo, Steve Whitaker, Ravenswood YMCA; Ken Gongol, Oak Park YMCA; Jerry Amber, Lawson YMCA; Art Brown, Roger Seehafer, Gayle Hunt and me.

I had played softball for a man named Jack Schatz who owned the Kenneth Allen Company. The company was based in Lombard, Illinois. I approached Jack and asked him if he would be interested in sponsoring a USVBA Men's Volleyball Team. Jack, being an enthusiast who loved all sports, agreed. And so, the Kenneth Allen Volleyball Club was formed in the summer of 1962. Jack was a great sponsor. He bought full uniforms, paid entry fees and even let us use his station wagon to drive to tournaments. He and his wife Carol were our great cheerleaders. They frequently attended tournaments and were banging on the bleachers, cheering for us. They were very gracious and generous people and spent much money over the years on sponsoring sports teams. Jack later became A.A.U. Chairman for youth volleyball and gave much of his time to the responsibilities of the job.

I found out that one of the men on our softball team was Harold "Whitey" Wendt, a great volleyball player from Chicago. Here was a man who was a five-time Most Valuable Player in the National Tournament, a man who was the USA top spiker for a European tour that lost only once, and a man with many All-American awards. His team won repeated National Championships, and he was elected to the Volleyball Hall of Fame. He never mentioned any of the awards he had won, and he was my teammate in softball for years. He had the credentials to brag, but he didn't say anything about them – just that he played volleyball. He had started playing in the late 1930s. In 1960, I had the privilege of playing on a team with him in a volleyball league in the western suburbs. He was much older by then but he still could hit. We won the championship. There is no question in my mind that if he hadn't been on our team, we wouldn't have won. I enjoyed that season and especially the championship so much.

Our team enjoyed some great seasons with many strong players. Some went on to become Olympic team coaches: Doug Beal, Terry Liskevych, Jim Coleman, Mick Haley and Bill Neville. The Kenneth Allen Volleyball Club had a successful inaugural season, winning eight tournaments in six different states. We tied for ninth place in the US Open Tournament in San Antonio, Texas and placed third in the National AAU Tournament in Wichita Falls, Texas. Jerry Amber, Gayle Hunt and I were named to the AAU All-American Team. These results were from the US Open: defeated

Midland, Texas 15-2, 15-0; lost to Hollywood, California 5-11, 1-15; defeated Denver, Colorado 15-11, 15-7; defeated Kansas City, Missouri 15-8, 15-5; and lost to Pasadena, California 6-15, 6-15.

The 1964 Nationals were played in New York and we tied for 12th place: defeated Woonsocket 15-11, 15-13; lost to Westside of California 1-15, 17-15, 8-15; defeated Toronto, Canada 19-17, 14-16, 15-2; and lost to Dean Movers 15-11, 6-15, 15-7. The 1965 Nationals were held in Omaha, Nebraska. We traveled over 6,000 miles that year to tournaments all over the country.

After the 1964 Nationals, which was an Olympic year, many of the top teams broke up or reorganized which resulted in a much weaker field in regard to depth. We tied for 12th in the US Open, but that finish does not tell the whole story of the season.

We had anticipated a better finish at the Nationals, but it was not meant to be. We went to the Nationals without three of our best spikers. Roger Seehafer, a collegiate All-American, could not go because of exams and a dissertation for an advanced degree, Jim Vineyard, who a few years later made one of the USA National Teams, could not go because his wife was having a baby at any moment. Finally, Bob Mosier, a top spiker who the next year would make Honorable Mention All-American at the Nationals, became ill for a prolonged time and could not go. This had to rank as one of the most disappointing finishes to a season, and all because of a set of circumstances that was out of our control. Our Senior team, all players over 35, finished third in the Senior Division Nationals. We defeated Omaha, Nebraska 15-8, 15-5; defeated Dallas, Texas 15-10, 15-12; and lost to Woonsocket 7-15, 11-15. Our Open team defeated National Poly of Mexico 15-4, 10-7; lost to Honolulu, Hawaii 7-13, 5-15; defeated Kansas City, Missouri 16-14, 14-11; and lost to UCLA 11-15, 7-15.

A Special Season

The 1966 season was something very special. We played in four different regions during the season and won 13 consecutive tournaments. The most remarkable thing about winning 13 in a row was that we were not at full strength at all the tournaments. Many times a key player could not go, but we won in spite of this. For this reason, I consider the 13 in a row one of the highlights of my playing career. After the regular season ended, we played in the National AAU Tournament in Elkhart, Indiana. We made it to the finals and lost in a three game match: 15-12, 6-15, 5-15. It was our first tournament loss of the season. The team that defeated us was the Sand and Sea Team from California. The 1966 National Open was held in Grand Rapids, Michigan. We finished a disappointing sixteenth. The opening round match with UCLA killed us. We lost 19-17, 12-15, 13-11. The match was so close and tight all the way to the end when time ran out. We defeated Grand Rapids, Michigan 15-10, 15-2 and lost to Sand and Sea 13-15, 10-15. A season that had so many successes ended so disappointedly.

Two Teams

In the late 1960s, the Kenneth Allen Volleyball Club had so many good players that we would at times enter two teams in tournaments. Our White team was our stronger team. Our Red team in the National A.A.U. Tournament defeated Dayton, Ohio; lost to the Olympic Club of California; defeated Edison Post; and lost to Ft. Wayne, Indiana. Our White team finished in fifth place, defeating The Armed Forces All Stars; defeated Los Angeles, California; lost to Outriggers from Hawaii; and lost to Westside of California.

The 1967 Open was held in Detroit, Michigan. Our Red team lost consecutive matches to Seattle, Washington 4-15, 10-15; and to Canoe Club of Hawaii 9-15, 11-15. Our White team finished in ninth place defeating Alleheny 14-10, 15-6; Westside, New York 15-4, 15-4; losing to Dallas 4-15, 15-3, 16-18; and Long Beach, California 12-15, 11-14. The 1968 Open was held in Portland, Oregon. Our team finished fifth. We defeated Stockton, California 13-15, 15-2, 15-6; lost to Outrigger, Hawaii 13-15, 9-15; defeated Santa Monica College 13-15, 15-6, 15-5; defeated Olympic Club of California 12-14, 15-6, 12-10; defeated Cisco Volleyball Club of

California; 15-8, 13-15, 15-5; defeated Church College of Hawaii 17-15, 6-15, 15-11; and lost to Westside, California 7-15, 9-15.

The 1969 Open was held in Knoxville, Tennessee. Our Senior team (players over 35) won the National Championship, defeating Outrigger, Hawaii 15-13, 8-11, 11-9; Staten Island 15-4, 14-16, 14-10; St. Joe of Youngstown, Ohio 15-3, 14-8; and Outrigger, Hawaii 12-10, 5-15, 12-10. Our Red team finished sixteenth losing to Westside of California 8-15, 6-15; defeated Indiana University 15-6, 11-8; and losing to Dallas 1-15, 5-15. Our White team finished seventh, defeating San Diego State 15-4, 15-12; losing to Cisco of California 5-15, 11-14; defeated U.C.S.B. 15-6, 15-8; defeated Lexington, Kentucky 15-3, 12-15, 15-8; defeated L.B. Pacific 14-11, 15-7; and losing to Olympic Club of California 15-17, 5-15.

A Tournament at George Williams College

We had a tournament in the late 1960s at George Williams College. Our White team, the "stronger one", was eliminated by playing poorly. I was on the Red team at the time and we surprised everyone by winning the tournament. Nobody expected us to win which made the victory so much sweeter.

The 1970 Open was in Honolulu, Hawaii. Our team finished third. We defeated Washington Athletic Club 15-2, 15-6; lost to Outriggers, Hawaii 14-16, 15-11, 11-15; defeated Santa Monica College 15-7, 11-9; defeated Wind Jammer, 15-13, 15-6; defeated C&H Gold 13-15, 15-4, 15-4; defeated Olympic Club of California 15-1, 15-6; defeated Armed Forces 15-10, 15-12; defeated Cisco Volleyball Club of California 17-19, 16-14, 13-7; and lost to Balboa Bay, California 6-11, 3-15.

The 1971 Open was held in Binghamton, New York. Our Red team finished sixteenth losing to Woonsocket 13-15, 6-15; defeated Kansas City, Missouri 15-8, 16-14; and lost to Long Beach, California 5-15, 3-15. Our White team finished fifth defeating Ukranian, New Jersey 15-11, 15-1; defeated Long Beach, California 13-10, 15-6; defeated Santa Monica College 12-9, 11-13, 13-11;

and losing to Armed Forces 12-15, 8-15. The 1972 Open was held in Salt Lake City, Utah. Our Red team finished sixteenth losing to Outrigger, Hawaii 15-11, 5-15, 9-15; defeated San Jose, California 15-7, 6-15, 15-9; and losing to our White team 4-15, 12-14. Our White team finished 9th defeating Reubens, Oregon 15-8, 15-6; losing to Santa Barbara, California 14-16, 4-15; defeating our Red team 15-4, 14-12; defeating Balboa Bay White 13-10, 16-14; and losing to Sand and Sea California 15-13, 12-14, 9-15.

At the 1972 Regional Championships, our White team won, which wasn't unusual, but our Red team finished third.

Last Year At the Open

1973 was my last year of competition at the Open level. The Open was held in Duluth, Minnesota. I always looked forward to playing in the Senior Division "over 35." It was a disappointment. We finished ninth when our best spiker couldn't play in important matches because he was needed to play on our White team also. We lost to Westside 6-15, 10-15; defeated Heart of America 14-11, 14-12; and lost to Dallas Athletic Club Texas 6-15, 11-13. Our Red team finished twelfth, defeating Spokane, Washington 15-3, 15-6; losing to Olympic Club 11-15, 9-14; defeated Latvian, Minnesota 15-6, 15-2; and losing to Bullys. Our White team finished 5th, defeating Baltimore 15-4, 15-5; defeated Armed Forces 13-7, 16-14, lost to Cattlemans 6-15, 3-15; defeated Columbus YMCA 15-8, 13-11; and lost to Outriggers 7-12, 13-11, 9-14.

I did get three more opportunities to play competitively, but at a lower level. In 1977 a former teammate of mine called and invited me to play on his team in a league at Wheaton College. It was the largest league in Illinois at the time, and I played in 1977, 1978 and 1979. Two out of the three years we won the championship, but that ended my career. Looking back I wish I had continued to play for many more years, but at this time it was hard to accept my declining skills. I was 42 years old so I retired. I really miss playing. I enjoyed every second of it. I am thankful to God for allowing me to play for so many years.

Marriage, Family and the Lord

I married my wife Marcia in June of 1965, and we had a son Paul in July of 1969. I had been raised in a church where good works and church attendance were going to get me to heaven. If my good works outnumbered my bad works, then I would go to Heaven, but if the bad outnumbered the good then I would go to Hell. My wife had been teaching in a public school close to our home in Oak Forest just before our son was born. She was saved as a little girl, but had drifted away from the Lord. The mother of one of the girls in her class invited her to come to their church, called Calvary Baptist Church at that time, which eventually became Oak Forest Baptist Temple.

She went to the church and rededicated her life to the Lord. At her prodding, I visited. While there I became confused because they said that a person could know for sure that when they died they were going to heaven. They used I John 5:13 which said, "These things have I written unto you that believe on the name of the Son of God; that ye may know that ye have eternal life, and that ye may believe on the name of the Son of God."

I was so confused, not knowing which church was right, that I decided to cover all my bases. I went to both churches every Sunday. This way if my church was right, I was going to heaven. If their church was right, I was still going to heaven. I couldn't lose.

A Patient and Powerful God

It took a long time for this hard headed young man, but God was patient and didn't give up on me. Marcia's church emphasized reading the Bible, backing up their beliefs with Scripture. God started to work on me, and thinking I was saved, I got baptized. I was home alone one evening watching an evangelist on television, and he was preaching a message on being sure you were saved. I got on my knees in front of the television, and with tears in my eyes asked the Lord Jesus to save me and He did. The Bible says, "Therefore if any man be in Christ, he is a new creature: old things are passed away; behold, all things are become new." (Second Corinthians 5:17)

My life changed dramatically. As I grew spiritually, I started to attend church on Sunday morning, Sunday evening and Wednesday evening. I began to read my Bible, pray consistently, tithe, and eventually go on church visitation to tell others about Christ. He allowed me to serve as a Sunday school teacher, superintendent and deacon. Being an introverted person, I knew it was God's power doing these things and not me. I was privileged to hear messages from pastors and evangelists from all across this country who came to our church. I thank God for all the wonderful things He has done for me.

A New Volleyball Opportunity

God did something very special for us. At the time our son was getting to be of school age, the church started a Christian school. Paul started kindergarten there and my wife began a long teaching career there also. In the 1974-75 volleyball season, I showed Mrs. Brown, the school's volleyball coach, a few things about volleyball. They went to the ACE (Accelerated Christian Education) National Tournament and won the championship. The next year, part way into the season, the coach's son committed some infraction and was expelled from school. She had to resign her position and so the team was without a coach. The principal approached me and asked if I would volunteer to take over the team for the rest of the year. I said that I would. You've got to remember that when you volunteer for a job in a Christian school, you'll probably have it for life or until the school ceases to exist.

We did not have a gym, so we practiced quite infrequently and only when we could find another gym. The rules only allowed eight girls on the team and we had a lot more. A large number of Christian schools are so small that many times anyone who comes out makes the team. I had to sit down with each girl and explain who made the team and who didn't and why I made the choices. It was a hard job to cut down to eight. The last two cuts were the most difficult. The ninth and tenth girls were sweet Christians. What made it more difficult was one girl's dad was the Director of Ministries in the church and the other girl's dad was a deacon. To their credit, they never complained about my decisions. I've heard of coaches who have had vehement complaints from parents whose daughters did not make the team, or were not starters, or did not get enough playing time.

The First Championship

Our team won the State ACE Championship in Somonauk, Illinois, and with that the right to go to Nationals in Lynchburg, Virginia. We won all of our preliminary matches to get to the Final Four. At this point in the tournament, they brought in some new referees. I had a freshman who had an excellent serve. On the first play of the game, she served a ball which they received about waist high with an overhand pass. There was no whistle. I knew right away we were in big trouble. In those days you couldn't get away with receiving overhand when the ball was below your chest. It was a best three-out-of-five game match and we lost the first two games. We fell behind in the third game and it looked like it was all over. I took the freshman out and substituted a senior in her place, and it turned the match around. We rallied to win the third game and blew them out in the fourth. The fifth game was nip and tuck all the way. We won the game by two points in dramatic fashion. On match point one of our spikers tipped a ball that was going way out of bounds. But a player on the other team touched it before it landed out of bounds. The ball wasn't even close to the line; it was at least three feet out. It was so exciting! People jumped up and down celebrating. To this day, that game remains as one of my top three thrills in coaching. After that match, the finals were anticlimactic with us defeating a team from Santa Fe, New Mexico, three to one.

The next year they hired a young lady, Pam Campbell, to coach the team. She left after that one season and the team was again without a coach. The administration again asked me to coach and

I agreed. I coached the team for the next 19 years until the church sold the property, moved and the sports program ceased to exist.

The Lord blessed me with some wonderful Christians and some very talented players. God supplied the players and without them, we would have done nothing. Our goal was to strive for excellence on the floor and to be a good testimony for the Lord. It was so good to see our girls pass out tracts and witness to the public school teams we competed against.

There is always at least one player on your team who brings unexpected humor to the court. We had such a player. I don't remember the specifics of this particular game which we were playing or what the score was, but we were playing in a tournament in front of many people. The ball was on our side and someone passed it to this particular player. She raised her arm, turned so that she was facing the back of the court, and spiked the ball at another player on our team. The whistle blew and a point was awarded to the other team. We were all looking at her with confused expressions, but she acted as if nothing happened. When a coach asked her during a timeout why she did that, she seriously thought that the pass had been the third hit and that the play was over. She was simply giving the ball back to our server.

One time a player turned to another and asked her what she thought about while she was playing on the court. The girl replied that she thought about being in the right position, using the correct techniques and following the ball. The first player with a puzzled and shocked look on her face said, "Really?"

Please understand that the accomplishments I am about to describe are not meant to sound as though I ever thought I could do anything in my own strength. The glory only belongs to the Lord. The accomplishments were because God blessed. He deserves the credit. I was only a willing helper.

Seven Years and 37 Consecutive Championships

The most amazing accomplishment for our team was during a seven year period, to win 37 consecutive tournaments. In that stretch there were two tournaments that were double elimination, and we lost in the winner's bracket. This forced us to play through the loser's bracket to again face the team that defeated us. Each time we had to defeat them four straight games to win the tournament. The talent pool had started to dry up. I knew at the end of the 37th tournament that the streak would end the next season and there was nothing I could do to prevent that from happening. I remember sitting on the bench at Maranatha Baptist Bible College when we were winning that last tournament. I turned to a girl who was my assistant and said that this was the end of an era.

I thank the Lord every day that He has counted me faithful by giving me so many opportunities to play and coach volleyball. The girls I worked with were such a blessing and an encouragement to me. Now I travel around the country conducting clinics and Christian volleyball camps eager to share the truth of Scripture that in everything we do, it is all for the glory of God.

Part 2
The Coach

Whether you are a brand new coach or a seasoned, time tested one, there are many aspects of this wonderful ministry that go way beyond strategy and the teaching of skills. Even if you aren't coaching right now, I pray God will use this section to open your eyes to the possibilities in Christian coaching and what an influence it can have in your life.

Chapter 4

The Rookie Coach

I've known many people who wanted to be volleyball coaches but I was not one of them. I remember as a player traveling down to Kansas City for a tournament. There were just three of us in the van: my teammate, Bill Neville, his wife and me. Bill asked me the question; "Don, did you ever think about being a volleyball coach?" My answer was no. I merely wanted to play and enjoy the game as long as I could. Looking back I'm so thankful that God had other plans. Bill related to me about his desire to become a coach. He eventually coached Olympic teams and wrote many books, including the classic, *Coaching Volleyball Successfully* and *Serve It Up, Volleyball for Life*. He is well respected not only in the United States, but all around the world.

Some of you reading this right now may think that coaching is the furthest thing from your mind. You might be saying, "There is no way I could or would want to do it." Don't be so sure. God may have other plans for you. Those of you who have played in high school or club ball, attended camps and clinics, or had a very knowledgeable coach have an advantage over those who have not. Start putting drills, techniques, systems, devotionals or anything else that you might use in the future down on paper. I have learned not to trust anything to memory but to write it down. That way if God does give you a coaching opportunity, you will have a running start.

Start Learning

Those of you who haven't had the benefits of having played or been around a knowledgeable person about volleyball should try to attend some clinics or camps in your area. There are many good books and videos available. Never be afraid to ask questions. Start observing other coaches and see how they handle different situations. You may want to start out by helping with your junior high team.

Some of the traits of a good Christian volleyball coach:
1. To be loving
2. To be prayerful
3. To be enthusiastic
4. To be patient
5. To be encouraging
6. To be gracious
7. To be honest
8. To be humble
9. To be faithful
10. To be teachable

Take a moment to read through the above traits, and then pray that God will give you the strength to develop these characteristics in your coaching and in your life. You can be the most knowledgeable coach in the world, and yet if you don't possess these qualities, you will never achieve spiritual success with your team. Ask God to give you the ability to take on these traits as you seek to become the greatest coach you can be for Him.

To be loving

Key Verse: Deuteronomy 6:5 commands, "And thou shalt love the Lord thy God with all thine heart, and with all thy soul, and with all thy might."

Your life should be a testimony of this verse. Your goal should be that your players will exhibit this also. You should love reading His word, praying, going to church, fellowshipping with other believers, giving financially and witnessing to others. These are the keys to successful Christian living, and your coaching will only be a reflection of your own spiritual growth. Remember, your players will not go any further spiritually than you.

You must stress First Corinthians 10:31 to your players, which I'm sure you are already familiar with from earlier in this book. Remember, you should be coaching to glorify God and not self. One of the thrills of coaching is working with players who really love God and love the game of volleyball. When you get a group of these players, you have something very special.

To be prayerful

Key Verse: James 5:16 instructs, "Confess your faults one to another, and pray one for another, that ye may be healed. The effectual fervent prayer of a righteous man availeth much."

Get in the habit of praying specifically for your players daily. Someone suggested to me many years ago to pray every day for my players, and I took up the challenge. This means not only the players on the team now, but the ones from the past as well. The list of players I pray for gets longer and longer as the years pass. It's my desire that my prayers have been and will be a blessing and encouragement to them. I had a player tell me back in the 80's that even her mom and dad didn't pray for her every day. Your team will not enjoy blessings without prayer.

To be enthusiastic

Key Verse: First Samuel 17:48 informs, "And it came to pass, when the Philistine arose, and came and drew nigh to meet David, that David hasted, and ran toward the army to meet the Philistine."

He didn't walk. He ran. Enthusiasm is contagious and you must be the catalyst. I love to be around people who are enthusiastic in what they do. You don't have to be around me for very long to know that I'm enthusiastic about volleyball. Enthusiasm leads to extra effort which leads to better performance. In practice have your players run for the ball, not walk. Have your players run onto the court for games. Have them show that they are excited about playing. The Christian life is exciting. Be enthusiastic about serving God.

To be patient

Key Verse: Ecclesiastes 7:8 shares, "Better is the end of a thing than the beginning thereof: and the patient in spirit is better than the proud in spirit."

Don't yell or holler at your players when they make a mistake. Help them to learn from their mistakes. Explain what they did wrong and how to correct it. Especially be patient with beginners whose skill development is slow. Someone has said that patience is a virtue. Many of us struggle with it. We've become an impatient nation. Who likes to wait in line for their food or for anything? We want things now, not later. Think about microwave ovens, drive up windows, instant potatoes, remote controls, minute rice, I-Pass lanes, rally scoring and ATM's. Be patient even when you know your players might not be giving as much as you think they could give. Remember, you don't know everything about their home lives or their disciplinary habits or even their ability. It takes time to develop a winning volleyball team; it doesn't happen overnight.

To be encouraging

Key verse: Deuteronomy 1:38 tells us, "But Joshua the son of Nun, which standeth before thee, he shall go in thither: encourage him: for he shall cause Israel to inherit it."

Use praise when it is deserved. Praise publicly and privately. Say things like, "I know you can do this." "I have confidence in you." "You practiced that skill yesterday and performed it well." "That was a great effort you made on that play." "I believe in you." "I am so proud of how you encouraged the other players on the court." "I'm so proud of the effort you made today." "I know you are giving your best and it shows."

This encouragement should go beyond the volleyball court. Strive to live for God and seek His guidance and stay in His will. Share with the team what you received from your devotions last week. Ask a player to share with you what she received from her devotional time. Tell the team what's happening in your life and encourage them to share with you from their own lives. Say, "What's happening in your life?" If you see one of your players say, "You seem down or extra happy today."

Good friends can be a source of encouragement. I had a partner for church visitation on Thursday evenings and we tried to be faithful every week, but one particular week our church also sponsored Neighborhood Bible Time, similar to a Vacation Bible School. We worked with the kids from nine to twelve in the morning. In the afternoon we worked a similar shift with different kids. We did this Monday through Friday. By Thursday I remember feeling tired and so was thinking of not visiting in the evening. My partner Wally said: "We're going visiting tonight, aren't we?" Of course, I agreed. I had the joy of sharing the gospel with someone that evening and seeing them accept Christ as their Savior. I was thankful for the encouragement of a friend.

When it comes to your team, sometimes your encouragement is what will keep them going in the Christian life. If you are an encouraging person, your team will respond to you in kind. If you are constantly berating them for their lack of performance or their lack of desire, then you will have a team that won't want to really try for you.

To be gracious

Key Verse: Ecclesiastes 10:12 explains, "The words of a wise man's mouth are gracious; but the lips of a fool will swallow up himself."

Don't look for a scapegoat to blame when you have a disappointing game or tournament. The reason your team played poorly wasn't the bad officiating, or someone cheating, or the poor court conditions, or the last mistake of the match. Acknowledge the other team played better and deserved to win. When someone compliments your team, acknowledge that God is the one Who deserves the credit first and then the team second. Remember when you blame other circumstances for losses, you are teaching your team to do the same thing. It is human nature to blame something or someone other than ourselves. Fight this tendency and your players will respond in kind.

We went down to a southern Christian university for a national invitational one year. After the tournament a man congratulated our team. I was gracious and thanked him. I told him the girls worked very hard. He said, "No, it is not how they played, it is how they are." I knew he meant the team's testimony. I couldn't have been more pleased.

To be honest

Key Verse: Second Corinthians 8:21 shares, "Providing for honest things, not only in the sight of the Lord, but also in the sight of men."

Explain to the players their roles on the team. Will he or she be a starter? Does the player have a chance to become one? Will he or she be a back row specialist, front row specialist or a server? Each player needs to know what's expected of them and just how he or she fits in to the overall structure of the team.

Don't be afraid to tell them what specific areas of their game need to be improved. But do this in an encouraging way. Share with them their past accomplishments, so they don't walk away feeling like they have let you down.

When it comes to honesty, your personal testimony must be impeccable. You can't be honest in some areas of your life and dishonest in others. And in turn, you must demand honesty from your players.

To be humble

Key Verse: Matthew 23:12 warns, "And whosoever shall exalt himself shall be abased; and he that shall humble himself shall be exalted."

Give God the credit for what is accomplished through the team. As the coach, you're simply the vessel. If you take the credit for all the victories, God will humble you. Pride will try to sneak in without you even realizing it. You must constantly monitor your attitude. Ask for God's help before He has to humble you. If you act in a humble manner, your players will see that and be just like you. God hates pride.

To be faithful

Key Verse: First Corinthians 4:2 says, "Moreover it is required in stewards, that a man be found faithful."

Here are the areas where you need to apply faithfulness:
To your God
To your spouse
To your children
To your parents
To your job
To your team
To your responsibilities

I think the best thing about faithfulness is that every Christian can achieve this goal. Not every Christian can be a pastor, deacon, pianist, soloist, Sunday school teacher, or a choir member, but every believer can be found faithful.

I can't imagine the feeling of those who will some day stand before God and hear Him say, "Well done thou good and faithful servant." I hope and pray that I will hear those words someday. Faithfulness means not quitting but keeping on even though you are tired, discouraged or fearful. It means always doing the right thing and not the convenient thing. It knows that God is always watching everything you do and you desiring first and foremost to please Him.

To be teachable

Key Verse: Second Timothy 2: 15 states, "Study to show thyself approved unto God, a workman that needeth not to be ashamed, rightly dividing the word of truth."

Whether you're young or old, a player or a coach, you should always be learning. Ask yourself after every game, "What can we learn from this victory or this defeat?"

A little hint–you'll learn more from your defeats than from your victories.

Ask yourself, "Is there something we can do different or better?"

Ask other knowledgeable coaches how they do things. Attend clinics, read books and watch instructional videos. Emphasize to your players how important it is for them to be teachable. Stress the importance of learning from the wisdom of older, godly Christians.

If you take these "be's" to heart, then you will find that your team will willingly follow you. And no matter what the outcome, that their ultimate purpose will be to glorify God with every serve, pass, set, spike and block.

Chapter 5
Coaching Strategies

Coaching volleyball can be a wonderful experience, but you will find that the job is sometimes difficult. It can even be frustrating. In this chapter, I want to share some strategies that will keep you going for the long haul.

Remember, for the ultimate success of a school's sports program, the longevity of the coach is the key. I have seen many schools go through various coaches and athletic directors to the point that the players almost don't know game to game who will be their coach. This breeds frustration in the players who in the end won't be able to achieve their potential. But you won't be able to continue coaching for the long term if you don't learn how to handle conflict and in a practical manner, teach the required skills.

When you begin coaching, you will go through a honeymoon phase where the team is happy to have a knowledgeable person coaching them. This phase can last anywhere from six months to two or three years, but at some point you will have to start dealing with problems on your team. And when you begin to deal with the team, these dealings will bring up other issues that were perhaps buried before.

Don't let an occasional bad attitude on your team ruin your own attitude. These things are going to happen, and I am going to give you strategies for dealing with potential problems that will help keep you coaching even if you feel discouraged for a short time.

But first, I'm going to cover some tips that will help you while you coach a game.

Momentum

If you're around volleyball even for a short time, you realize that it's a game of momentum. It's so great when you really have the momentum. The sets, passes, spikes, blocks, digs and serves are executed correctly, and every decision you make as a coach seems to turn out well. You are on top of the world. The game plays like an orchestra with all the instruments coming together making beautiful music.

Suddenly, something happens. Someone makes a mistake or the ball drops between a group of players who make no attempt to move for it. In a matter of seconds, you lose momentum and everything collapses. The team that looked like champions, now looks like they never saw a volleyball before in their whole lives. It's like that same orchestra warming up while all playing different parts and sounding terrible.

Once you lose the momentum, it is hard to get it back. Similar to a snowball going downhill getting bigger and bigger, after awhile it's very hard to stop.

The momentum is now on the other side of the net. The opposing team gleefully serves and smashes their spikes into huge holes on your side. Just minutes before, the other team couldn't hit the ball to save their lives.

Here are some things you can do to get the snowball back to your side of the court before it gets any bigger:

1. Someone on your team makes a very good or exceptional play.

2. Substitute a player.

You can substitute for a player who is making mistakes, or you can substitute for any player to achieve your goal. One coach I know uses the one, two, three; you're out system when a player is making mistakes. The player stays in for the first two mistakes, but if she makes a third, she comes out. If the player after one or two mistakes makes a strong play, the slate is wiped clean and she stays in.

Changing lineups in subsequent games must be done carefully. If you go into game two with a lineup you've never used before, your players can become confused and frustrated as they try to play in positions they are not used to. Substituting one or two players is more helpful and will give you guidance during later practices when you are deciding on your future lineup.

3. Call a time out.

Time outs are very important. Some coaches believe they should be used quickly before the opposition starts a long run of points. Others use them after about a five-point run. I believe that experience is the best teacher in this regard. The longer you coach, the more you have the feel of the proper time to use them. You may have a team that can rally by themselves. If so, a time out is a waste, better used closer to game point, when it can really help your team win. A younger, less experienced team will benefit from you calling time outs at an earlier time in the game before the other team takes every last bit of momentum left.

If you call a time out, use the whole time. If the opposition called the time out, get on the court in position before the official signals the time out is over. Having so few to use means that we must make sure we don't waste them.

Have your stat person keep accurate track of the number of time outs used. Delay calling the time out until it is close to the referee signaling the serve. During time outs, try to get your players to get or keep control of their emotions and focus on the next play. Give them one good thing they can do to change the momentum of the game. Don't yell at your players during time outs, as this is counterproductive. I've seen volleyball teams of men or boys do better after being yelled at in a time out, but with girls, it is better not to yell. I don't know that it is the best thing for boys either but when girls get yelled at during pressure situations, many times they will fall apart even more. Remember, even if they are playing poorly, they still feel they are playing their best. Games are not the times to correct major playing errors; use practices for that. Instead, while in the time-out, focus on the next good serve, pass, set or spike your team can make.

4. Change a strategy.

Here are some tips that might save the game:

Move someone over to help with serve receive

Move receiver over, in or back

Simplify your attack – nothing fancy or high risk

Move players over to cover areas where most balls are being spiked or tipped

Conflict Central

Sometimes you will come across situations when you need to confront a player or group of players. Don't run from this conflict, or it will come back to haunt you later. Spend time in prayer before you deal with a player so that your dealings reflect the leading of the Holy Spirit and the love you have for the athlete. Seek advice from other established coaches or your administrator if the conflict is a potentially volatile situation. Perhaps there are other factors in the player's life such as a rough home life or difficulty with relationships that are partly to blame for the situation.

However, in the end, you must go to the player and share your concerns. Here are some key points to remember when dealing with conflict:

1. Conflict is normal and not something to get all worried about.
2. Always confront the player privately. Don't call her away from a group of her friends in a stern manner, as that will embarrass her more than the actual point you need to talk to her about. Remember this basic rule of management — praise publicly; confront privately.
3. The only exception to the above rule is if the player makes a rebellious comment about the team or you as a coach in front of the team. If you don't say anything at that moment, you are communicating to the rest of the players that you tolerate rebellion. A quick comment like, "Let's go talk privately about what you just said" is usually sufficient in that situation. Take the player to a private corner and talk to her there. If this happens in between games or during a time out, bench the

player immediately. Don't allow one player to spoil the game for everyone. Especially remember this rule if the player is one of your best athletes and your team won't win without her. If you don't deal with her attitude, the rest of the team will resent you. We all know that a good attitude is more important than winning; yet many coaches communicate a completely opposite viewpoint to their teams.

4. When you confront the player, share that you are doing it out of love. Communicate appreciation for the player and the contribution she makes to the team. Share your concerns and what you feel she needs to do to change the situation. End the session with more praise for the player. Remember, no matter how mature or strong the player seems, she is still young and possibly did what she did or said what she said because of immaturity. Show grace in these types of situations.

5. The next time you see the player, make sure you look her in the eye and say you are glad to see her. This is crucial to your relationship with the player. Whether or not she acts like she notices, she does notice and cares deeply what you think about her.

6. When you coach in a Christian school, often you have many different ages on your team. This age difference brings added potential conflicts into the mix. The older girls won't like the younger girls hanging around them and will usually have no problem saying so. It is important to manage this problem before it starts by assigning your key older, spiritual players to some of the more annoying, younger girls. Share with the older player that she is to help the younger player by being nice to her, occasionally warming up with her before a game and just generally being a spiritual example to her. If a few of your key players are doing this, then the rest of the players will be less inclined to ostracize the younger players and your team will have a harmonious spirit.

7. Be careful that you don't always sit with a certain player or a group of players. The other athletes will notice this and resent you for it. Make it a practice when at games and tournaments

to single each player out to ask how he or she is doing and how you could help him or her that day.

8. As a coach, you have to go by ability when it comes to who starts and who plays. Yet, you will face inevitable conflict by practicing this philosophy. Sometimes you will have older players who get upset because they feel they should play. Often it isn't the players who get as upset as the parents. Sometimes, you will get in trouble when you play a younger player—not by the player, but by the other younger players or their parents. They might feel that their daughters or sons should play if an athlete the same age as theirs gets to play. Handle these conflicts carefully. Be as honest as you can be about what you feel the player needs to do to get to the point of starting.

   Share with the team that no one "deserves" to start. Begin each season with a clean slate, sharing that you have no starters except those who work hard and deserve it. Don't let the players assume they will be starters without having them prove it to you and to the team.

9. You will have a lot less conflict if, from the beginning, you prove to the team that you are fair and just. You recognize ability and seek to strengthen each player's capability and skills. Sometimes this means going to a player privately and sharing something specific with her. Perhaps you feel she would be a good setter or middle hitter. Practice with her after practice to help achieve that goal. It is up to you to have the entire team function as a harmonious whole. You need to be constantly looking for areas where an individual player can develop her talents so she can contribute. If you are working to develop every player, regardless of ability, then the parents and the athletes will regard you as fair, and you will avoid many problems throughout the season.

10. One of the key ways to avoid criticism by fans and parents is to substitute fairly. If you only take out a certain player when she plays badly, but fail to take out a strong player when she does the same thing, you are asking for criticism. If you get your players used to substituting, you won't have as much trouble as the season goes along. This is not to say that you can't keep

your starters in when the going gets tough. But if you develop your bench throughout the season, you will have some depth during key games at the end.

Encourage Good Nutritional Habits

Inform and encourage your players to develop good nutritional habits. Many people in our churches have poor health because of eating improperly. It's very hard to serve God effectively if you are sick. If you are eating properly, you'll feel better, play better, coach better and serve God better.

It all begins with having your players start reading labels on their food products. Ingredients are listed in a particular order for a reason. The ingredients listed first are the ones that comprise most of the product; therefore, if sugar is listed in the top three, then there is probably far too much sugar than is healthy. Remember, there are other names for sugar in those ingredients such as high fructose corn syrup, dextrose or sucrose. If you see a lot of those terms in a particular product, you are getting a large amount of sweetener. Health care practitioners warn that sugar is one of the major culprits in causing health problems.

Here are some other principles I've gleaned through the years:

Eat whole grain cereals, not those loaded with sugar.

Eat whole grain bread rather than white or rye.

Eat fresh fruits.

Eat fresh vegetables. The darker the color of fruits and vegetables means greater nutritional benefits.

Cut back on white flour.

Avoid fried foods. Baked or broiled is better.

Consider vitamin supplements after consultation with a health practitioner.

Give up soda. It's easier than you think.

Eat fish regularly. Salmon and sardines are very good. Ocean fish is better than lake fish because there is less pollution.

Drink water, water, water. Don't wait until you are thirsty to drink.

Drink eight glasses a day.

Avoid products that list partial hydrogenation on their ingredients. This process increases the shelf life of the product but is harmful to one's health.

Chicken and turkey are good sources of protein if you discard the skin.

Romaine, red leaf and green leaf are better than iceberg lettuce.

Give handouts to your team about healthy eating.

Avoid products containing Monosodium Glutamate, Aspartame or NutraSweet.

Care about Everyone

Show a special interest in every member of your team, not just the stars. Make every player feel they are important and a part of the team. This will result in good team harmony. Share with the team that it takes a lot of humility to be a good bench player and that you need the bench as much as the rest of the team. Teach the bench players to pay attention to the game and to help the other players during time outs by giving them towels and water bottles. Teach your bench to pray for the team that is playing. And teach your bench to anticipate your next play so that they are ready to go in at a moment's notice.

Condition Year Round

Encourage players to work on conditioning in the off season. I used to give my players empty calendars every month during off season. I encouraged the players to fill in each day what they were doing to become better at volleyball.

Stress Stretching

Explain the importance of proper stretching before games and practices. Many players don't realize how important these exercises are.

Setting Goals

Have the players set team goals. Get together with the team and ask them to volunteer goals for the entire team to accomplish. Encourage specific goals rather than broad, general ones. Rather than writing, "Win every game this season", write, "Improve serving accuracy by 30%". Break the game into tangible goals that everyone can accomplish. Don't aim so high that no one can reach them, but don't set such easy ones that everyone can reach them without trying.

Have the players set individual goals. Talk to each player and ask him or her to share with you his or her personal goals for volleyball. Be encouraging during this time. Express what you've seen the player accomplish so far but also share with the player what you would like to see her accomplish in the future. When she reaches a goal, be sure to notice and compliment the player.

Team Verse

Select a team verse for the season. Have the team memorize and recite it throughout the year.

Prayer Partners

Pair the girls up and have them pray together every few practices or so. Have each girl pray for the other regularly and ask if there are any specific needs she can pray about.

Rewarding Practices

Give small rewards in contests among your players. Have them hit certain targets with serves, spikes or passes. Quarters work well if you don't have anything else. Once a year take ten single dollar bills and put them on the opposing side of the court. If a dollar is hit by a serve or a spike, the player can keep the dollar. Make drills and scrimmages gamelike. Plan every practice. Do drills that involve every player. Keep drills fast paced and fun, awarding points for exceptional play.

You will do a lot better job as a coach if you use honey as motivation rather than vinegar. If you constantly yell at your team, they will become discouraged and feel like they can't do anything right.

One coach had her team practice serving and told the players that when they missed a serve, they had to do five push ups. One thing she hadn't counted on was the fact that the push ups made the girls arms even weaker so that they were even more likely to miss serves. The coach realized this when the girls came up to serve and instead of serving, did five push ups. They didn't even want to try because they knew they would fail. Obviously, this method wasn't working very well so the coach changed her method to a rewards based program awarding points for drills executed well. She saw an amazing change in her team's spirit and work ethic.

Focus Factor

Don't allow distracting talk during practices and games. Stay focused on your goals for each drill and for each practice. This doesn't mean that you are always serious, but it does mean that you should make every moment of practice count.

Negativity Can't Rule

Don't allow negative attitudes. Ban the team from saying, "I can't." Remind the players of Philippians 4:13, "I can do all things through Christ which strengtheneth me." Share with them that even if they feel as though they can't, God will help them take baby steps until they reach their goal.

Rest

Encourage the team to receive proper rest. The girls might think they are superwomen but they won't play well if they are tired.

Visualize

Practice visualization. Have them see themselves performing skills perfectly. Have them think through each step of their skills and imagine them performing them well.

De-Stressing

Practice relaxation. There are many books and tapes that you can purchase.

Volleyball Camps and Clinics

Take your girls to a Christian college volleyball camp in the summer. They will come back with new determination to play well for the glory of God.

Wear Out a Volleyball

Encourage your players to get their own volleyball and try to wear it out. Give them drills they can do at home and individual goals they can work on in their spare time. Compliment them when you see them attaining their goals. Purchase jump ropes to give to your girls to use in the off season. I did this and gave them out at the end of one season. Just before the next season was about to start a player decided not to play. She returned her rope to me. It was still wrapped in the cellophane. She hadn't even opened it.

Leather Volleyballs

Buy leather volleyballs not synthetic leather. Teach the team not to sit on the balls or leave them outside. Teach them not to kick a volleyball.

Safety Awareness

Emphasize safety with your team. My pet peeve is water spills. Just a little moisture (water, perspiration or juice) on the floor can cause serious injuries. Another problem area is sweatshirts or other articles of clothing and extra volleyballs lying on the floor near the playing area. Have all players stay on extra alert in jumping drills.

When extra balls are rolling near those players, have the girls yell loudly – "Ball! Ball!" Instruct your players never to jump when they hear these yells.

Serving practice is another area where being alert prevents players from getting hit in the face or head. Always make sure injuries are checked out before allowing players to return to action. It's much better to err on the side of caution to avoid problems in the future.

Fund Raisers

Fund raisers like car washes help provide money for the team. To increase income for the volleyball program, have each girl get pledges from people such as a dime or quarter or half dollar for every car washed. This money plus what's given as you wash cars could be used to pay for the girls to go to a volleyball camp.

Sponsor your own volleyball tournament. Tournament booklets with sponsoring businesses in your community will pay for officials and awards.

A quarter page ad could be $10. A half page ad could be $15. A full page ad could be $25. A double spread could be $50. Along with the tournament booklet, charge each participating team a reasonable fee to cover trophies, etc. Sell concessions during the tournament.

Local Coverage

Call in your match results to local newspapers. This is not to seek glory but to stimulate interest and excitement.

Devotional Time

Assign each varsity player a date when she is responsible for sharing a devotional with the team. This would be on game days or tournament days.

Emphasize Fun

Stress to your players that some day they will end their playing careers. Share with them that they should have fun and enjoy each day that they get to practice and play. All too soon it will be over.

Encourage Christian College

Encourage your players to pray about attending a Christian college or university after high school.

Training for the Future

Remember that the players you are now coaching may someday become coaches. Make the experience meaningful. Be a godly example. Your influence will be felt not just by your strong players, but by your players that had to work hard to get better. Teach your athletes to practice like they want to play and they will see results both on and off the court.

Part 3
Skills

Teaching the skills of volleyball successfully is almost an art form. The learning curve is a bit higher than in some other sports but once the skills are properly learned, the players are going to have a whole lot of fun. As I coached, I enjoyed teaching each skill because of how they build on each other. This ties in so beautifully with the Christian life and how we learn God's principles line upon line and precept upon precept.

Chapter 5

The Forearm Pass

As the building block on which the rest of the elements of the game rest, the forearm pass must be learned correctly and practiced diligently for any team's success. This skill is commonly referred to as the bump. Without a good consistent pass the whole attack system breaks down. A great amount of time must be spent on this skill. The key to its success is proper technique.

It is essential because once a bad habit is formed, it is difficult to break or change. For this reason this skill must be taught correctly at a very young age. If a person could really master this skill there would be a place for them on any team. Just think of the number of times as a coach or a player you have said or thought "If we could just get one good pass up, we could run our attack and take control of this game or match." Think of the number of games or matches lost just because the passing fell apart. It is usually the first thing that does fall apart, though often the serving falls apart at about the same time. If a good pass can't be achieved, no other skill in the game can be executed.

When I began my career many years ago the great majority of balls received over the net were not forearm passed, but rather overhead passed. Because this way was the accepted technique, there were many thumb and finger injuries trying to receive the floater serves. I am still reminded of this by a strange looking right thumb with a bone protruding at an angle from just that type of situation.

These occurrences made overhead passing painful for weeks at a time until they healed. Some time in the early 1960's our national men's team went to a foreign competition. We received the first serve with a perfect overhead pass and the foreign official blew the whistle. Every time we attempted to receive the serve overhead, no matter how perfect it was, the official would blow the whistle. Our team was forced to forearm pass every serve received. The world officials had decided that this is the way the game would be called. Consequently, when our team returned to the United States everyone began to receive serves forearm style.

A few years ago the cycle turned when serves could once again be received with the overhead pass. Some of the overhead serve receives I've seen at Division I college games left me shaking my head. Balls were sloppily handled time and again with no whistle.

The movement of the feet to get into proper position to perform the forearm pass is very important. At top levels of volleyball, because of the speed of the game, balls are often taken from the side of the body. However at beginning levels of volleyball this results in poor passing. Many of these balls could be played directly in front of the body with just the effort of moving the feet to get into position. This lack of movement directly affects the accuracy of the pass.

Elephant Swings

At beginning levels there are lots of what I call, "elephant swings." The arms are together and pointed toward the floor. When the ball comes to the right or left of the player the feet do not move. The arms swing like an elephant's trunk and the pass ends up all over the gym.

Another common error is the bending of the arms like chopping wood or priming a pump. The elbows are bent and the hands are brought up close to the chest. You get a continuation of arms straight then bent again and again. This unnecessary movement takes time and uses muscles in wasted effort.

The Arms

The straighter the arms are held the more accurate the pass. Without bending the elbows you can react more quickly to balls hit to you with speed. Another error is to hold the arms very close to and sometimes even touching the legs. Or some people swing at the approaching ball with a long upward swing resulting in the ball either bouncing off the ceiling or going beyond the other team's end line. The approaching ball will supply enough of the power needed to pass it accurately.

The Feet

The feet should be approximately shoulder width apart. One foot is slightly in front of the other. One of the reasons I recommend this is because at beginning levels it is so difficult to get players to move their feet. If you do this at any level when the balls are hit to you, you are already close to them without taking an extra step. If the feet were parallel, it would require taking that extra step which would take more time. Consequently, you can reach more balls with this foot position. The body weight should be on the ball part of the feet and not the entire foot. Too many beginning players plant their feet and stand flat-footed. The legs should not be locked straight but should be slightly bent at the knees. The body should be leaning forward, not backward or directly over the body's center of gravity. The heels of the feet should be slightly off the floor with the seat down. The arms are completely straight and extended in front of the body and not close to the legs.

The Hands

When standing and waiting for the ball the hands are apart and not together. When you decide to forearm pass the ball and are in the right position, the hands are put together in one of three accepted ways. The hands must be put together to avoid balls bouncing from one arm to the other resulting in double hit calls by the official.

One method places the fingers in an interlocked position. The fingers on both hands are brought together. They intertwine so that the bases of the fingers are locked tightly together. The top parts of the fingers fold over and cover the top of the opposite hand. The thumbs are side by side and touching each other. One thumb should not be on top of the other. The thumbs then point down towards the floor. This action causes the arms to become perfectly straight.

The second method is to take your right hand and make a fist so that the thumb is straight. Take the left hand, which is open, and go around the right hand, closing your fingers around that fist. Thumbs again are side by side and they again point down toward the floor, straightening the arms.

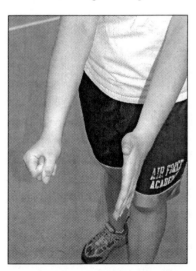 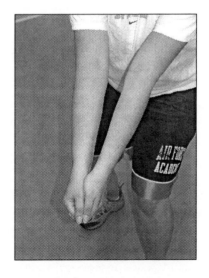

The third method is the one I learned so many years ago. The hands start apart from each other. The fingers and thumbs are touching each other. The palms point upward. The fingers, thumb and hand are not straight but slightly curved, forming a small cup. The right hand is placed partially over the left. The fingers of the right hand cross over and cover the fingers of the left hand. The hands are now in a bowl or small cup position. The thumbs are brought together side by side and pointed toward the floor resulting in straight arms.

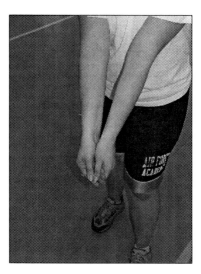

All three of these methods work well. It's a matter of individual preference. I personally recommend the last one. In all three techniques the pointing of the thumbs and hands downward is the single most important thing. As the ball approaches, the head is held erect with no movement. The eyes are focused on the ball. The ball is contacted on the forearm about 3 to 6 inches above the wrist. Any ball contacted higher or closer to the elbow will result in a whistle by the officials. Any ball contacted near the hands will result in poor accuracy. Many beginning players make this mistake.

Some young players separate the thumbs and contact the ball on the inside fleshy part of the forearm. This is poor technique.

The blood vessels are close to the skin near the wrist. Contacts on that area are painful and result in black and blue marks. The contact should be on the top of the arm bone. At the contact point, the arms are first brought down towards the floor and then up. The harder the ball is hit the more the arms are brought down at contact to absorb some of the force of the ball and slow it down.

It's not like a bat meeting a ball. It is more like a person jumping on a trampoline. The elasticity allows a person to go down first and then up. This method is extremely important. The arm swing is very short covering only a matter of inches. The knees are bent at contact.

Up or Down?

There are two schools of thought on the next point. Some coaches say that you should extend up with knees straightening. Others say you can stay down with the knees bent throughout the play. There are coaches that teach that as the ball contacts the forearm the entire body stays in the same place on the floor.

Other coaches teach that as the ball is contacted the passer takes steps forward. You could call this moving through the ball or run-throughs.

Right or Left

If the ball is coming to your right or left, the best thing to do is take a step hop to get into the proper position. Take a quick side step with the foot that's nearest to the flight of the ball. After that step take a hop going in the same direction with both feet. Both feet leave the ground at the same time and then land at the same time. If the ball is farther away from you, it is best to take a crossover step first.

In this maneuver the foot farthest away from the flight of the ball crosses over in front of the other foot. This is allowed by the step hop already explained.

The quickness of these movements will hopefully get you directly in line with the flight of the ball. When you are passing you should if possible have your shoulders in line perpendicular to the flight of the ball. Make sure you aim for a specific target, not just a big general area. Getting the ball to a more specific spot makes the setter's job so much easier.

At lower levels of volleyball forearm passes are usually inconsistent. Beginners should be instructed that if you have to err it's better to err by passing the ball farther off the net rather than very close to the net.

Helpful Passing Hints

1. Call for every ball that you are going to pass.
2. Use proper technique.
3. Attempt to get the ball directly in front of you.
4. Avoid long hard swings at the ball.
5. Stay low.
6. Use step hop or crossover step hop on balls to your right or left.
7. Expect every ball to come to you.
8. Practice! Practice! Practice!

Passing Checklist

- Position of eagerness; shifting weight to toes
- Eyes locked on server after a glance at target (setter)
- Instant movement of feet after server's contact to get completely behind the ball if possible
- Knees bent
- Arms completely straight with loosely-cupped hands together, wrists bent toward the floor
- Contact made above the wrist
- Very slight movement of the arms (to direct the ball) as body moves up

- Arms must pull back to cushion hard-hit balls to keep them on the correct side of net. On hard-hit balls to the side, arms are shot out completely straight to the side
- A good pass is to the setter, about 10 feet above the height of the net, and not tight to the net

Passing Errors and Corrections

Error	Result	Correction
Hands coming apart	Double hit or one-armed hit	Loosely lock the hands or fingers
Contacting ball on thumbs	Wild hit	Make contact higher up on forearm and bend wrists down
Contacting ball on biceps	Lift violation	Step back to make contact lower
Swinging the arms to side	Wild hit	Move the feet to get in front of it, or shoot out the arms
Swinging the arms up	Ball hits ceiling or overpasses	Slight arm motion on contact; more leg lift
Passes shooting over setter's head	No spiking because no setter	Pull back arms on contact of hard hit serves; tilt them upward more
Not getting to the ball	Aced	Movement begins before and during the serve on the balls of the feet
Not calling the ball	Confusion between teammates	Quickly yell that the ball is yours

Chapter 7

The Set

The setter has been described as the quarterback of the volleyball team. Some basic traits of a good setter are:

1. Good hands
2. Quick feet
3. Confidence
4. Leadership ability
5. Quick mind
6. Intelligence
7. Level headed—not easily excited or flustered, able to think clearly in pressure situations
   These last two traits are like frosting on the cake.
8. Tall
9. Left handed

When I first started playing volleyball many years ago, all of the tall players were spikers and all of the short ones were setters. That has changed dramatically. Now you see very tall players exhibiting all the traits for setting that years ago only the short players possessed.

Getting to the ball quickly is the key to making good consistent sets. A setter can never go to sleep on the court but must always be thinking what spiker is hitting where, how the defense lines up, where their best blocker is, what spiker has the hot hand, what the score and the situation is, where a weakness exists in the defense and which spiker likes a set a little higher or a little lower.

As you can see, intelligence in a setter is very important. If I had a choice of either having a great spiker or a great setter, I would take the great setter. Some people think I make this statement because I was a setter and not a spiker. That's not true. It's just that if the setting is poor, then every aspect of the team will suffer. The passing will look worse than it is and the hitting will be non-existent.

The Right Place

Very few things help a team more than when the spikers know that the sets are going to be in the right place or position almost every time. This increases their confidence and consequently their effectiveness. If you have a great spiker but no one can get a good set to that spiker, what good is it?

A great setter makes the spikers better — a fair spiker becomes good; a good spiker becomes very good; and the very good spiker becomes excellent. Speaking from experience of a setter, the spikers really appreciated the good consistent sets. I can remember putting up the perfect set and the spiker burying the ball. The crowd would ooh and ahh at the spike but most spectators would not acknowledge or understand that the great set made it all possible. It was a great feeling as a setter to know that when I did my job, the spiker was able to do his. The teamwork between the setter and the spiker was and is a wonderful part of this great game.

The Feet and Legs

The feet should be about shoulder width apart with one foot slightly in front of the other. Most right handers favor the right foot advanced forward, but I have talked to some who prefer the left. The weight is on the ball part (front) of the feet with the heels slightly off the floor. The knees are in a bent position and not lock-legged. The hips are lined up with the shoulders.

The Arms and Elbows

The arms are resting against the sides of the body with elbows bent and the hands are higher than the elbows and pointing forward. The elbows are pointing backward. As the ball approaches the arms are raised with the elbows pointing out away from the body.

The Hands

The fingers are spread and round. Some have suggested that the thumbs and index fingers form a triangle. Others say the hands are in a bowl position. The hands are higher than the eyes with the thumbs pointing back toward the eyes. By keeping the elbows out the hands are able to be positioned correctly. I've seen some beginners raise the elbows to such an extreme that the fingers are lined up, pointing toward each other resulting in poor sets. The ball should be contacted as much as possible directly in the center plane of the body.

The Contact

Contact is made approximately 8 inches from the forehead. Many beginners make the mistake of contacting the ball too far away from the forehead. With the contact this far away, they have no arm extension to set the ball. Contact is made on the pads of the fingers with the thumbs, index fingers and middle fingers doing almost all of the work. The last two fingers on each hand do very little. Contact is made more to the sides of the ball than the back of the ball. As the ball makes contact with the hands they are brought back toward the forehead. It's the same effect as a diver on a diving board.

I can remember occasionally as a player when the ball would actually touch my forehead when I was setting. It was a very slight brush of a touch. I say this to emphasize when working with beginners that the hands come back before moving forward.

Face the Target

The setter should always try to face the target. It helps to have the shoulders perpendicular to the net on good passes. If that is done you can see with your peripheral vision how far from the net you are standing. That aids in guiding you in regard to the set and the distance it should be from the net. The more the shoulders drift away from perpendicular the more the sets drift away from the net.

I keep telling my setters to square off and face the target. When they do that the sets don't drift. As the hands come forward the arms extend or straighten. With young beginners I always tell them to fully extend the arms so that there is no bend in the elbow. This important follow-through helps to correct any mistake in hand position when setting. With this extension of the arms, the legs are extended, also assisting in sets that have to travel farther. Lastly, the fingers are pointing out toward the ball as the ball is released from the hands.

Length of Contact

At times, I've been asked how long the ball can stay in the hands before it is released. The rules state that the ball cannot visibly come to rest. It's like the old saying that beauty is in the eye of the beholder. One person says that a thing is beautiful while another says that it is not but something else is. Some officials are strict and some are more lenient. Some teachers and some parents are the same way in their approach to child training, strict or more lenient.

If you get called for a carry, simply make sure you release the ball a little quicker. The lower you let the ball come down the more of a chance that you will be called for a violation. I've seen some setters bring the ball down below the chin and even to shoulder level and not get called. If you keep it in the range of your forehead you won't be called on it.

The set should come out as softly as possible with no spin or rotation on the ball. Any spin on the ball makes the spiker's job much more difficult.

Contact More on the Sides of the Ball

I mentioned earlier about contacting more on the sides of the ball than the back. Every setter, at some time in their career, has had a ball slip through their hands while setting. It happened to me when we were playing the Hollywood California Stars, the defending champions in the National Tournament. But if it ever happens just make sure the next time to close your the hands a little more than the last time.

Setting Height

The height of the set and the distance from the net are determined by a few things:
1. Spiker performance. Some athletes like it higher and some lower. Some like it closer to the net and some like it deeper.
2. Blockers. What kind of blockers? Are they tall or short or do they jump high or low?

The Backset

The backset is used for different reasons at different skill levels. At higher levels it is used for deception. The setters try to isolate so only one blocker can get to the spiker. The statistics show that if one spiker goes against one blocker, the spiker has a greater chance for success. If two blockers go against one spiker, then the blockers have a greater chance for success. It becomes a guessing game between the setter and the blockers and whoever wins is most likely to win the game.

At lower levels of volleyball the backset is used not for deception as much as trying to get the set to the best spiker in the clutch situations. If your team only has one good spiker at the net and the setter gets stuck facing the other spiker, it's time for the backset to the best spiker. My philosophy has always been to feed the horses, meaning make sure the best hitters get the most sets. If we must lose, we'll do it going with our best.

At lower levels I recommend that the ball is contacted not off the forehead, but back farther. The elbows must be out from the body and not inside. If the ball spins when it comes out it means that the elbows were in and not out. At this level many setters arch the back. Instead of going forward, go backwards. The full extension of the arms is extremely important along with the extension of the legs. This enables the ball to travel farther. Making sure that one foot is slightly advanced makes balance so much better.

Remember, after you put up that beautiful set, don't stand there admiring it expecting the spiker to bury it down. Get down low and play defense by covering the spiker.

Setters are very important to the success of any team. They must put in extra time setting outside of practice. All the extra work will pay huge dividends. My best setters were the ones that put in the extra work. It's hard to describe the feeling when you put up that beautiful set and your spiker puts it away. It's teamwork with each person needing the other, just like life.

Error	Result	Correction
Not bending the knees	Low, shallow sets	Use legs to push up/out the sets
Not facing the destination of the set	Setting over the net or behind spiker	Face the target spiker
Slapping at the ball	Lift violation	Use fingertips only with elbows out and rounded hands
Hands uneven	Double-hit violation	Make contact with both hands at the same time
Hot potato set	Low set	Follow through toward target
Ball too low to set with hands	Abundance of forearm passes	Get planted before pushing off toes and knees

| Using normal form for backset | Low, shallow backset | Contact the ball higher on the head and bend back and follow through toward target |

Chapter 8

The Spike

Poised at the net, the player is ready; waiting to perform what is arguably the most dramatic moment of the game. The ball is passed to the setter. The setter gives a high set to the waiting player. Leaping at the net, the arms are drawn back as far as they can go, and then brought up while the hand contacts the ball with full force. The crowd gasps as the ball catapults into the middle of the opponent's court, untouched.

No question about it, every good coach desires a good hitter, someone who can really put the ball down. Every coach really wants more than just one good hitter but teaching this skill to even athletic players can be difficult. Imagine trying to teach this skill to every player on the team, even those who are not so gifted.

It is possible. Every player can learn proper spiking technique. Every player can learn how to hit the ball with confidence. It just takes knowledge of the proper techniques, and a thorough understanding of the process, plus a willingness to practice.

The Volleyball Slam Dunk

Spiking attracts people to the game of volleyball. It is comparable in excitement to the slam dunk in basketball. If you see two low skilled teams bumping the ball back and forth over the net, after a short time it will get quite boring. You might not feel this way if your children are involved but nonetheless, passing the ball back over the net practically assures that until one team makes a major error, play will continue for a long period of time. This wears the players out and after a while, even the ability that was once there starts to wane. The game starts to depend on a player's mistakes rather than their smart choices.

However, if you walk into a gym and see a spiker jump high and hammer the ball down into the other court, that same game becomes charged with excitement. You want to see more and you desire to be able to perform that skill too.

Learning the skill is very difficult because of the inaccuracy of the setters at beginning levels. At top levels the sets are so precise that the spiker's job is made much easier. Learning to hit a golf ball is difficult, but you have the advantage of having your feet firmly planted on the ground to assist you. Learning to hit a softball is difficult, but you again have the advantage of having your feet planted on the ground. In spiking, you are up in the air with gravity pulling you down. If you find out that the set is not where you expect it - too close, too far or too low in relation to the net - you must make corrections without the leverage of the feet assisting you.

Many young players can perform the arm swing, the steps, the hip turn and the jump individually. The problem begins when they try to put all these parts together to spike the ball. I have found that it is important to separate each component of the spike and work with each component until the athlete has mastered that aspect of the skill. Breaking it down also makes it easier for the player to mentally digest the process. Some coaches have confessed to me that when they first started teaching spiking, they tended to teach a new way every other week or so. This was because they were reading every available book and watching sports videos in which different methods of learning spiking were taught. Through my coaching clinics, they have expressed their relief to me at seeing a teaching approach that really works. It helps so much to break this skill down to the point where even the youngest, most inexperienced player can learn it.

Phase One-The Feet

Let us start with the feet. Some coaches recommend a 3-step approach, while some prefer a 4-step approach and others a 5-step. I personally favor and recommend a 4-step approach. It is very symmetrical and easy to learn with the first two steps doing one part of the process and the last two doing something else. For right-handed players, the steps must be right-left-right-left. For left handed players, the steps are left-right-left-right. These steps must be in that sequence to allow the hips to line up properly.

If a three-step approach is preferred, just take out the first step. For right-handed players, it is left-right-left, while for the left-handed players it is right-left-right.

If you prefer a five-step approach, just add one step to the beginning. For right-handers it is left-right-left-right-left, while for lefthanders it is right-left-right-left-right.

In the 4-step approach, the first two steps are long gliding steps covering a long area. The feet land on the ball part (front) of the feet. The last two steps are shorter and quicker with the landing taking place on the heel part of the foot first. On steps three and four the hips turn approximately 40 to 45 degrees to the right for right-handers and to the left for left-handers. This turn allows the hitting shoulder to line up properly and the help get the hips ready for a forward rotation. As steps three and four are planted on the ground, the knees are bent and the feet which have first landed on the heels, quickly flatten out with a rolling motion to the toes. The toes push off the ground as the spiker jumps. Beginning spikers must be careful to jump more upward than forward to prevent foot faults. The take off is with both feet at the same time. This is the exact opposite of a lay-up shot in basketball. The only time the take-off is with one foot is when advanced players execute a special attack called a "slide."

Phase Two-The Arms

The arms start in front of the body. During the first two steps they are brought backward rapidly. The back swing for women is somewhat shorter than for men. The arms are behind the body and fully extended. The arms swing forward as the body leaves the floor. The left arm, fully extended, points to the volleyball. The right elbow is bent and the hitting arm is pulled back, bringing the hitting hand behind the head. The hitting elbow comes forward first with the hand reaching high so that at contact with the ball, the arm is fully extended. The hand is held, not closed, but open. The degree of the spread of the fingers varies with the hitter. The greater the spread, the more contact with the ball. The ball is contacted in front of the hitting shoulder. Contact is first made on the heel part of the hand. As the hitting arm is reaching up, the other arm is starting to pull down. This pulling down motion helps the hitting shoulder and arm to be raised higher. As the heel of the hand makes contact with the ball, the hand rolls over the top of the ball. The fingers are the last to make contact with the ball as the wrist snaps forward and down. This snapping motion puts top spin on the ball, causing it to go down into the court instead of sailing out of bounds. This top spin effect works just like a curve ball in baseball.

As you come down from the spike, cushion your landing by bending your knees. Stay low and keep you hands in front of you so you are ready to play a ball that is blocked back to you. By staying low you buy more time to play those blocked shots. Note the following spiking form.

Overcoming the Block

Spikers at more advanced levels try to go over shorter blocks, through holes in the block or around the block. Some spikers become proficient at tipping the ball just over the block. If you are going to tip the ball, it must be disguised. It must be done at the last possible second to catch the defense back on their heels expecting a hard spike. This is accomplished by doing everything as if you were going to hammer the ball, but at the contact point, the arm stops and the fingers tip the ball. If you are spiking and your setter yells "Tight," it means that the set is too close to the net. You must change your follow through by either pulling your hand back quickly to shorten your follow through, or by following through parallel to the net, as in a cut shot.

Understanding the Terminology

The terminology in volleyball has changed over the years. It started out that for right-handers, the left side of the court was called the "strong side." Sets to the other side were called "weak side." Then the strong side became the "on side," while the weak side became the "off side." Then, the "on side" became the left side and the "off side" became the right side. For left-handed hitter, it is the exact opposite. Most right-handed spikers feel it is easier to hit on the left side because the set is hit before the ball crosses the center plane of the body. On the right side the set passes the plane of the body before it is hit. This creates a timing problem for many hitters, making it more difficult to execute the attack properly.

Also, spiking and hitting are now interchangeable words so a spiker could also be called a hitter.

The Middle Hitter

Many spikers use a three step approach when hitting a middle hit. The three step approach allows the hitter to achieve a quicker approach for the lower sets that are usually received in the middle position. The main difference in the approach for a middle hitter and an outside hitter is that the middle hitter's arm swing is not quite the same. The middle hitter's back swing will not be as large as an outside hitter's. With the quicker sets in the middle, there really is not enough time for a very large back swing.

With a "two" set in the middle, (the number two is commonly used to denote a set to the middle) the middle hitter will probably have enough time to fully extend both arms on the forward swing and contact the ball with his/her hitting arm fully extended. With a very quick set in the middle, known as a "one", the hitter may not have time to fully extend his/her hitting arm to a straight position. Everything else in the arm swing will need to be the same, including the snapping of the wrist and the abbreviated follow through used for a tight set. The footwork is the exact same as mentioned previously, as well as the hip turn. The only difference really is in the arm swing. This quick arm swing will allow the middle hitter more success in hitting the ball past a blocker who may not be ready for a quick middle hit.

The Outside Hitter

On outside hits, the first step should be more to the outside of the court, not to the inside. The reason for this is if the set is pushed farther out to the sideline than expected, there is not enough time to correct. You cannot commit inside and then get outside and still be able to hit back inside. It is much easier to commit outside and then adjust inside if the set is not pushed out far enough.

Tips for Hitters

1. Stay Alert for Defense
It is important for the spiker to know what defense the opponents are playing. Is the middle person playing middle up or middle back? Is the line left unguarded? Are they blocking with one or two? A spiker has to be constantly thinking. Good spikers vary the speed of their hits and change the direction of their hits to beat the defense.

2. Stay Positive

Spikers should always compliment their setters and share the praise with them. This cannot be stressed enough. The spikers that were the easiest to set to were the ones that acknowledged the good sets and did not complain about the bad ones. The spikers that were the hardest to set to were the ones who complained about the sets that were not perfect. A good spiker realizes that they need a good setter, and a good setter realizes that they need a good spiker. This lesson can be easily transferred to the Christian life. Just as we need each other on the volleyball court, so we need each other to make it in our walk with the Lord.

Are you ready to go out and try the skill of spiking? Congratulations! Are you already accomplished in this skill but just want to learn how to teach others? Then, I hope this chapter has been helpful for you. As you continue to train, the following list will help you to know how to correct errors common to spiking.

Spiking Checklist

Spiking Error	Result	Correction
Poor approach/not pulling back fast enough	Late to the spike	When the ball comes over to your side, pull back to 10 ft. line to be prepared for a set
Not getting far enough outside	Ball sails overhead/cannot be reached effectively	Begin approach from sideline or even off the court to close-in on the ball
Overrunning the ball/hitting behind the head	Cannot be reached effectively/ no power	Keep ball in front of hitting shoulder

Slow approach	Low vertical leap	A fast, aggressive approach and transfer of power upwards
No bend of knees at plant	Low vertical leap	Use leg muscles to their fullest
Dropping hitting elbow	Ball sails into net	Reach up to the ball to get on top of it
No wrist snap at contact	Ball sails out of bounds	Hand, fingers and wrist need to get on top of ball to apply enough snap to impart topspin on the ball
Not lifting non-hitting arm	Low vertical leap	Use both arms to swing up to meet the ball
Not turning hips during approach	Low power on spike; physical shoulder problems	On the last 2 steps, a right-hander should plant right-left powerfully to spring into the spike
Improper footwork at plant (one foot or wrong sequence)	Low power on spike because it hinders the hip turn	On the last 2 steps, a right-hander should plant right-left powerfully to spring into the spike
No heel-toe motion at plant	Low vertical leap	Roll from heel to toes to use legs to elevate
Leading with hand instead of elbow	Slow, mechanical arm swing; no power	Lead the arm swing with the elbow so that it straightens on impact with the most power

Hand/wrist not held firmly	Ball pushes hand back	Strengthen hand muscles for attack Widen the spread of fingers to direct the ball to its destination
Fingers too close together	Erratic control of ball	Widen the spread of fingers to direct the ball to its destination
Letting the ball drop too low below the net when attacking	A net spike	Make contact at the highest point reached in order to drive it downward
Surprised by a set	A down ball or poor spike	Anticipate that every set could be coming your way
Ignorance of the blocking opponents' number	A blocked ball	Be aware of the of blockers, abilities, where they are set up, and any holes to hit through
Poor estimation of a tight relation to to-the-net set	Center line or net violation	Be aware of the ball's closeness to the net (and remind your setter to communicate to you) to know when a poke or tip is a better strategy
Poor estimation of a far-inside set	Out-of-bounds or net spike	These sets call for adjustments of angled approach and arm swing, and body control
Same target each time	Defense picks up spikes	Mix up spikes by hitting line and angle and using dinks occasionally

Hand too flat on contact	Ball squibs off fingers; push violation.	Slightly cup hand over ball and contact the ball first with heel of hand, then fingers snapping over
Coming down too early	Net spike	Wait to approach until setter releases the ball in order to meet it at the right time
Net or center line violation	Side out	Jump up, not out, for the ball so that you have a controlled landing
Not jumping high on tight set	Ball tipped into the net or blocked	Leap as high as possible and punch at the ball with fist or knuckle to get it high above blocker and net
Slow motion elbow	Weak spike	Pull hitting arm behind head to allow plenty of room to attack the ball

Chapter 9
The Serve

The skill of serving has been compared to the free throw in basketball. You are in total control of what's happening and no one can guard you or stop you. Every time a serve is missed in regular scoring, it's like rolling the ball to the other team and saying, "We can't score on you, why don't you try to score on us?" When I coached, missed serves caused me so much frustration. At times, it got to be like a germ going around the court. The first person would miss the serve and we would win the ball back only to miss the next serve. This would continue for three or four rotations. In my frustration, I can remember hollering, "Throw it over!" I used to tell my girls that every time you miss a serve, you are missing a target that is 900 square feet.

Diligent Practice Required

I think one of the major reasons for poor serving is because it is not practiced diligently. I call serving practice "checkout time" because the body is going through the motions, but the mind has checked out and is not doing what it should be doing. The practice server hits one in and then one out or maybe two in a row in and then one in the net. This continues with no consistency at all. Before each serve is hit in practice, the server must say to themselves, "this serve is match point." You must force your mind to focus, realizing how important this serve really is. This forced concentration will help them in game situations. Many times when a serve is missed in practice, the server just hits another one without thinking. If you miss a serve, you must analyze what went wrong. Was the toss too low or too high, too far in front or behind? Was the stride wrong?

Was the ball contacted on the wrong part? Was the arm swing too slow or too fast? After you figure out what went wrong, you correct it and serve the next one. You continue this process, and the more you do this the more consistent your serve will be.

Key Times to Make that Serve

There are special times when the serve must be in the court.

1. The first serve of the game.

Everyone is excited about the match. Your team is warmed up and expecting to play well and the game starts. Your first server misses the serve which is like sticking a pin in a balloon. Your team will be discouraged and your opponents are encouraged. It's a bad way to start a game.

2. The serve after a timeout.

Your team is running points and things are really clicking. The other coach calls a timeout. After the timeout, your server misses the serve. You lose the momentum and once you lose it, it's hard to get it back. You may wind up losing the game, and you can usually trace it back to that missed serve after the timeout.

3. Game point.

It looks like the game is yours. You have game point, but your server misses the serve. The other team rallies and wins the game. If you miss that serve, nothing good can happen. If you had made that serve, many good things could have happened. The receiver could have mishandled the ball, the setter could have botched the set, the spiker could have blown the spike or touched the net. The other team could have watched it land on the floor thinking it was out, or the official could have made a mistake and whistled one of their contacts. But because you missed the serve, you opened the door for the other team.

4. The serve after a teammate has just missed a serve.

By getting the serve in, you stop the possible spread of that germ that caused the next person to miss and the next also.

5.   The serve just after someone on your team has made a great play.

I remember watching the two best teams in the country playing in a national tournament. A player from the Hollywood Stars ran back full speed way past the end line and stuck out his arm to hit the ball back over his head very high. The ball went over the net and looked like it was going out, but the backspin caused it to land just inside the opposite end line. It was a great play. The team that made the great play served the next ball into the net. They went from the high of the great play to the low of the botched serve.

Concentrate

In the above five situations, the serve must be kept in the court. If you practice serving diligently, your team will be successful. I do think that serving dynamics have changed since rally scoring has been implemented. In the past, players would tend to mentally dismiss the botched serve, because it didn't mean a point for the other team, simply a side out. Now, players realize that every serve counts, and a missed serve can even mean the end of the game.

The Underhand Serve

Begin by facing the net at least more than a stride behind the end line. Make certain that you leave a little room between the line and where your stride will finish. There is never an excuse for a foot fault on a serve. The line doesn't sneak under your foot while you are not looking. The closer you finish to that end line, the more it increases the chance that the line judge will call a foot fault, especially at low levels of volleyball where line judges are known for their lack of concentration.

Hold the ball in the open hand. Right handers hold the ball in the left hand and vice versa for left handers. Because the majority of people are right handed, it will be explained from that perspective. If you are left handed, just reverse the procedure.

The ball is held waist level or lower. A common error is to hold the ball higher. This results in very high serves that either hit the ceiling or go over at such heights as to give the receiving team more time to get to the ball and play it. The ball is held 9 to 12 inches away from the body. This distance stays the same throughout the serve. A common error is to push the ball farther away from the body as you stride.

The Step

The left foot is advanced forward of the right foot. The right hip is back farther than the left. The angle is probably 30° to 45° to the right. The left foot is almost straight toward the net. The right foot is turned comparable to the shoulder turn. The hitting hand can be open, but I recommend a closed fist. There are two possible contact spots from which to hit.

1. The fist is closed with the thumb on the outside.

The area on top of the fist with the thumb and index finger are made as flat as possible. The ball is contacted on this flat spot on the top of the fist.

2. The fist is closed, but the hand is rotated to the right so that the palm is pointing up. The contact is made with the heel of the hand.

The Arm Swing

The ball is held to the right of the body, not in the center. The best way to explain the arm swing is to compare it to a grandfather clock. The bottom part of the pendulum swings straight back and forth. The arm swing should be a copy of that pendulum. The most common error of the swing is to bring the arm back and then bring it behind the back like a letter J. The swing should go straight back and then straight forward.

Here is a little thing you can do to help the server realize if the swing is correct or not. Stand directly behind them, and extend your arm straight with your hand pointing to their back. Have them serve, and see whether or not the back swing touches your arm or not. If they touch, they know they are doing this J motion.

The Feet and the Shift

The left foot strides toward the net, shifting most of the body weight from the right foot to the left foot. The ball is not thrown up but is hit from the hand. Beginners throwing the ball before hitting it results in more missed serves. The principle here is that it is easier to hit a standing target rather than a moving one. The ball is contacted more to the back of the ball instead of the bottom. After you contact the ball, do not stand back there admiring your beautiful serve. Move quickly into the court and be ready to play balls that are returned to your coverage area.

The Floater

One of the most difficult serves to return is the float serve. It acts the same way as a knuckle ball in baseball. It is hit directly in the center of the ball. The idea is to hit the ball so that there will be very little or preferably no spin on it at all. When hit this way, the ball will dip or dive not moving in a predictable path such as one that spins. This happens because the valve in the ball changes the weight and the effect of the air pushing against the ball as it moves through space.

I've seen balls served that have acted like a kite in a hurricane with them breaking many inches. Some servers prefer to hold the ball so that the valve is in the position on top of the ball, while others prefer it on the side.

My preference was on the bottom. Simply by experimenting, you can find which way causes the most movement of the ball. When you figure out your personal best position, stick with that way.

Need More Power?

Servers that are always short with their serves and need more power to get them over the net can try these hints:
1. Increase the speed of the arm swing.
2. Increase the length of the back swing.
3. Increase the speed of the stride toward the net.
4. Take a three step approach - left, right, left. (Make sure you back up to allow room for the three steps.)

One major point about the stride toward the net is that it must be straight toward the net. A common error is to step to the right or the left resulting in poor serves. A good underhand serve is one that clears the net very low and one that is served deep toward the back end line. This makes it more difficult to pass the ball to the setter and run their attack.

The Overhand Serve

Some of the principles of the overhand serve are the same as the underhand:
1. The stride toward the net
2. The shift of body weight

3. The position of feet and shoulder angles
4. Moving into the court immediately after the serve
5. Low and deep serves are best
6. Can use the three step approach

The margin of error on overhand serves is greater, because now you are hitting a moving target, not a stationary one. The ball is held at chest level. The holding hand's elbow is bent with the ball held about 12 to 18 inches from the chest. The hitting arm's elbow is bent and drawn back. This elbow is higher than the hitting hand. Almost all servers make contact with the ball on the heel or bone part of the hand. The hand is open with fingers spread.

When I learned to serve many years ago, there weren't all the videos and instructional books to give me guidance for hand position. I developed a serve where my hand was cupped with the fingers close together. My contact was on the cup formed by the hand. I don't know of anyone else who uses or teaches this technique. The reason I think it's good is because if the open hand hits the ball and the fingers make more contact than the heel; the ball will not have enough power to go over the net. The cup provides more strength to get the serve over.

The Toss

The holding hand moves upward to toss the ball into the air. This arm should not go down first and then back up. It only goes upward. As the ball is released, the left foot strides forward, shifting the body weight. The ball should be tossed above the head about 12 to 18 inches. The higher you toss the ball, the more serves you will miss. The hitting hand is brought back behind the head. The hand is then brought forward with the elbow leading. The shoulder rotates from back to front. The ball is contacted in front of the hitting shoulder. As the ball is contacted, the hand slows with very little follow through. The more follow through, the more spin on the ball, the less chance of a good floater serve. Note the following serving demonstration.

Please note the cup position of my hand in the following picture. This was how I learned to serve overhand and it has served my players well when they need more power in their serve.

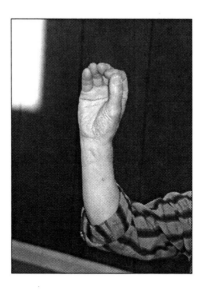

The Jump Serve

Some players use a jump floater serve. All these principles are the same except the ball is contacted while the body is in the air. This allows the ball to be hit from a higher level, changing the angle that the ball crosses the net. At very high levels of volleyball, the jump serve is used quite often. It takes a great amount of strength, timing and practice to master this technique. This serve is hit just like a spike, but with the spiker taking off from behind the end line. Usually the ball is tossed very high to enable the ball to be contacted at the highest point possible.

The Best Place to Serve

Servers can now serve from anywhere behind the end line. When I played, we could only serve from the right side no more than ten feet from the sideline. Later in my career, they let us serve from anywhere behind the end line. Some years went by, and they changed it back again to the right corner. Now it's back to anywhere. Who knows what it will be tomorrow? Just remember that if you have a player who serves from the far left to remind her to quickly return to her position or have the other players cover her spot.

The Serve as an Offensive Tool

Good servers try to serve in the seams between players and to serve away from where the best spikers are on the court. Keeping the serve far from the best spikers makes it more difficult for the setter to get the ball to that hitter. The mental part of serving is very important and can never be minimized. The servers must think positively and not allow negative thoughts to enter their minds.

While waiting for the official to blow the whistle signaling your serve, take a deep breath. Scan the opposing court and select the best place for your serve. Concentrate on perfect execution no matter what is happening around you. Then you will experience success at the single event in volleyball over which you have full control.

Serving Checklist

Serving Error	Result	Correction
Hitting left side of ball	Ball goes right	Contact the center back of the ball
Hitting right side of ball	Ball goes left	
Hitting top of ball	Ball goes into net	
Hitting bottom of ball	Ball hits ceiling	
Slow arm swing	Ball does not get over net	Speed up the arm
Stepping over service line	Foot fault violation	Start farther back so you don't get close to the line

Serving off the wrong foot	Inconsistent service: lack of power	Foot opposite the hitting hand must plant at contact
Dropping ball before serving underhand	Not hitting ball cleanly	Keep the ball stationary; hit it out of hand
Pulling ball away from body while hitting it	Just hitting ball cleanly	Keep the ball stationary; hit it out of hand
Tossing too high or too far away	Inconsistent point of contact	Keep toss low and to the right of the head
Hitting ball with fingers only	Lack of power	Contact with heel of hand
Hitting the ball with fist	Inconsistent serves	Contact with heel of hand
Not bringing hitting arm behind head	Lack of power	When ball is tossed, bring elbow back like an archer

Chapter 10

The Block

The block is the first line of defense to stop the attack. Successful blockers not only intercept the ball and return it to the opponent's side for an immediate point, but they also give the defense a chance to counterattack by channeling the attack into an area of the court that is well defended or slow the ball down and keep it from getting buried.

The three most important facets of blocking are technique, position and timing. If even one of these three is not performed correctly, the block will be ineffective. Technique is how you execute or perform the skill. Position means your body and hands are in the correct place. Timing is jumping at the correct time with the hands being where they should be at the correct time. The following four tips are essential for good blocking:

1. Watch the spiker, not the ball.
2. Shrug the shoulders.
3. Jump a little later than the spiker.
4. Favor blocking the cross-court shot.

There are two basic kinds of blocking: control blocking and stuff blocking. There are more advanced blocking techniques such as stack blocking which is used at higher levels of volleyball, but I'm only going to consider the two basic ones.

Control Blocking

In control blocking, usually used by smaller players or players with limited jumping ability, the object is to keep the ball in play by deflecting it back into your own court so you can still get your pass, set and spike.

Stuff Blocking

In stuff blocking, used by taller players or players blessed with good jumping ability, the goal is to contact the ball on the opponent's side and deflect it down into the opponent's court to terminate play. In blocking, you try to cover an area so the ball will either be blocked and not hit into a certain area of the court, force the spiker to hit into an area where your digging strength is positioned or force the spiker to hit a shot that is not their best, most comfortable or favorite shot. A good rule of thumb is to make sure you are blocking the cross-court shot. At lower levels of volleyball, blockers are usually too far to the outside, and the spiker beats them by going cross-court.

Blocking Technique

Blockers stand approximately arm's length from the net. Blockers do not run forward to the net to block. Their only two movements are to either slide sideways along the net or to pull back from the net to dig. Running forward to the net to block results in net violations, center line violations and possible sprained ankles. At higher levels of volleyball, blockers stand with hands held higher than the head to be ready for the middle attack. At lower levels when opponents do not use the middle quick, the hands can be held about shoulder height with arms pressing against the sides of the body. The feet are approximately shoulder width apart with knees slightly bent. The blocker should watch the ball as it is passed to the setter. Next, glance to see where the spiker is approaching from as soon as the ball leaves the setter's hands. Take your eyes off the ball and watch the spiker. The spiker will go directly to the set. Move quickly to that spot. By watching the spiker, you can see where the body and shoulders are facing. Go into a deeper knee bend and begin the jump. You should jump a little later than the spiker. Thrust your arms straight up to maximum extension. As the arms are lifted, the fingers are spread. Girls are taught to be dainty, but not when blocking. Fingers are firm.

If you are control blocking, the hands are tilted back with fingers pointing back away from the net. As contact is made with the ball, take your eyes off the spiker and quickly try to locate the ball. Pull the hands down quickly, being careful not to touch the net. Cushion your landing by bending your knees on contact with the floor. Stay low until you locate the ball. You have to teach young beginning players that the blocker can touch the ball again right after touching it on the block without penalty. The block does not count as one of the three allowable contacts before the ball is returned.

If you are stuff blocking, instead of tilting the hands backward, they are tilted forward with hands over the net in the opponent's court. As the ball is contacted, pull the hands quickly back to avoid touching the net when coming down from the jump.

Very low skilled teams who have no spikers do not need to block. As skill levels increase and there are players who can spike, some teams put up one blocker and use other players as diggers. One reason why blocking is not very good at lower levels of volleyball is because there are not many good spikers on those teams to be able to practice that skill.

If one blocker cannot stop the spiker, then you need to block with two people. In two-girl blocks, the outside person (the one closest to the sideline) sets the block. The other person closes in on the outside person. This eliminates collisions by blockers.

Blocking Discourages Your Opponent

A team that can block very well discourages the spikers on the other team by not allowing their best shots to be put down. A good tight block helps your diggers to be more effective because they know where the spike won't go. A blocker should have the confidence to say to herself, "no matter what shot you use against me, you're not going to get through my block!"

Diligently teach your team to block and then teach those around the blocker to dig for the ball. The game level and excitement will increase to new levels as you master this important skill.

Blocking Errors and Corrections
Blocking Checklist

Error	Result	Correction
Hands cupped	Not much area above net covered	Spread fingers as wide as possible
Hands too far apart	Balls goes between them	Close them to a ball-width distance
Flying into the net	Net violation	Since it's not a forward, but an up motion, get set at the net before jumping.
Flying alongside the net	Running into another blocker	Get set at the net before jumping
Hands tilted off the court	Blocked ball goes out of bounds	Tilt hands into opposing court
Blocking too far from net	Blocked ball falls on your side	Penetrate hands over the net
Loose wrists	Blocked ball falls on your side	Lock shoulders, elbows, wrists and fingers
Jumping straight-legged	Lack of vertical jump	Bend knees and push off toes
Watching the ball	Missing the block	Watch the spiker at the last few seconds
Swinging arms into block	Net violation	Shoot arms up

Chapter 11
The Defender

Putting up a perfect set and watching a spiker bury the ball is very exciting. Serving the ace that wins the game or match is also very exciting. However, the best excitement is digging and getting up the opponent's best hit. Digging is what I did best. I just loved to dive on the floor and make saves. Early in my career, I played in an era when there was not much instruction in digging. Much of what I did I learned through trial and error. I believe that one important thing that helped my quickness in digging is because of my background in table tennis. It was great training for moving to the ball quickly. I would highly recommend starting to teach table tennis at a very young age.

The Three D's

The three D's of digging success are desire, determination and dedication.

The dictionary states that desire is "a wish, a longing for, a craving for." When I was in a digging position, I wanted the ball to be hit to me. Determination is "firmness of purpose; a decision or result thus arrived at." Dedication is "to commit oneself to a particular course of thought or action." Desire says, "I want to be a good digger." Determination says, "I will be a good digger." Dedication says, "I will do *everything* possible and become a good digger."

I have seen players that wanted to become good diggers. I have seen others who have said that they would become a good digger, but never achieved that goal because they lacked the determination. To achieve the "D" of dedication is the most important.

Digging Position

When digging, it is most important to be in a position that is low and close to the floor. There are three reasons for this position:

1. You can move quicker from that position.

A correlation would be a sprinter in a track meet. By starting low, he or she moves quicker.

2. The next reason is safety.

If you have to fall to the floor, you do not have as far to go.

3. The last reason is that the lower you are, the more time you buy to reach balls that would otherwise hit the floor.

When going to the floor for a dig, the movement should be parallel to the floor, not like a tree falling in the forest.

The body and foot position are similar as described in forearm passing. One of the biggest mistakes commonly made by diggers is focusing only on the ball. Before the ball is set, you must know which attackers are eligible to hit and what position they are approaching from. Watch the approaching spiker and line your body up so that your shoulders are perpendicular to the spiker. Quickly move to the defensive spot on the floor. As the spiker contacts the ball, watch their shoulder to see if there is any turn. If you see a turn, adjust your shoulder and body position to expect the hit in the direction of that turn. If you miss this shoulder turn because of focusing only on the ball, you will not be in the right position to dig the ball. As a digger, you must always be on the alert for the possibility of a dink. Some spikers, when they are going to dink with one hand, telegraph that fact by slowing down their arm swing or just raising that arm up instead of in a normal spiking swing. Spikers that dink with two hands in an overhead set position usually do the same. A good digger looks for that and as quickly as possible reacts, knowing that the spiker can no longer hit down with power.

You Can Receive Every Ball

When digging, you must think that you can get to every ball. I can remember in college when I was playing "pepper" with a teammate, and I was doing the digging. There were times when I felt that there was no way possible for him to hit the ball past me. I do not know if it was the adrenalin flowing or just getting psyched up, but what a great feeling it was!

The harder the spiker hits, the more you must "give" at contact with the ball. The arms are brought down toward the floor and then brought back up. This motion minimizes the power of the shot and allows you better control. We used the same principle when we were kids playing softball. We did not use a glove back then. As the softball hit our hands, we would pull them back towards the body, thus taking the sting or power away.

When it becomes necessary to extend beyond your area of reach to get to the ball, you can either use sprawls or rolls. Sprawls are usually used for balls in a frontal position, although some players do use this method on balls to the side. Rolls are used mostly for balls that are out to the sides.

Sprawls

1. Player starts in position low to the floor
2. Body moves forward
3. Right-handers extend right hand
4. Right knee is bent and turned outward
5. Left hand and arm cushion on floor to act as shock absorber
6. Left arm bends when hand contacts the floor
7. Contact on floor is with abdomen and inside of right thigh
8. Make sure that the chin is up and not close to the floor
9. As the body slides across the floor, the right arm is fully extended and the ball is contacted with the back of the hand in a flick-type motion
10. Player quickly gets up, ready for the next play

Rolls

There are two types of rolls: rolling over the back of the neck and rolling over the shoulder. I was never a tumbler, and I was not proficient in front or back somersaults so I used the roll over the shoulder. I personally found it much safer and easier to master. A large number of players perform the other method.

Shoulder Rolls

This example is on balls hit to the right of your body:
1. Start in low position.
2. Move parallel to floor.
3. If ball is close to you, both hands can make contact.
4. For balls farther away, the right arm is extended.
5. Some players contact the ball with the back of their hand, while others close their hand with their palm up for contact.
6. The good part of the roll is that many times you can use both hands as shock absorbers.
7. Make sure arms bend at elbow when hands contact the floor.
8. The right shoulder dips.
9. The contact with the floor is made on the back of the shoulder.
10. The other shoulder follows and does the same.

11. The right side of the body touches the floor, but most of the contact is with the hands and the right shoulder.
12. As the roll starts, the right leg whips forcefully over in the direction the body is moving. This helps speed up the roll.
13. After completing the roll, extend arms to push off the floor to get up quickly, ready for the next play.

Digging Checklist

Error	Result	Correction
Falling flat from upright position	Injury	Begin low and move parallel with ground
Using one hand when you can use two	Inconsistent digs	Get two hands on any ball possible
Giving up on any ball	Opponent gets point	Hustle for every ball until whistle is heard
Standing up during an opponent's spike	Inconsistent digs	Get low to the ground and lean forward
Swinging at the ball	Overpassing to opponent	Pull back on impact to cushion hard-hit ball
Falling on elbows	Injury	Cushion with hands and roll
Slowly getting off the ground	Lack of readiness for the next ball	Pop back up after digging

Chapter 12

Offensive and Defensive Systems

I have always believed that the skill level of the players you have determines the type of offensive system you use. I have seen teams try to use a particular system, but do not have the personnel to run that system, and in the end, that team suffers disappointing results.

At top levels of volleyball, because of the great skill level, there are more options of systems to use. But if you have low skilled players or even players of medium skill, I suggest that you keep things basic and simple.

Why? I have had great success with a basic offensive system. The players could run it in their sleep; they understood it so well. Balls didn't drop to the ground because of basic movement errors, and we were able to turn the opponent's attacks into attacks of our own on a consistent basis.

The Regular 4-2 and the International 4-2

The most basic system is called the 4-2. The number four refers to the spikers and the number two to the setters. There are two variations of this system, Regular 4-2 and International 4-2. The major difference in the International 4-2 is that there are no backsets. The setter is in the right front position and always faces the spikers. (See Diagram 1)

Because the spikers are hitting from the left front and middle (or slightly right of middle front) they do not have to adjust to hitting from right front. This eliminates the timing adjustment of trying to spike after the ball has crossed the center plane of the body.

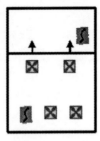

Diagram 1

One disadvantage of the above system (Diagram 1) is that the opposition blockers have less distance to travel, because they know the set will be in usually only two spots—left front or middle (or slightly to the right of the middle position). This makes blocking against this system easier.

In the Regular 4-2, the setter usually goes to the middle front position or slightly to the right of that position. From this position, they can either front set or back set. See Diagram 2.

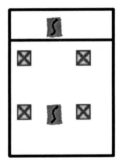

Diagram 2

In both of these systems, the setters must line up opposite one another to insure there will always be a setter at the net.

Multiple Attack Systems

The following systems are also referred to as multiple attack systems. If you have an outstanding setter, you may want to use a

5-1 system. Every ball is set by the same person and it also allows an additional attacker at the net in the following positions:

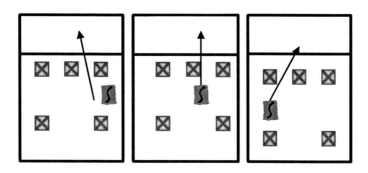

Diagram 3

In Diagram 4, we see that the next three positions in the 5-1 system has only two attackers at the net.

Diagram 4

Many top volleyball teams use this system. They add the option of setting to back row attackers who must take off from behind the three meter (ten foot) line. There are two ways to bring your setter up in the 5-1 and 6-2 offensive systems. In both of these, the setter drops back to the right back position when the opponents are attacking.

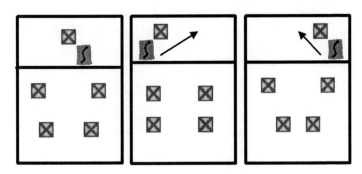

Diagram 5

In Diagram 5, the back row setter is positioned close to the net. Many teams use this method. The advantage is the setter is close to the net and does not have to move very far.

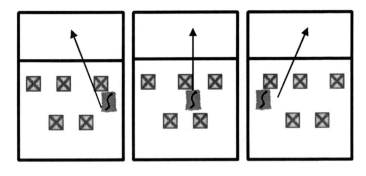

Diagram 6

In Diagram 6, the setter starts back away from the net and moves forward as the
ball is served. There are two disadvantages to this method. The first is the setter has much further to move, and the second is the opponents may serve to the place where the switch is taking place to create confusion.

The 6-2 System

Another system is called the 6-2. Those teams that use this system have two excellent setters who are also excellent spikers. Every time a setter is in the front row, she becomes a spiker. The back row setter always comes up to set. The advantage of this system is you always have three attackers at the net.

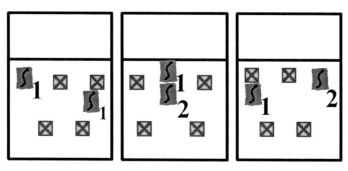

Diagram 7

In Diagram 7, S1 comes to set from the back row, and S2 in the front row is now an attacker.

Blocker Power

Top level teams strive to get two blockers on one attacker. If they can get three blockers up, it is a real blessing. At lower levels of volleyball, a team strives to get one blocker up against one attacker. There are two variations of the defense—middle-up and middle-back. If opposing teams rarely dink or hit, the middle-back position might be a better defense. Notice in Diagram 8 the court coverage when blocking with two blockers in the middle-back position.

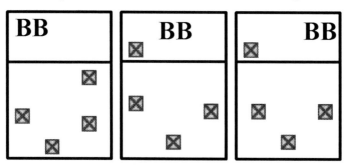

Diagram 8

Diagram 9 shows defensive court coverage with two blockers in the middle-up position.

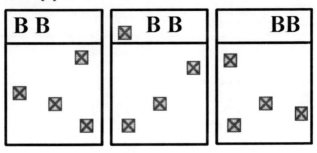

Diagram 9

Diagram 10 shows defensive court coverage with one blocker in the middle-back system.

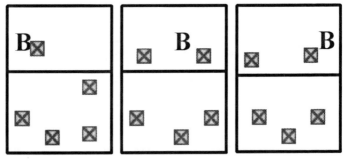

Diagram 10

Diagram 11 shows defensive court coverage with one blocker in the middle-up position.

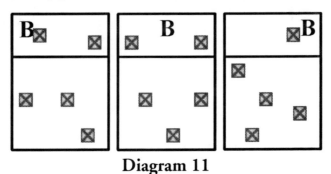

Diagram 11

Diagram 12 shows how the court should be covered when your team is spiking.

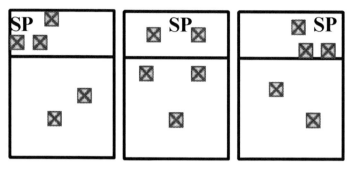

Diagram 12

Diagram 13 shows basic serve receive patterns.

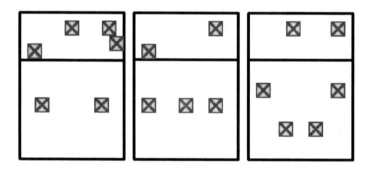

Diagram 13

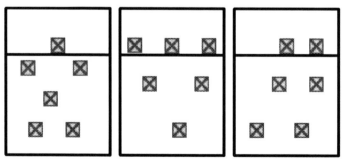

Serve Receive

5 Player Serve Receive   3 Player Receive Option   4 Player Receive Option

Part 4
Drills

After teaching skills, it is time to bring exciting, game-like drills into your practices. When you use a drill, you are enforcing the skills concept that you recently taught and can practice over and over again the same skill. This reinforces learning and helps the players in games and tournaments.

Chapter 13

Movement Drills

Drill 1

Players spread out on one side of the court. Coach points in a direction – right, left, front or back. Players quickly move in that direction. Coach rapidly points in different directions forcing players to shift and change directions quickly.

Drill 2

Players spread out like previous drill. Coach says "Go," and all players try to run quickly in 5-foot squares making sure to square the corners. See how many complete squares can be completed in 30 seconds or 20 seconds for younger players. The second time through have players move in opposite direction.

Drill 3

Line up 7 cones in the shape according to Diagram 14. Players line up in a single file line at first cone. Cones are about 10 – 12 feet apart. The players are instructed to go as fast as they can to each cone and not short it, and stay as low as they can. The players go through the "WV" course eight different times. The first player shuffle steps forward to first cone and then backwards to second cone, doing the same thing until they reach the last cone, then returns to the end of the line. The second player starts when the first person gets past the second cone.

The second movement is side slides.

Then cross over steps to each cone.

Next, a zigzag run.

Followed by running a complete circle around each cone.

Now instruct the players to jump over each cone with a two foot jump and to raise their arms as high as possible on each jump.

Next, back and forth hopping over each cone.

Lastly, the players try to get one of each of the previous moves in a single time through.

If you have a small number of girls, they may need some rest time between turns. With a large number of girls, you may not have to rest in between.

Players line up here

1st Cone

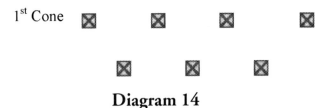

Diagram 14

Drill 4

Get a rubber deck tennis ring from a sporting goods store. Tie a clothes line to it. Have players make a circle about 9-10 feet away. Swing the rope so that the ring reaches the players. They are to jump over the rope or ring, trying to avoid it touching them. If it does touch them, that player drops out. Continue to eliminate players. Vary speeds to challenge the jumpers. If the rope or ring touches a player and continues to touch other players, just the first person hit goes out. When swinging the rope do not turn your body, but hand rope to other hand behind the back. Be careful at faster speeds so players don't fall. Make sure players jump straight up and down and are not leaning in any direction. Stop after a few people are out, and then have everyone return to try again.

Drill 5

Use an elastic or Chinese jump rope that comes in 8 or 16 foot circles. The 16 foot is best. Emphasize safety so ropes do not snap and hurt someone. If you have enough ropes, put 3 people to a rope. Two people put the rope around the back of their heels and move backwards from each other so the rope is off the floor. In each different movement, have them do 20 jumps. The third player stands with both feet inside the rope, facing either one of the holders. This player jumps into the air, spreads feet apart and lands with each foot outside the rope. They immediately jump back inside to starting position. They repeat until completing the 20 jumps. The jumps should be as fast as possible. The jumper trades places with a holder and that person does the jumps; then when finished, switches with the remaining holder and they jump. This set of jumps is called "Apart-Together."

The second set of jumps is called "In-Out-In-Out". The original jumper stands outside the rope, again facing one of the holders. This player jumps with both feet sideways into the middle and then jumps out the other side. Then jumps back into the middle and out to the original side. After 20 jumps, switch with any holder.

The third movement is called "Over-Over." The first jumper stands outside the rope and tries, with a sideways jump, to go completely over the rope to the other side and then jumps over to original side. After 20 jumps, trade places again. If the players are in great condition, you can increase the number of jumps. You can probably come up with other jumps, using turns and twists.

The last movement uses only one rope. Coaches put the rope by their heels. Have all the players make a single file line facing the rope. One player at a time jumps forward in and then out of the rope, and then returns to the end of the line. If the player touches the rope, they drop out of the drill. All the other players take turns jumping through the drill. When the first person in line returns to the front, have the coaches raise the rope a little on their legs. Continue jumping. After completing the drill at this height, raise the rope again. When the coaches get to the back of the knees with the rope height, make sure the players are not leaning when they jump. Be careful not to trip on the rope. Use discretion on how high the rope should go. Stress safety.

Drill 6

Players line up at the left front position at the net. They run and jump for the block, pull back for the approach, and jump for the spike. Next they slide to the middle position to do the same – block, pull back for the approach, and make the approach. They then slide to the last position at the right front, execute a block, pull back, approach and spike. After completing all three positions, the player goes to the end of the waiting line. The second player in line starts when the first player finishes the spike in the first position.

Drill 7

Players start at the end line very close to where the end line meets the sideline. Coach has a supply of balls and stands near the center of the court. The coach hits the first ball and the player tries to pass the ball back to the coach. The coach then tosses a ball along the sideline, forcing the player to roll or sprawl to get the ball up. The player gets up quickly to spike the coach's next toss which is near the net. The player then moves to the middle net position and tries to set the next toss. Then the player runs to the net near the sideline and attempts to block with no ball involved. Next, the player moves down that sideline and rolls left without a ball. Finally, the player turns to face the sideline and rolls right without a ball to complete the circuit.

Drill 8

Line up three cones in a straight line about 10 feet apart. Line up players in a straight line about 6 feet away from the first cone. The first player charges forward, stops at the cone, and goes through the motion of forearm passing a ball without the ball. The same player takes a quick step-hop to the right and does the same. The player quickly step-hops to the left near the first cone and does the same. The same player repeats the process to the second cone and finally to the last cone, then proceeds to the end of the line. When the first person gets to the second cone, the second person starts.

Drill 9

The coach stands near the net with a supply of balls. The first player lines up behind the end line, near the sideline. The coach tosses the first ball, making the player run forward toward the net trying to play the ball and run right through it without hitting the floor. Coach tosses the second ball back towards where the player started. The same player runs to play the ball. The coach throws a third ball across the end line. The fourth ball is tossed towards the net along the other sideline. The last ball is tossed back toward the end line. The goal is for the player to get to every ball, pass the ball back to the coach and run through it without diving for any of them. After the fifth ball is tossed, the first player is through with the drill, and the second player steps up.

Drill 10

Similar to the previous drill, except the players line up in a single file line at the net facing the end line. The coach tosses the first ball, forcing the first player to run down towards the end line. The coach should push the players to work hard to reach the ball without diving for it. That player then goes to the end of line. Toss to the second girl in the line and so on.

Chapter 14

Passing and Digging Drills

Drill 1

Players pair off with one ball per group. One person gets in forearm passing position. The partner holds the ball with two hands on the forearms of their partner. The partner with the ball on their forearms shuffle-steps from one sideline to the other, while the holder uses pressure to keep the ball in that position. When they reach the sideline where they started, change positions and repeat.

Drill 2

One partner holds the ball loosely on the sides, while partner hits the ball from hands with the proper forearm pass. Do ten hits and then change positions.

Drill 3

Partners stand about 12 to 15 feet apart. One partner tosses the ball to themselves and then forearm passes the ball to their partner. The partner catches the ball, tosses to themselves, and forearm passes the ball back to their partner. Keep repeating the same procedure.

Drill 4

Similar to the previous drill, except the partner tosses not to themselves, but to the other partner. That partner forearm passes the ball back, and the ball is caught and tossed again. After 10 tosses the players switch positions.

Drill 5

Same as the previous drill, except that the person tossing throws the ball to the left or right of the partner, forcing them to move and then make the forearm pass. The partners should switch after 10 tosses.

Drill 6

Partners try to forearm pass back and forth without catching or tossing. Count how many good passes are made in a row without a mistake.

Drill 7

Have players line up in three single file lines at about mid court, facing the net. One line is in the middle and the other two near each sideline. Have three coaches or players on the other side of the net, near the net with a good supply of balls. These people hit balls to their respective lines. Place one player in the setting position to act as a target. Players try to pass to that setter. After the ball is passed, that person chases the ball, returns it to the hitters and goes to the end of the next line. The hitters can also back up to mid court and hit.

Drill 8

Players partner up with one ball per group. The players stand about 2 to 3 feet away from their partner. The goal is to call every ball and not let it hit the floor. Every ball should be forearm passed.

Drill 9

Players break up into groups of six to eight players. Form two equal lines facing each other about 12 to 15 feet apart. The player with the ball forearm passes to the other line and runs to their right to the end of that line. The person in the other line who receives that pass forearm passes the ball back to the original starting line, runs to their right, and goes to the end of the other line. See how many correct forearm passes can be made in a row.

Drill 10

Five players line up directly under the net, equal distant apart. The other players line up behind the line leaders. Five other players line up on the 10-foot line facing the players under the net. The players on the 10-foot line throw the ball with two hands to their lines. The players under the net forearm pass the ball back to the tosser. After ten passes, they become the tossers, and the person tossing the ball goes to the end of the waiting line. The next players in the waiting line go to the position under the net to continue the drill.

Drill 11

Players partner up with one ball per group. On the signal "Go," the players forearm pass to themselves at about net height. Their partner counts the number of good passes for sixty seconds. The counting partner takes the next turn.

Drill 12

Partners stand about 12 to 15 feet apart with one ball per group. The player with the ball forearm passes to them self, turns 90 degrees, passes to them self, turns another 90 degree turn, passes to them self, turns another 90 degrees, passes to them self, turns another 90 degrees, and then passes to their partner. The partner then does the same. (Quarter-turn passing)

Drill 13

Line up players at the wall with waiting lines. The number of lines depends upon the available wall space. Players forearm pass to a target on the wall ten times. They then go to the end of the line, and the next player steps up to attempt ten in a row. When everyone has had an attempt, lower the target. Keep lowering the target until it is lower than head level.

Drill 14

Bounce, pass and catch. Make groups of three with one ball per group. Form triangles about 12 to 15 feet apart. Player with the ball bounces it down on the floor with two hands. The receiver forearm passes to the third player. The third player catches the ball and bounces it to the first player who now forearm passes it to the second person. The second person catches it and bounces it to the third person. After a few times around, reverse the direction of the flight of the ball.

Drill 15

Break up into groups of three with two balls in each group. One person is picked as the first worker. The two tossers are about 12 to 15 feet apart. The worker lines up directly in front of one of the players tossing the ball. The tosser throws to the worker who forearm passes the ball directly back. The worker then quickly side slides across to and in front of the second tosser who does the same. The worker side slides back again. Make ten passes before switching positions with one of the players tossing the balls. The goal is to pass accurately and side slide as quickly as possible.

Drill 16

Form a single file line with players near the sideline, facing into the court. The coach, with a large supply of volleyballs, stands near the opposite sideline. The coach tosses a ball to the first player, making the player run forward to about mid court. This player must forearm pass the ball over the net simulating a third hit. That player chases the ball, returns it to the coach and goes to the end of the line. After each player has gone about 10 times through the line, put the line where the coach was, and move the coach to where the players were. After 10 times through, change positions again. The coach moves to the net, facing the court the players are on, and the players move to the end line, facing the net. For this portion, the players face the net and put the ball directly over the net. The next variation entails the coach and the players switching places - coach at the end line and players at the net. This time the players have to hit the ball backwards into the opponent's court.

Drill 17

Two coaches or tossers must stand near the net: one at the middle of the net and the other near a sideline. The players are in a single file line about 8 feet from the end line. The tosser in the middle position tosses to the line leader making them come forward. This player passes the ball to the second tosser near the sideline. After the pass, the player goes to the end of the line. The person tossing near the sideline tosses to the next person in line who, in turn, passes to the first tosser.

Drill 18

Players partner up with one ball in each group. The player with the ball tosses it high to their partner, making them play the ball with cupped hands over their head. After ten tosses, change positions.

Drill 19

Same as previous drill, except tossing player throws the ball over the head of the partner. The partner is forced to spin quickly, run to the ball and pass the ball back over their head to the partner. Change positions after ten tosses.

Digging Drills
Drill 1

All players make a huge circle on one side of the court. Most of the players are off the court. Pick one to stand in the middle. The outside people have a supply of at least 8 balls. They feed balls to the coach who tosses the balls far from the center person. That person must run to play each ball. The coach rapidly tosses the second ball in another direction. The player chases that ball down. The turn is complete when eight balls have been played. The outer circle people retrieve the players' balls from the center to make the drill safer. The tosses should really extend the player.

Drill 2

Same as previous drill except that the coach spikes balls rapidly at the middle player instead of making them run for the ball.

Drill 3

To get maximum benefit, the players should have pretty good ball control skills. If not, then more time is wasted chasing the balls. Pair off 2 players. Players hit back and forth at one another. They should practice hitting with top spin and varying the speed of the hits, as well.

Drill 4

Groups of three players are in a triangle position approximately 15 feet apart. The player with the ball passes to second person.

The second person sets back to the first person, who then hits with top spin at the third person. The third player passes the ball to the second player, and the drill continues.

Drill 5

Players line up in a single file line with the first person in the middle of the court. The coach stands on a table or chair on the other side of the net, near the middle of the net. The coach needs a few players to feed balls. Coach hits a ball to the first person in line. They try to pass to the setter position. The player immediately side slides to the right sideline, touches it with the outside hand and then quickly slides back to the middle of the court where the coach hits a second ball. The player passes the ball and side slides to the left sideline and touches it with the outside hand again. The player then slides to the middle for the last hit from the coach, and then goes to the end of the line. The second player steps up and repeats what the first player did.

Drill 6

The coach stands on a table or chair at the net in the right side position. Players line up as defenders in three lines: one guarding the sideline, one line covering the middle, and one covering the cross court. The coach hits balls at any line, and the players attempt to pass the ball to the setter position. After a player plays a ball, they go to the end of a different line. A second version is with the table or chair in the middle of the net and lastly with the table or chair at the left side position.

Drill 7

Similar to the previous drill except there are two coaches on chairs or tables. One is at the right side position, while the other is at the left side position. This time the players line up in two lines; each one set up to take the cross court shots. The coaches alternate hitting at the players, and they are only hitting to the cross court players. After the player passes the ball, they chase it and return it to the holder to feed the coaches. The players then go to the opposite line.

Drill 8

The coach stands on a chair or a table at the net in the middle hitter position. Two spikers on the other side of the net get in position to begin their approach. One spiker should be on the right side while the other is on the left side. Two diggers stand about 6 to 8 feet apart near the middle of the court. The coach hits to either one of the diggers. The digger tries to pass to the partner who, in turn, tries to set to one of the spikers. The spiker approaches the ball and hits. There should be a waiting line in both the spiker and digger positions. The goal is to make a good dig, set and hit.

Drill 9

Same as previous drill except there are no spiking lines. The coach hits to either player, who passes to the partner, and who tries to set the ball back to the passer. The passer then attempts to attack the ball.

Drill 10

Coach is near the net with helpers supplying balls. The players line up in a single file line at the end line. The coach is on the same side of the net with the players, facing the players. The first person in line lies down on their stomach. The coach slaps the ball allowing the player to get up quickly. The coach then bounces the ball off the floor while the player tries to make a play with the ball before it hits the floor again. The player goes to the end of the line after their turn. The coach should vary the height of the bounce and distance away from the player to make them really hustle.

Drill 11

Split the players up into groups of about five. Pick a reliable hitter in each group who has good control. The four players form a semicircle around the hitter, and the hitter spikes at each in the circle in random order. The players should try to keep the ball moving continuously without hitting the floor and becoming a dead ball.

Drill 12

Same as previous drill, except that the diggers line up in a single file line in front of the hitter. The hitter spikes to the first digger in line. If the digger makes a good return, then the spiker hits the ball to them again. When the digger fails to make a good dig, they go to the end of the line.

Drill 13

Players stand at the net in blocking position. The coach stands at the sideline about 15 feet behind the player, slaps the ball and the blocker quickly turns to face the coach. The coach spikes the ball at the player who tries to pass to the target area near the center of the net, but a few feet off the net. The next player steps up and the drill continues.

Drill 14

After having taught sprawls and rolls, have the players practice on mats without volleyballs. Then hit or tip balls to the players, who sprawl and roll to get the balls, while still on the mats. If players are skilled and ready, have them practice the skills on the floor without mats and without balls. Lastly, the coach hits and tips to players on the floor without the mats. Make sure the skill level is good before attempting this on the floor without mats.

Drill 15

Players line up on one side of the net. Three players are at the net with the middle person as the setter. All of their backs are to the net. Three diggers are in defensive position. The goal is for the setter to set to one of the spikers who hits the ball at their own diggers, who try to get the ball to the setter. The setter then sets the ball to one of the spikers who hits at the diggers again. Try to keep the ball moving without letting it hit the floor.

Drill 16

Players line up at the end line in three single file lines. The coach is on the same side of the net near the middle of the net. At the slap of the ball, all three line leaders charge forward. The coach spikes at anyone. That person digs the ball back to the coach. They run back to the front of the line. The coach slaps the ball again, and the same three charge again. They do this three times, and then go to the end of a different line. The next time players move up and do the same.

Chapter 15
Setting Drills

Drill 1

Pair off with a partner. One volleyball per pair.
1. Player A lies on their back on the floor; Player B stands to the side of player A near their head.
2. Player B drops ball over the head of player A.
3. Player A tries to set the ball straight up.
4. Player B catches the ball and repeats the entire procedure 10 times.
5. Partners change positions and repeat the drill.

The dropping partner looks to see; if the ball is contacted near the forehead, if the arms are fully extended after the set (elbows straight), if the fingers are pointing outward in the follow through and if the ball is held or cleanly set (not visibly coming to rest). The dropping partner encourages their partner and tells them what was done correctly and what should be corrected.

Drill 2

Pair off with a partner. One volleyball per pair.
1. Player A sits on floor cross-legged facing Player B (who is standing and holding the ball) about 12 feet apart.
2. Player B tosses the ball to player A.
3. Player A tries to set the ball back to player B using proper technique.
4. Player B catches ball and repeats the entire procedure 10 times.
5. After 10 tosses, players switch places.

Drill 3

Pair off with a partner. One volleyball per pair.
1. Player A is on one knee facing player B about 12 feet apart.
2. Player B tosses ball underhand to player A.
3. Player A sets the ball back to player B.
4. Player B catches the ball and repeats procedure 10 times.
5. After 10 attempts, players switch places.

Drill 4

Pair off with a partner. One volleyball per pair.
1. Both player A and player B stand facing each other about 15 feet apart.
2. Player A holds the ball in a setting position near their forehead.
3. While holding the ball in this position, player A throws the ball to player B in a setting motion.
4. Player B catches the ball and puts it in a setting position near their forehead.
5. Player B then throws the ball to player A in a setting motion.

Everything is the same as a regular set. Keep checking to see if the toss starts from the forehead. Many will start at their chest and wind up doing a two handed chest pass like in basketball.

Drill 5

Pair off with a partner. One volleyball per pair.
1. Both player A and player B stand facing each other about 15 feet apart.
2. Player A tosses the ball over their own head and then sets to player B.
3. Player B catches ball, tosses it to them self, and then sets to player A.
4. Repeat 10 times.

Drill 6

Pair off with a partner. One volleyball per pair.
1. Both player A and player B stand facing each other about 15 feet apart.
2. Player A tosses the ball directly to player B.
3. Player B sets to player A.
4. Player A catches the ball and then tosses it again to player B.
5. After 10 tosses, switch places.

Drill 7

Pair off with a partner. One volleyball per pair.
1. Both player A and player B stand facing each other about 15 feet apart.
2. Player A tosses the ball to the left of player B, forcing player B to move to the ball.
3. Player B squares off to face player A and sets the ball back to player A.
4. Player A catches the ball and tosses it to the right of player B, forcing player B to move to the ball.
5. Repeat for 10 tosses; then switch places.

Drill 8

Pair off with a partner. One volleyball per pair
1. Both player A and player B stand facing each other about 15 feet apart.
2. Player A tosses the ball over their head and then sets to player B.
3. Player B sets the ball to player A without catching it.
4. Player A sets the ball to player B without catching it.
For beginners, see how many consecutive sets can be made before there is an error.

Drill 9

Pair off with a partner. One volleyball per pair
1. Both player A and player B stand facing each other about 15 feet apart.
2. Player A sets the ball high so that it lands on the floor halfway between the players.
3. Player B lets the ball hit the floor and bounce up, then tries to get into a crouch position to get under the ball and set it so it will land on floor halfway between the partners.
4. Repeat exactly.

The ball is not tossed or caught. Partners should keep repeating the drill. The main purpose of this drill is to make an attempt to get under every ball before you set it.

Drill 10

Form groups of about 8 players. Each group of 8 makes 2 lines about 15 feet apart. Have one line of 4 facing the opposite line of four. The first player sets the ball to the person opposite them and then runs to their right to the end of that line. That person sets to the line where the first set came from, and they go to their right to the end of the line they just set to. Continue this until the ball is mishandled. Count the number of consecutive good sets (not mishandled). Repeat the drill again, trying to break the record.

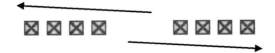

Drill 11

Form 3 lines. Have one line in the normal setting position. Have one line at the opposite sideline with the first person on the sideline. The rest of that line is off the court. The third line should line up behind the coach, with each person holding a volleyball. The coach is near the center of the same court, facing the net. The first player holding a volleyball hands the ball to the coach, and she moves to the end of the setting line. The coach tosses the ball to the first player in the setting line. She sets the ball to the line on the sideline, and then goes to the end of that line. The person on the sideline catches the ball and moves to the end of the coach's line. The coach should keep tossing the balls at a good tempo to keep the players moving.

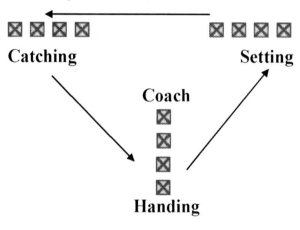

Drill 12

Players partner up with one ball for every 2 players. Players should be approximately 15 feet apart. The player with the ball sets to their partner. That person forearm passes to them self, and then sets the ball back to their partner. Their partner repeats the process. The goal is to try to make as many continuous plays as possible without ball handling errors.

Drill 13

The player with the ball sets to their partner who forearm passes to them self, makes a 90 degree turn, passes to them self, makes another 90 degree turn, passes to them self, makes another 90 degree turn, passes to them self, makes another 90 degree turn, and then sets the ball to their partner who does exactly the same.

Drill 14

Similar to Drill 13, except the first player sets the ball to them self, does a 180 degree turn and backsets to their partner who then sets to them self, turns 180 degrees, and backsets back.

Drill 15

Similar to Drill 14, except the first player forearm passes to them self, turns 180 degrees, and backsets to their partner. That player then does the same.

Drill 16

The first player sets the ball to their partner and quickly bends down and touches their fingertips to the floor. Their partner sets the ball back to them and then touches their fingertips to the floor. Repeat. Do this for a short period of time because it is tiring.

Drill 17

The first player forearm passes the ball to them self, and then sets the ball to their partner, quickly gets down and touches their seat to floor, gets up ready to receive the set from their partner who does the same thing.

Drill 18

One player sets the ball to their partner, quickly takes two steps forward and two steps backward to their original position. The partner does the same. The second time they set the ball to their partner, they take two quick backward steps and then two quick forward steps back to their original position. The partner does the same thing. The third time they set the ball to their partner, they take two quick side steps and two steps back to their original place. The partner does the same. The last time they set the ball to their partner, take two quick side steps in other direction and quickly go back to their starting point. The partner does the same.

Drill 19

Partners stand very close to each other. The first player sets to them self and then to their partner. Immediately they run around their partner and back to their starting spot. The partner sets to them self, then to first player and runs around the first player back to their original position. Each set must be high to have time to run around and get back into place.

Drill 20

The first player sets to their partner and immediately runs forward and stands very close to their partner. That partner sets a short set to the first player at the close position. That player sets a high set back to their partner and then back peddles to their original spot. The partner then does the same. Make sure the sets are high so there is time to back peddle to the original position.

Drill 21

Form groups of three players in a triangle position about 12 to 15 feet apart. One player bounces the ball hard on the floor, so it rebounds up to the next player. That player quickly turns to face the third player, squares their shoulders to them and sets the ball to that person. The third person catches the ball that has just been set and bounces it to the first player, who in turn faces the second person, and sets to them. The drill continues with bounce, set and catch. After a few minutes of going clockwise, reverse the direction and go counterclockwise. Bounces must be high and exact.

There is another variation of this drill, using two volleyballs with the same triangle formation. In this version the first and third players hold the volleyballs. The first player bounces it to the second player. As soon as this happens, the third player tosses her ball to the first player who catches it. While this is going on, the second player is setting the first ball to the third person. The first player bounces the second ball to the second player. Players change positions after the setting player gets ten sets. Again, begin going clockwise and later switch to counterclockwise.

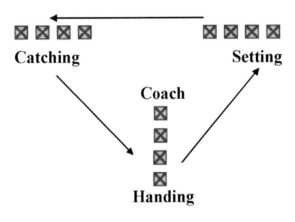

Drill 22

Players line up at the sideline close to the net with each person having their own ball. The first player walks along the net, setting the ball to them self at a height slightly above the net. When they get to the other sideline, they cross the net and return on the other side doing the same thing. The second player may start as soon as there is room between them and the player in front of them, so many players can be moving at the same time.

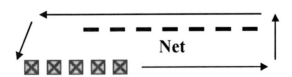

Drill 23

Players divide up into groups of three. Two players stand about 12 feet apart, each holding a volleyball. The setting player lines up directly in front of one of the tossers about 10 to 12 feet apart. The person with the ball in front of her tosses a high ball to the setter. The setter must set the ball back to that tosser and quickly side slide to the front of the other tosser. The second tosser throws a high ball and the setter sets that ball back to the second tosser. The setter slides back to the original spot for the next toss. After ten sets, the players trade places.

Drill 24

To start this drill, position players at the end line in three lines, facing the court, but behind the stripe. Have three tossers stand with their backs right up to the net, each holding a ball. One tosser throws the ball to the first person in line, making the toss inside the court, forcing that player to run in and set the ball back to them. That person goes to the end of the line. Tossers always catch the ball, and then toss it to the next player in line. Setters must not run into the court until the person tossing the ball has released the ball.

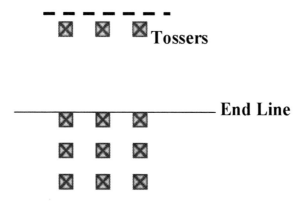

Another variation of this same type of drill is called "W's". The setting players all line up in one line. This time the line is behind the end line close to one of the sidelines. The tossers are in the same positions. The first tosser throws, forcing the setter to move into the court to set the ball back to them. The setter immediately back pedals on a diagonal back to the end line. As they reach the end line, the second tosser throws the ball forcing the setter into the court to set the ball back to them. The setter immediately backpedals to the end line diagonally, where the third tosser throws the ball. The setter enters the court, sets that last ball back to the final tosser and then goes to the end of the waiting line. The first tosser controls the tempo of the drill. This person should make sure that more than one person is working on the court at all times, but also that there is not a backup of players at the second or third position.

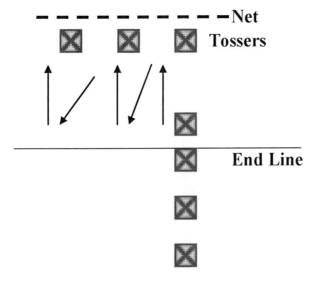

Drill 25

Have players partner up with one ball for each group. Spread players out on both sides of the net. Have one player from each group set the ball to them self at a height slightly above the net height. Have them set for one minute, counting the number of sets in that time. After one minute, the players should switch.

Drill 26

Have players line up against the walls with about three people in each line. The first person in each group does ten wall sets, aiming at a spot on the wall about 10 to 12 feet high. Every player in each line does ten sets and moves to the end of the line. If the players are beginners, they can toss the ball to themselves, set it to the wall, then catch it and repeat. If the players are more advanced, the first person sets the ball to the wall and quickly moves to the end of the line. The second player moves up quickly and sets that ball that is bouncing back, quickly moves out of the way and the third player moves to set the ball to the wall. See how many consecutive sets can be made for each group.

Drill 27

Players line up at the basketball baskets. The first player in each group slams the ball down hard on the floor with two hands. When the ball bounces off the floor, they try to set the ball into the basket. The next person in line steps up and repeats what the first player did.

Drill 28

Form lines of players with about 6 to 8 in each group. First player sets the ball above her own head very high and quickly goes to the end of the line. The next player in line steps up and does the same. See how many consecutive sets each group can make.

Drill 29

A more advanced drill. Player sets the ball just above her head. While setting to self, the player drops to her knees. Keep setting from this position and try to return to a standing position. Next, move down into a sitting position while still setting the ball, and then try to return to a standing position again. Lastly, try to go down to a laying position while setting the ball and then return to a standing position.

Drill 30

Line up in groups of three in single file lines facing the same direction. The first person in line takes three walking steps forward while setting to self three times. After her third set, she backsets to the second person in line, and then goes to the end of the line. The second person does the same, followed by the third person. Repeat the drill.

Drill 31

Groups of four players line up in a square position about 10 feet apart. Number 1 sets to number 2 and runs to switch places with number 3. Number 2 sets to number 3, who should now be at number 1's original position. Number 2 switches with 4. Number 3 sets to number four and number four sets to the new number one. After setting the ball, the player must always switch with that same person, not the person to whom the ball was set. Solid arrows designate player's running motion; dotted arrows designate ball's motion.

Drill 32

Line up with 4 players. Have two at the net (one at each sideline), and two about mid court, about 8 feet in from the sidelines. Number one sets to number two, number two sets to number three, and number three sets to number four. Number four reverses the flight of the ball by setting to number three. Number three sets to number two, and number two sets to number one. Go through this cycle twice. Stop the ball and players move one spot clockwise. Start the drill again. After twice through this cycle, the players switch positions again. Dotted line denotes first ball motion; solid line denotes reverse ball motion.

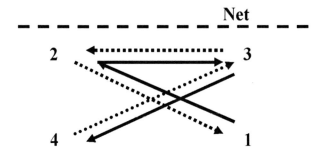

Drill 33

Line up in groups of three with each player about 10 feet apart. Player number one sets to number two, and follows that set to the end of where number two was positioned. Number two sets across to number three and follows that set to the end of where number three was positioned. Number three sets to number one and follows that set to where number one was positioned.

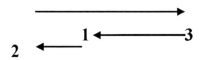

Drill 34

Four players line up at the net, equal distance apart. Number one sets to self and then sets to number two. As soon as number one sets the ball, that player runs to the ten-foot line, touches it with her hand, and returns to the original position. Number two sets to self and then sets to number three. Number two then runs to the ten-foot line, touches the line with hand, and returns to original position. Number three does the same. Number four sets self and then sets the ball all the way back to number one. Number four runs to ten-foot line, touches the line with hand, and returns to the original position. After going through one complete cycle, the players change positions. Number one goes to number two's spot, two goes to three's spot, three goes to four's spot, and four goes to number one's spot.

Drill 35

Players line up in sets of three about 10 feet apart. Outside person tosses the ball to the middle person who backsets to the other player. This player catches the ball. The middle person turns and faces the player with the ball. The one holding the ball tosses it to the middle person who backsets the person who started the drill. After ten backsets, have the players trade positions. If players are higher skilled, the tosses are all replaced by sets so the players will continuously be setting, and there will be no catching involved.

Drill 36

To run this drill, use the same starting position as previous drill. This drill is for more highly skilled players. The balls are all set; no catching and tossing. This drill makes people think and move.

The ball may be set to any of the other two players. Sets can be front sets or backsets. No one changes positions unless the set comes from the middle position. Every time the middle person sets to someone, they change positions with that person after that person has set the ball.

Drill 37

Players pair up into partners, with one ball per group. One player sets the ball nice and high to the partner and takes two quick steps to the right, touches the floor, and returns to the starting position. Partner does the same thing. After one cycle, the player moves to the left, then back. The ball must be set high to allow time for movement.

Chapter 16
Spiking Drills

Drill 1

Players line up in hitting line. Each person has a tennis ball. First player in line takes full approach, jumps at net, and throws tennis ball over net into other court. First person chases ball and second person does same. Each person who throws tennis ball should use spiking motion with arm and not just use wrist snap. After a few times through, move line to middle and repeat drill. Lastly, move line to other sideline and repeat drill.

Drill 2

Players line up in hitting line. First player tosses ball very high to self. Staying on floor, she hits ball with wrist snap to topspin ball, trying to hit cross court. Second player does the same. After a few times through, move to middle and repeat drill. Finally, move to other sideline and repeat. Must emphasize a high toss in order to execute this drill since players usually throw ball too low.

Drill 3

Same as previous drill except players jump up to hit their own toss with topspin.

Drill 4

Same as previous drill except players bounce ball hard off floor before jumping to hit with topspin. Players should bounce ball close to themselves to execute drill correctly.

Drill 5

Coach holds ball with right hand on the fingertips while standing on a chair. Players line up in a single file line just to the left side of the chair. If they are left handed, they stand to the right of the chair. The first player stays on floor with no approach and no jump. She moves upper parts of body from waist up and using proper arm swing, hits ball down from coach's hand. Ball should be hit on top, not the back of the ball. Coach releases ball a split second before it is hit by dropping hand straight down quickly. For coach's hand protection, it is best to release ball too early rather than too late. After player hits ball they chase it and return to the end of the line. The next player steps up near chair for next hit.

Drill 6

Same as previous drill except players jump to hit without an approach. They jump from same position as in previous drill.

Drill 7

Same as previous drill except players take a full approach, jump and hit from coach. On this drill, coach holds ball higher to force players to jump high.

Drill 8

Have players line up in spiking line for outside hit. The first few times through, the setter underhand tosses to spiker who hits.

Drill 9

Same as previous drill except the setter tosses to self and then sets to spikers.

Drill 10

Same as previous drill except the spiker first tosses the ball to the setter who sets back to the tosser to hit.

Drill 11

Same as previous drill except setter tosses ball to spiker who forearm passes to setter who sets to spiker to hit.

Drill 12

Same as previous drill except spiker tosses ball to setter. The setter hits ball with topspin to spiker. Spiker forearm passes to setter who sets to spiker. Spiker hits.

Drill 13

Players line up in three hitting lines: two outside and one in middle. Setter starts in setting position at net. Coach stands near middle of own court with supply of balls. Coach tosses ball to setter who sets any line. As soon as play is over, Coach throws another ball and controls the tempo of the drill. All three attackers take approach on every set. If your line is set, the hitter chases the ball and goes to end of different line. The two hitters who don't get the set quickly pull back to front of their same lines and approach again with the next toss.

Drill 14

Same as previous drill except every set must be dinked.

Drill 15

Players stand about seven to eight feet from wall. Use as many players on wall as you have accessible space. Each player has a ball and tries to hit it from other hand to floor, close to wall, so that the ball hits the floor then the wall and rebounds to the hitter. If they are beginners, they catch ball and repeat. Players should be using proper arm swings on every hit while trying to get topspin on the ball.

Drill 16

Same as previous drill except players toss ball up before hitting it.

Drill 17

Same as previous drill except players don't catch ball on rebound from wall, but try to make continuous hits.

Drill 18

Another variation of this drill is to have lines at the wall with about four to a line. First player hits to wall and quickly goes to end of line. Next player quickly steps up and hits ball as it rebounds from first player. See how many good hits in a row a line can make.

Drill 19

One spiker lines up on outside. Setter underhand tosses to spiker who approaches and spikes the ball. Same hitter quickly pulls back while setter tosses a second ball. Spiker approaches and hits and quickly pulls back. Spiker is not finished until they have hit six to eight consecutive hits. Next hitter does same thing.

Drill 20

Spiker lines up at net in outside position in blocking stance. Setter holds ball while standing in setting position. Setter slaps ball.

Setter tosses to spiker who forearm passes back to setter. Setter sets to spiker who approaches and hits. Next hitter steps up to net in blocking position, ready for the slap of ball.

Drill 21

Place either cones or hoops on other side of court in various spots. Spikers try to hit these areas when spiking.

Chapter 17

Serving Drills

Drill 1

Divide group in half. One group stands between one end line and the other group on other side. Using many balls, players serve from each side. No penalty if serve is good. If serve is missed, that players immediately sprints to net, touches center line with hand, and runs back to same end line. Another variation is to do five sit-ups after each miss.

Drill 2

Silent serving. Players line up as in previous drill. There is silence for the whole time this drill is used. Penalty for talking is any number of laps that coach chooses.

Drill 3

No miss serving. Players line up as in previous drill. Coach says start and times for 30 seconds. Players try not for aces but just to get the serve in the court. Count the number of missed serves for this team for each 30-second time frame.

Drill 4

Players partner up with one ball per group. Players line up opposite each other on opposite sidelines. Players try to serve back and forth to each other using same technique as if hitting over net. Goal is to hit serve right to partner to they can catch ball without moving from spot.

Drill 5

Three coaches or players stand on chairs at net, one on each end and one in middle. They are on the same side of the net holding hoops just above net. Players serve from opposite side only, trying to serve through hoops. Give 10 points for each through-hoop or 5 points for hitting hoop.

Drill 6

Players stand 30 feet from wall. Have marking on wall 7'4 ¼" high. If limited wall space, use lines of players. Goal is to serve to wall above the line as close to that line as possible.

Drill 7

Players partner up and stand opposite each other across the net on opposite 10- foot lines. Each group of two has a volleyball. They serve back and forth to each other trying to hit it to partner so she can catch it without moving. When serving from this short distance they are to use same serving technique as from end line. The only difference is they hit it softer. After a few minutes, the coach tells all players to take a few backward steps. They now serve from there. After a few minutes have them take a few more backward steps and serve from there. Keep doing this until players are behind the serving line.

Drill 8

Players partner up with one on each side of net. Serving will be done from one side only. Use many balls. Servers will serve as soon as they have a ball, not one at a time. They serve 10 times. Partner on other side of net count and tell them how many good serves they had out of 10. After 10 serves, they change places and continue. Counters retrieve balls and roll them under the net back to the serving people.

Drill 9

Place all servers on one side of net behind end line. Place hoops on opposite side of net in different positions. Place three players on side of net with hoops to retrieve balls. The retrievers roll the balls back to the serving lines after they hit floor. Give points to all serves landing inside of hoops.

Drill 10

Place equal number of servers behind opposite end lines. Use many balls. On signal from coach, servers quickly serve ball with the goal to be the first to make 15 good serves. Give a reward to the winners.

Drill 11

Line up servers behind serving line. First player serves to a specific spot, chases ball, and returns to end of serving line. As soon as first player has served the second person steps up and serves. Continue through serving line many times.

Drill 12

Players line up with three receivers on each side of net in a line across the court. Each side has a waiting line of players off the court near the receivers. The third group stands behind each serving line. The servers alternate serves one side to the other. Every time a receiver puts up a good pass, she goes back to the serving line. One server goes to the end of waiting line. The first person in waiting line takes the place of the person who put up the good pass. Coach points to serving side each time to keep drill moving.

Chapter 18
Blocking Drills

Drill 1

Players line up at wall with lines of about three per group. First players are about an arms-length from wall. These players do 10 wall blocks. Start from crouching positions, jump fully extended, and touch fingertips to wall at the highest reach possible. Be sure to emphasize landing with cushion and bending the knees. Do not hurry. Get in ready position and jump again. After 10 jumps, go to the end of the line. The next person then steps up. Make sure they are not jumping forward into the wall. Do about three to four sets before drill is completed.

Drill 2

Players line up in single file line facing the net. Position is near the sideline and perpendicular to the net. First player gets in blocking position. This player goes up to block. If she is tall or has a good jump, she reaches hands over the net for a stuff block. If she is short, she tilts hands backward for a control block. When this blocker lands, she side slides to middle of the net and blocks a second time. She then side slides to the end and blocks a third time. The player then returns to the end of the line. The second person in line blocks in the first position when the first person gets in position for the second block in the middle of the net. After everyone has been through three sets, the line moves to where the third blocking position was, and now blocks will move in opposite direction.

Drill 3

Make two single file lines perpendicular to the net at the sideline, one line on each side of the net facing the net. Put taller players on one side, and shorter players on the other. First players on each side of the net try to jump at the same time and touch fingertips over the net. They come down and slide to the middle of the net and repeat. They then slide to the end and make a third jump, again attempting to touch fingertips. The second players in line jump in the first position as soon as the first jumpers move to the center position. Emphasize no net touches. After three sets the line switches to the third blocking position. Repeat the drill with slides going in the opposite direction.

Drill 4

Line up same as in previous drill except that it does not matter if taller players are on one side or if players are mixed. One line on one side of the net is the designated jumper's line. The other side is the reactor. The first person in jumping line goes up to block. The reacting line leader tries to jump with that jumper. The jumper slides toward the middle of the net and anywhere along the net jumps a second time. The reactor tries to jump at the same time. The jumper moves farther and jumps a third time. Again the reactor tries to jump at the same time. The jumper and reactor go to the end of the opposite lines for the next turns. When the whole group finishes the set, the jumper becomes reactor and vice versa. Reactor always tries to touch the fingers of the jumper. Do three sets in the same direction and the last sets in the opposite direction. Jumpers should vary the spot of the jumps so it is not all the same.

Drill 5

Line up in two lines, one on each side of the net. One side is the blocking side and one side is the spiking side. In this drill you must emphasize that the spiker needs to stay on his own side of the net and does not jump over the centerline. They must be careful to avoid sprained ankles. The first person in the spiking line takes a normal approach to the net, jumps, and pretends to spike a ball. The blocker is instructed to block the power alley (cross court), and jump slightly later than the spiker. The spiker walks back to where middle spike approach would start, while the blocker moves over toward the middle block position. Spiker takes an approach and spikes at the middle. The blocker jumps for the block. Spiker walks back to the third spiking position at opposite side of court. Blocker follows. Spiker approaches and jumps for the spike. Blocker jumps to attempt a block. Blocker goes to end of the spiking line, and the spiker goes to the end of the blocking line.

Drill 6

Line up with three players at the net in blocking positions - one at the left sideline, one in the middle, and on at the right sideline. The person in the middle position has a line of players behind him/her waiting to move up. Coach stands at the middle of the net on the other side of the net. Coach points to either the right or the left and the middle blocker quickly slides to the end blocker. The two players jump to form a double block. When they come down, the end person goes to the end of the middle waiting line. The girl who slid from the middle takes the end position. The girl in front of the middle waiting line moves up to the net. The coach points again in either direction, and the drill continues.

Drill 7

Three coaches or players are standing on chairs on one side of the net, at the net – one at the left sideline, one in the middle, and one at the right sideline. A line of players will make a single file line on the other side of the net. The first person is ready, and in blocking position. You will also need three feeders to give balls to the chair people to keep the drill moving. The person in the first chair hits the ball down into the court while the blocker tries to block the ball. The same blocker slides to the middle. The middle chair person then hits, and the same blocker attempts to block. At this time, the next person in the waiting line steps up to the net. The player in first chair hits to that blocker. By this time the first player should be blocking the person in the last chair. When the player finishes, she moves to the end of the waiting line.

Drill 8

Same positions as in previous drill. This time the chair people hold the ball above the net with two hands, one on each side of the ball. First blocker lines up at the net and jumps, trying to push the ball back out of the holder's hands without touching the net. This blocker slides to the middle and does the same in the middle, and then slides to the last chair to finish off the drill. This player then goes to the end of the waiting line, as the drill continues. Again, you will need feeders to supply balls to the holders.

Drill 9

Same positions as in previous drill. This time the blocker jumps up and grabs the ball from the holder without touching the net. The player moves the same way as in the two previous drills.

Drill 10

Players line up along the net, facing into their own court. Players are about six to seven feet from coach. First person stands without jumping, fully extends arms up in blocking position. Coach throws ball into the hands of the blocker. Blocker keeps hands still and lets the ball hit the hands without trying to direct the ball. Player goes to the end of the line. Coach throws to the next player. Drill continues. After a few times through, the players try to direct the ball toward the floor as soon as it hits hands.

Drill 11

Same as previous drill, except coach now hits ball into the blocker's hands.

Drill 12

Put the hitters into a spiking line. Place one blocker on opposite side ready to block. Spiker approaches, hits, and blocker attempts to get hands on the ball. Spiker then switches to become the blocker, and the blocker goes to the end of the hitting line. A variation on this drill would be to use two blockers for a double block.

Drill 13

This drill helps the blocker to focus on the hitter instead of the ball. Place a blocker at the net ready to block. Place a spiker on the other side of the net, ready to spike. Coach stands behind blocker and throws ball over the net so that the spiker can approach and hit. Blocker goes up to block. You can do this same drill with two blockers. Players change places after each spike.

Chapter 19

Combination Drills

Drill 1

Coach stands on one side of the net at the net with supply of balls. Two players stand on the other side of the net at the net, side by side, facing the net. There are two waiting lines, one at each sideline off of the court. Coach slaps the ball. The two players at the net pull back quickly. The coach tosses the ball into the court. Player closest to the ball calls for it and passes it to the second person who sets the ball back to the person who tries to spike the ball into the court. If ball cannot be spiked, it is passed over the net. These players chase their ball and go to the end of the waiting line. First player in each waiting line steps into position at the net, and coach starts again.

Drill 2

Players line up in a single file line, behind the end line, near the sideline, facing the net. Coach is on other side of the net with supply of balls. Coach slaps the ball allowing first three players in line to charge into the court. The coach tosses the ball into the court. The three players on the court try to perform a pass, set, and hit (All three do not have to touch the ball each time.). After the play is complete, they chase their ball and go to the end of the line. The next three get ready to run.

Drill 3

Three players are on each side of the net while coach tosses the ball over the net. The three must try to work in a pass, set, and attack with the only stipulation being that the set must be put behind the 10-foot line. The three on the other side try to do the same. As in a game, when the ball hits the floor, the play ends. Coach then tosses the ball over the net from the other side.

Drill 4

Three players stand on the end line, about 6 feet apart. The coach stands on the same side of the net on the sideline and against the net. Coach spikes the ball against the floor. The three players run into the court and try to work a pass, set, and attack. After play, they chase their ball and go to the end of the line, and the next three players get ready.

Drill 5

Two players stand at the net. They pull back, pretend to pass a ball, move to the sideline, approach, and spike a pretend ball. They go to the end of the waiting line, and the next two players step up to the net.

Drill 6

A team of six players line up on one side of the net. Coach stands on the other side of the net with a supply of balls. Coach tosses a ball into the court. The players work a pass, set, and attack. As soon as the ball crosses the net, the coach throws a second ball into the court. Players play that ball. Again, as soon as the ball is over the net, the coach tosses another ball into the court. Continue for about 10-15 attempts. Put six new players in the court or rotate, and repeat the procedure.

Drill 7

Line up six players on one side of the net. Place three in position at the net. The coach hits the ball into the net. Net players try to retrieve ball out of the net and get ball over the net. They have only two hits to accomplish this because coach's hit counts as the first hit. The three at the net move away, and the next three take their place at the net.

Drill 8

Put tape on the floor so each court consists of 15 feet from the net to the tape. Sidelines are still the regulation 30 feet. Play triples with three on a side with official rules. Each team tries to use three hits to get the ball over the net on this short court.

Drill 9

Make a single file line of spikers back away from the net. Coach serves a short serve to the first player in the line who tries to pass serve to setter. The setter sets the ball back, and the player attempts to spike the ball. The player goes to the end of the line, and the next person steps up.

Drill 10

Position a setter at the net. Make a single file spiking line ready to pass and attack the ball. Have another player toss the ball from the opposite side of the net, and then sprint to the net to get in blocking position. The spiker attempts to pass the toss to the setter who sets the ball back to the spiker. The spiker attacks the ball, while the tosser tries to block. The spiker and the tosser go to the end of opposite lines. The next in line move up to become the spiker and the tosser.

Drill 11

Put six players on one court in defensive positions. Three players line up on the other side of the net, at the net. A tosser stands behind the end line of the court with the six players. The tosser slaps the ball, and two of the three players on the other side of the net pull back to pass the ball. The coach tosses the ball. The two players attempt to pass the ball to their setter, who sets the ball to either one. They attack the ball, trying to put the ball down on the six defenders. The defenders play the ball and try to put the ball down on the other side. Continue until the ball is dead. Switch two more spikers into position on the three-player side.

Drill 12

Variation of Drill 10 - the tosser stands at the net, and not behind the end line.

Drill 13

Put six players on each side of the court. The ball is thrown over on first play. Each team must play three hits to get ball over and every play must be a legal overhead pass.

Drill 14

Place 4 people at the net on the same side, two lined up at each sideline. Place two spiking lines and a setter on the opposite side of the net. The spiking lines should be on the right side and the left side. The coach tosses the ball to the setter who sets either spiker. The spiker hits the ball and the blockers on the other side of the net attempt to block the ball. Switch around to give others the chance to hit and block.

Part 5
Team Devotions

Throughout the years, I've developed short reflections from God's Word that I've shared with my teams. I've also used them at volleyball clinics and camps around the country. I tried to make the devotions apply to volleyball and the different issues those players face and then to show how the Bible has the answer for their every problem.

Occasionally, you might find some thoughts that are repeated but since it is by repetition that we grow in Christ, I chose to keep them as I originally used them. I pray that, as you use and modify these reflections for your own teams and their unique needs, God will bless your players with spiritual growth.

Chapter 20
Setting for the Lord

Not only is the setter the most important link to the makeup of a team, but getting set up for effective Christian service will reap dividends of heavenly rewards. The acrostic SETTING will help you better remember these character traits that can make you a better volleyball player and servant of God.

S is for sacrifice.

Setters give up part of themselves for the good of the team. Think about a typical game and who gets the praise. Is it the setter? Usually not. The spikers generally get the glory for a kill. It is not very often that someone says, "Look at that great set" after it is killed by a spiker. And yet, we all know that if it weren't for that great set, there would be no kill in the first place. So, a setter isn't about self; rather a setter first and foremost thinks about the good of the team.

The setter also sacrifices time, energy, and effort by setting a ball in her backyard day after day over and over and over again to develop the touch and control. The team and its success become more important than what the setter thinks or wants. A true sacrificial setter knows that it doesn't matter who starts or who plays as long as God gets the glory.

I had a player some years ago who was a senior, and she came to me on game day as the teams were starting to warm up. She said that she had forgotten her jersey, but since a younger girl named Julie didn't play much, she wondered if she could use Julie's. She said this loud enough for Julie to hear, which didn't go over too well with her. One of my other players overheard this conversation and said to me, "Coach, why don't you let her use my jersey. I'm just a sub on the team and don't play that much." I immediately thought to myself, "Here is someone very special. She is willing to sacrifice a chance to play in the match by giving up her jersey. The team and its success were more important than her getting to play. This girl later became the captain of my team, and she was one of the best examples to all those with whom she came in contact.

Many times players would rather play in an individual sport than on a team because he functions much better when he only has himself to worry about. While this is often not a bad thing, it can be very beneficial to play on a team because of the other players. The other players bring relational issues to a team. But the conflict that others bring can be beneficial to a player. Throughout your life, you will be mostly in situations where you have to deal with other people. Participating in team sports teaches you valuable lessons about teamwork, concern for others, and how to be a leader. Mostly, you learn sacrifice when you play on a team. No matter what your level, you learn that you aren't the most important commodity; the team is.

The greatest example of sacrifice in the Bible is the Lord Jesus. He went through agony, suffering in our place. He willingly gave up His life so we could have eternal life. Remember, Abraham was willing to sacrifice his son to obey God, too. The Bible says that greater love hath no man than a man laying down his life for a friend (John 15:13). How about those missionaries who sacrifice for the Lord? These are people that are willing to give up every earthly comfort so that other people can hear about Christ.

Let's make it personal. Are you willing to sacrifice for the Lord? Would you be willing to go to the mission field, teach or be a pastor's wife? If you are willing to do whatever the Lord wants you to do, then the least you can do today is sacrifice for your team and do your part.

E is for enthusiasm.

Enthusiasm is showing the joy of the Lord. Someone has said that enthusiasm, or the lack of it, is contagious. As a setter you must be enthusiastic even when things are going wrong. You can't get on the court and have the attitude of not wanting the ball. You have to have the attitude of "Hit the ball to me! I can do it even under pressure."

I Samuel 17:48 talks about David hurrying toward the army to meet Goliath. Picture David facing a giant and showing the enthusiasm by running to meet him! How much enthusiasm do you show on the court, especially at practice? More importantly, how much enthusiasm do you show in your Christian walk? Is it drudgery to go to church or your chapel services, or do you go eagerly expecting a blessing? Is it easier to read notes from friends or emails than your Bible? Do you pray with enthusiasm? If your pastor says there is a financial need, do you give begrudgingly, or are you eager to give out of a heart of love?

The first T is for technique.

Technique is how you do something. In setting, it's the hand position, body movement, and all the things that result in good performance. How many of you work diligently on your technique to be a better player? I mean not only at team practice, but also on your own. Jesus told us how to do things. There is a way to do something to reach a goal. God's Word tells us to go into all the world and tell others. Getting people to do this is a problem. Most people, probably out of fear of personal inadequacy, don't do it. But, since as a Christian witnessing is not an option but a command, knowledge of the Scripture is key for when the time comes to share Christ.

The second T is for training.

Training is preparing to perform those techniques you have worked on for use in the future. A large number of volleyball players waste the summer goofing off. The summer is the best time to really improve your skills and conditioning. You have more time along with the better weather for outdoor workouts. I'm convinced most players at lower to middle levels of volleyball don't train enough. The Chinese women's Olympic team worked out 8 hours a day for 7 days a week! I attended a clinic by Mike Hebert, an excellent college coach, who said he wanted his setter (at the college level) to set 2,000 balls a day.

In the Bible, Elijah trained Elisha. Paul trained Timothy. Jesus trained the disciples. After I was saved, Pastor Karl Gehrig took the time to train me in regard to visitation and soul winning. He invested part of his life in training a shy, frightened and nervous introvert. In your Christian walk, are you training someone by your walk and talk, and are you letting someone disciple you?

I is for initiative.

Initiative is recognizing what needs to be done and doing it before you are asked to do it. It's taking the first step. In volleyball, the first step is crucial. How many times do you see players see a ball coming and then, too late, react to it? They should anticipate and move, not react seconds later. How many of you have helped chase balls down, put up posts and nets, or cleaned the gym after practice without being asked? How many of you saw a weakness in your game or physical condition and had the initiative to do something about it?

How many of you have volunteered to do something in Christian service without being told to? The Christian life is not about pew-sitting, but about winning the lost, helping the needy, and encouraging the weak. Those things take action! They take initiative. Do you have this essential quality?

N is for nutrition.

Nutrition is a process where we take in food for promoting growth. Of course, you've been told this your whole life; however, I believe a lot of volleyball players don't play well because they don't eat well—the old hamburger and fries routine. Someone has said you are what you eat. Some nutritionists disagree on some points but are in total agreement on others. All are for the value of fruits and vegetables, whole grain cereals and breads, chicken, fish, and salads. Baked or broiled foods are better then fried. Low fat is recommended. There is too much sugar in a lot of our foods. Soda is loaded with sugar.

Something really neglected is water. Eight glasses of water are the minimum every day. On game day, you should be drinking water all day! Some players wait until they are thirsty and then drink. I believe in the value of vitamins because a lot of our food is processed. Since most players don't eat a well-balanced diet, at the minimum, they should be taking a multivitamin every day. Vitamins C and E are very good along with the B's.

Look at First Corinthians 10:31, "Whether therefore ye eat, or drink, or whatsoever ye do, do all to the glory of God." Do your eating habits glorify God? Just as nutrition promotes growth, how much growth have you seen in your Christian life this past year? Are you doing something to promote that growth—like daily Bible-reading and prayer, accountability with an adult or godly friend, or service to others? If not, then start improving your spiritual nutrition today!

G is for Godliness.

The last letter in SETTING is for godliness, and it pretty much is a summary of the others. Do you show godliness on the court, during games, practices and before and after them? Do you guard your attitude and your mouth? (Psalm 141:3) If you touch a ball that a referee doesn't see, are you honest enough to call it? Before you step on the court, do you pray for help to glorify God in all situations?

A Christian coach told me he trained his girls to go out of the way to look for opportunities to show godliness. God's Word tells us to have certain attributes, and the best example was Jesus, Who showed love, joy, peace, longsuffering, gentleness, goodness, faith, meekness, and temperance (Galatians 5:22-23). Take a minute and think about our acrostic again.

Sacrifice
Enthusiasm
Technique
Training
Initiative
Nutrition
Godliness

Even if you aren't a setter on the volleyball court, I'm sure you would want to be a "setter" in real life: a person who is willing to sacrifice, be enthusiastic, have the proper technique, train hard every day, take the initiative, make good nutrition a daily goal, and above all else, strive for godliness in every aspect of your life. It takes work to be a setter, but the results are worth it. Won't you take the time to put these characteristics to work today?

Chapter 21
Decisions

I'm reasonably sure that the great majority of Christians pray before making important decisions. I think this happens when big things are involved – Where will I go to college? Should I marry this person? Should I take this job? What church should I attend? How should I treat this illness? What are my gifts and the best way to serve God?

I think that many times Christians fail to pray in what may be called lesser decisions – Should I go to a certain place? Should I listen to this kind of music? Should I have this person as a close friend? Should I wear this type of clothing?

I believe that we should pray for all decisions – nothing is too small to ask God's help. Asking God for help in decisions reinforces our dependence upon him. He's never too busy to help when his children come to him in prayer.

There are some questions we should ask ourselves before making a decision. Will this decision please God or displease Him? Will it honor Him or dishonor Him? Will it bring me close to God or push me away? Will others see my love for God or see my love of self?

Godly Counsel

Before we make decisions, we should first seek godly counsel. The Bible says there is wisdom in a multitude of counselors. In your church or Christian school, you know who the godly people are. Their lives speak so loudly it expresses their love and obedience for God. Some of you may have godly parents to go to, but some of your parents may not be Christians. If there is some doubt whether or not to do a certain thing, then give God the benefit of the doubt and don't do it.

In First Kings 12 we have a king making a foolish decision, one that some young people make even today. Rehoboam, Solomon's son, takes over as king when Solomon dies. Jeroboam and the congregation of Israel come to speak to Rehoboam. In verse four, they say, "Thy father made our yoke grievous: now therefore make thou the grievous service of thy father, and his heavy yoke which he put upon us, lighter, and we will serve thee." The king answers, "Come back in three days and I will have an answer for you." In verse six, the king consults with the old men that stood before Solomon and asks their advice. He says, "How do ye advise that I may answer this people?" Verse seven states, "And they spoke unto him, saying, 'If thou will be a servant unto this people this day, and wilt serve them, and answer them, and speak good words to them, then they will be thy servants forever'." In verse 8, Rehoboam consults with the young men that were growing up with him. In verse nine, he said, "What counsel give ye that we may answer this people . . ."

Remember in verse six he said "that I may answer this people" – now he says "that we may answer this people". I believe by saying we, he is affiliating himself with the young men and ignoring the older men. In verses 10 and 11, they advise to add to the burden and make it harder. The people gather after the three days to hear the king's answer. In verse 13, "And the king answered the people roughly, and forsook the old men's counsel that they gave him." He told the people he was going to make it harder, not easier. The people left and when the king sent Adoram to collect the tribute (or taxes), all Israel stoned him so that he died. King Rehoboam fled to Jerusalem and the kingdom was divided because of a foolish king listening to the counsel of the young men.

Over the years I've heard about young people who seek advice from their peers and ignore seeking counsel from older Christians. Many older Christians, through experience, are wise and would give them good counsel.

How would you feel if you had to fly to a certain destination and you had a choice of pilots? You could pick a pilot on his first solo flight. Or another pilot who had flown 1,000 times in all weather conditions without incident. Which one would you choose to fly with? Or if you had to have surgery and you had a choice. You could pick one surgeon doing his first surgery on a live person. Or the second surgeon who had performed it 1,000 times, and it was always successful. Which one would you choose to operate on you?

I read an article in the paper this year that said you have a 60% more likely chance to die with balloon angioplasty surgery if your doctor rarely does them. The same article said in regard to bypass, back, and cancer surgery, you are several times more likely to die if you have an inexperienced surgeon. Why would you want to use someone who has no or little experience? The same thing holds true in regard to seeking counsel from young, inexperienced people in regard to spiritual things.

Wavering on the Brink of a Bad Decision

I have two personal examples in my coaching career that are a perfect example of this principle. Player X had just finished her junior year. We had some workouts during the summer, and I heard a rumor that she was considering leaving school to go to the local public school for her senior year. I sat down with her and confronted her about what she was going to do. I told her that if there was a problem at our Christian school, then there was another Christian school not far away that she could attend. I told her I believed she should be in a Christian school. There would be chapel services with messages from God's Word, godly teachers as examples, and a curriculum based on God and helping young people to conform to the image of Christ. I told her to pray about it. She left without saying much. A day later her mother called me and said, I don't know what you said to my daughter, but she came home in tears, and spent time in prayer and Bible reading. She has decided to come back to school.

I later learned that some co-workers of Player X were trying to get her to do some things that she knew a Christian shouldn't do. The story has a happy ending with her graduating from a good Christian university, but the story doesn't end there.

A year or so later, I was doing a volleyball clinic at a Christian school in northern Illinois. I gave this devotional before one of my sessions. At the lunch break, the athletic director came up to me and said we have a problem. He said he had a girl who was a junior who was thinking about leaving and going to a public school. He said she probably thought I fed you that information so you would say what you did. She had to be assured that I knew nothing about her situation. I later learned that she did come back and finish her senior year at the Christian school. The story doesn't end here.

After the clinic I went back to our school and as I was walking through the hallway, I met Player X's father. I enthusiastically shared the experience with him and that I used his daughter as a positive example. I thought he would be excited to hear that. I later learned that he was at school that day for the purpose of pulling his son out of the Christian school to go to the public school.

Player Y had just finished her freshman year. I had worked with her since about fifth grade. Again, it was summer and she had not come to our workouts. I heard the rumor that she was going to pull out of school and go to the local public school. She finally showed up at one of the last summer workouts and told me she was going to switch schools and go to the local public school. I asked her if she had prayed about it. She said yes. I asked if she had sought some godly counsel. She said she had asked her youth pastor (He had graduated not too many years ago.), and he thought it would be okay. She graduated from the public school and attended a Bible college for about a semester before dropping out. I do believe that her chances of finishing college at that Christian institution would have been greater if she had stayed in the Christian high school.

The part that disappointed me most is she did not come to me and seek my counsel.

I plead with you not to make the same mistake as the second player I mentioned. Seek wise, godly counsel and you'll see God work through the decisions you make.

Chapter 22

Serving On Target

In volleyball circles, it is called one of three things: serve, service, or serving. They all mean the same thing. Many years ago I took a high school team down to a southern Christian University for a national invitational tournament. As I passed the Christian bookstore on that campus, a book caught my eye. It was titled *Improving Your Serve.* I immediately thought my girls could sure use that book because our serving was really poor. Of course, the book was not talking about volleyball serving, but about serving God. How do we as Christians show the love of God? By serving others. In Matthew 25:36-40, Jesus said, "Naked, and ye clothed me: I was sick, and ye visited me: I was in prison, and ye came unto me. Then shall the righteous answer Him, saying, Lord, when saw we Thee an hungred, and fed Thee or thirsty, and gave Thee drink? When saw we Thee a stranger, and took Thee in? Or naked, and clothed Thee? Or when we saw Thee sick, or in prison and came unto Thee? And the King shall answer and say unto them, Verily I say unto you, Inasmuch as ye have done it unto one of the least of these my brethren, ye have done it unto Me."

I had a girl on my team years ago named Debbie. She was a short girl, a defensive specialist who served underhand. She had a very good serve and kept it in the court consistently. Her main responsibility was to come off the bench and serve when we really needed a good serve in the court. That was her area of service on our team.

I had another girl named Becky. Becky started school at Oak Forest Christian Academy when she was very young. Her dad took a position at Northland Baptist Bible College and the family moved up north. Some years later her dad passed away and the mother and two daughters moved back to Illinois. Becky was going to be a senior when she came back to school. She came to our first practice and I could easily tell that her skill level was not going to be good enough to earn a varsity uniform. This was the year we were really loaded with talent. The team eventually finished undefeated at 41-0 in matches and won six tournaments. The whole season they only lost three individual games. Becky later related to me that after she went home from the first practice, she cried, realizing her skill level was not as good as the rest of the girls. She had come from a team up north where she was one of the best players on the team, and now it was the opposite. I talked to her and explained the situation that I didn't have a varsity jersey for her and asked her to consider being a servant to the team and being our manager. I asked her to pray about it. She came back later and said she would, and she did a great job for us and the rest of the story is the best part.

Later that season we went to a national invitational tournament in Tennessee, and one of our girls couldn't go—so Becky not only got the chance to wear a varsity jersey, but she also got the chance to play. I think it was God's way of rewarding a servant's heart. Years later Becky married one of our volleyball referees, a fine Christian man.

I think that we as adults have not emphasized enough to our young people that life is not all about just enjoying yourselves and having fun activities, but in serving others. For example, if we said we have two busses outside, one is going to the best amusement park in the state and the other is going soul-winning in some neighborhood, which bus would most of our young people fill up? Would they serve self or others?

Initiate Play

In the *National Federation Volleyball Rule Book*, Rule 8 is entitled "The Serve". Article 1 says that a serve is contact with the ball to initiate play. The word "initiate" means to start or begin. If the referee blows the whistle to serve, and the server holds the ball over five seconds, the ball is awarded to the other team. If this same thing happens again and again and again, there would be no game. Someone has to initiate play.

In the Christian realm, your parents, pastor, friends, or teachers can all encourage you to serve God. But until you initiate it and start, it will never happen. You must decide to serve God.

Article 2 says that the server shall serve from within the serving area. You can serve from anywhere behind the end line without making contact with the line or stepping over it at the time of contact.

Let me ask you a question. What is your area of service? Is it singing, playing a musical instrument, teaching Sunday school, working with little children, visiting the sick, or spending time with the elderly? You should have an area of service to bring glory to God.

Article 3 says that a team's term of service begins when a player assumes the serving position behind the line.

How many will serve God if they are in front singing a solo, or playing the piano, or something where they are in the limelight and receiving the praise of men? How many will still serve God in a back position where no one praises them, such as cleaning toilets, vacuuming the church, washing windows, or helping someone in need?

Article 5 says that a re-serve shall be called when the server releases the ball for service then catches it or drops it to the floor. In other words, if you see your toss is bad, you can let the ball drop and you can re-serve again with another five second limit.

How about in your Christian life? How many of you have dropped the ball? You once served God but you got discouraged, or maybe no one thanked you, or you just quit. Just like the serve in volleyball, you can pick it up and start serving God once again.

Greatest Example of Service

Who was the greatest example of a servant in the Bible? I think it was the Lord Jesus. The word "deacon" means servant. Are the deacons in your church humble servants, or do they consider themselves important people above everyone else? Matthew 20:27 states, "And whosoever will be chief among you, let him be your servant." Galatians 5:13 states, ". . . but by love serve one another."

This following article appeared in Our Daily Bread and is entitled "Love Makes the Difference . . . By Love Serve One Another." I believe it eloquently expresses what love really means.

"The Bible tells us to love our neighbors as ourselves. Often we feel we have fulfilled this command when we help others, even though it is done in a grudging routine manner. But God requires more of us than that! Heartfelt, unstinting zeal must be evident in our efforts. That's why the apostle Paul exhorts us to 'serve one another' with a warm and genuine interest.

"The *Sunday School Times* told of an elderly Christian who was a shut-in. She said, 'I have two daughters who take turns cleaning my small home. Jean comes and makes everything shine. Yet she leaves the impression that I'm an awful burden. But when Mary comes, no matter how dull the day or how low my spirit, she's so cheery that my heart is tuned to singing. Above all, she makes me feel she loves me. They're both good Christians, you understand, but what a difference in their attitudes! Mary has the extra touch of grace that this old world so badly needs. She does everything with a loving heart.'

"Both daughters deserved praise for the care they showed to their invalid mother. But one of them brought much more blessing and consolation. She did her work with compassion – as if she were serving the Savior in person. Her labor will receive abundant reward.

"Let me ask you some questions. How much time do you spend helping others? What is your attitude in performing such duties? Do you aid people grudgingly or with heartfelt devotion that leaves them uplifted and blessed rather than feeling they're a burden? For Jesus' sake, 'serve one another' with love."

O I want to serve like Jesus —
Willingly He came from Heaven above;
On the earth He lived for others,
Spent His life in kindly deeds of love.
– Peterson

Thought for the Day: Live for others if you would live for God.
– Seneca

Chapter 23

How the Christian Life Applies to Spiking

I'm going to take the body parts in what they do in spiking and tie that in with spiritual application.

The Hand

The hand is held in an open position: that is, fingers are spread, not together. If held together there is less control over the spike. Hand is not flat but curved. Contact with ball is made with the heel of the hand at first contact.

Ecclesiastes 9:10 shares, "Whatsoever thy hand findeth to do, do it with thy might." In my years of both playing and coaching volleyball, I've seen many players give a half-hearted effort. If you are going to play volleyball, give it your best effort or don't play at all.

The Fingers

The fingers roll over the top of the ball to create topspin to bring the ball down into the court.

We've all heard the phrase, "He won't lift a finger to help." It is possible that the term had its origin in Luke 11:46 where it says, "Woe unto you also, ye lawyers! for ye lade men with burdens grievous to be borne, and ye yourselves touch not the burdens with one of your fingers."

How many of you are helping someone that has a heavy burden? There are people in your church and school that are carrying these burdens. Seek out those individuals and help them carry the burdens. It will take time and effort, but it will be worth it.

The Wrist

The wrist snaps forward, helping to create more topspin on the ball.

We've all heard the term "weak wrist" or "wimp". Just as the wrist snaps forward in spiking, how many of you are going forward in your Christian life? How many of you are parked in neutral? Or worse yet, how many of you are going in reverse or backsliding? Examine your life and ask yourself, am I closer to the Lord now than I was a year ago, or am I farther away?

The Arms

The arms speak of strength. How many of you have seen your brother in front of a mirror making a muscle? In spiking, the back swing of the arms and the lifting of the non-hitting arm are most important.

When I think of arms and strength, I think of the army and being armed. A policeman is armed with his gun. We are to be armed with the Word of God. Ephesians 6:17 explains, "Take the sword of the Spirit, which is the Word of God." How many of you are going out and sharing the Word of God with the lost of this world?

The Elbow

The elbow must be up. When you drop the elbow, the spike will go into the net.

In the Christian realm we have to keep our spirits up. It is so easy to become discouraged. I had arthritis problems a few years ago, and I was really down. If you're down and discouraged, you can't be a blessing to others because your focus will be on your problem and not on others.

Secondly, the elbow must lead in spiking. Some beginners try to spike with the hands and upper arm leading first and the elbow last. There is no snap and no power.

What leads us as Christians? Psalm 23 says "He leads me." God is the One Who leads – but we must be willing to follow. We should want to please Him and bring glory to Him.

The Position of the Ball

The position of the ball should be forward of the hitting shoulder. You should be able to reach forward to hit the ball. Don't overrun it and let it get even with you or behind you.

Philippians 3:13 ". . . forgetting those things which are behind, and reaching forth unto those things which are before." Forget your past mistakes and don't let those handicap you in your Christian life or on the volleyball court. If you have asked God to forgive you then move on. I've seen players make a mistake on the court and dwell on that mistake and then make more mistakes because they are still focusing on that first mistake. When you make a mistake on the court, quickly analyze what you did wrong and then forget it and concentrate on the next play. We should be looking forward to the coming of the Lord.

The Hips

The hips turn approximately 45 degrees when spiking. We should turn away from our sins. The whole battle in life is whether we try to please God or try to please ourselves. We were put on this earth to please God. Revelation 4:11 says, "Thou art worthy, O Lord, to receive glory and honour and power: for Thou hast created all things, and for Thy pleasure they are and were created."

The Legs

They speak of power. Two major problems in spiking: (a) lack of speed in approach, and (b) lack of knee-bend in jumping.

I heard a testimony of an evangelist named Tim Lee, an ex-marine who lost his legs stepping on a landmine in Vietnam. He said he was running from God, and God had this tragedy happen to get him to stop running. He said he was happier without his legs in the will of God rather than to have his legs and be out of the will of God. We can also remember the story in Genesis 32:25-31 where Jacob wrestled with God and limped from that time on.

Isaiah 47:2-3 states, "Take the millstones and grind meal: uncover thy locks, make bare the leg, uncover the thigh, pass over the rivers . . . thy shame shall be seen." I know that this speaks of the humiliation of Babylon. Girls, the more of your legs you expose, the more you contribute to some guy lusting. I remember years ago going into a bank, and I saw a female teller with a slit skirt and immediately my eyes were drawn to her legs. I had to look away because I didn't want to sin. God's Word says in Matthew 5:28, "But I say unto you, that whosoever looketh on a woman to lust after her hath committed adultery with her already in his heart." Modesty is key.

The Feet

In the four-step approach, the first two steps are on the front or ball of the foot and on the last two steps, the heel lands first.

Do your feet take you to places that cause you to sin? If you are not sure you should go somewhere, give God the benefit of the doubt and don't go. We are commanded to use our feet to go and tell others about Christ. This is not an option, but a command.

The Toes

Toes are little things, but without them you couldn't jump very high.

When I was a young man, there was a basketball player in the Big Ten who was a great scorer named Robin Freeman. He had a lawnmower accident and lost some of his toes. He tried to play after the accident and couldn't do it. Something as little as his toes had stopped him.

How about little sins in our lives? Are they really little to God? Toes are sort of ugly. Sometimes you girls polish your nails to cover them and make them look better. You can't cover up those sins without them coming up again. Remember the example of David – how he thought his sin was hid until II Samuel 12:7, "And Nathan said to David, thou art the man . . ."

I had a player years ago when I had three teams, Junior High, Junior Varsity and Varsity, working at the same time. While we were doing our exercises, I noticed she wasn't there. I found her in the hallway with the explanation that her mother was about to pick her up. I didn't make a big deal about it. A short time later at one of our practices she wasn't there again. This time I found her hiding in a stairwell because she didn't feel like doing the exercises. Needless to say, this girl never contributed to our team. She would always sit next to me on the bench and ask if she was going to play, and I would say "No, you don't really care about the game by your example." Number 32:23 explains, "be sure your sin will find you out."

The Challenge

I'd like to challenge you. Examine your life and make sure some little sin is not holding back God's blessing from you. If there is a sin, confess it and forsake it.

If you take all of these principles to heart, then your life will be blessed. Maybe they will make a difference the next time you go to spike a volleyball!

Chapter 24

Confidence

When you think about it, what can you really put your confidence in?

How about the government?

We have come through some prosperous times, but how many of you or your parents wonder if social security money will be there when they retire? I saw a bumper sticker which read "I love my country; it's the government I don't trust!" The lies come from everywhere, including the President and all the way down the line. One of the news programs on TV in Chicago has a section called "The Fleecing of America", in which they go into the details of how millions and millions of tax dollars are wasted on frivolous things.

How about education?

I read that over half of the Chicago public school eighth graders failed the test to get into high school. The reason, I believe, that public education fails is because they took God out of the schools. Prayer and the Ten Commandments were thrown out because they said it was a conflict of separation of church and state. They forgot that this country was founded on God and biblical principles.

How about religion?

Religion sends more people to hell with so-called "clergy" denying the teaching of God's Word and not telling people how to get saved. Jesus spoke about religion negatively.

How about business?

What about the gouging of oil companies, chemical companies, gas companies, and pharmaceutical companies? I have an article in my files about legal drug prices. In the United States, a tube of Retin-A costs $80 while in Mexico the same product costs $13; prescription Zantac is $60 in the United States and $22 in Mexico; and Prozac is $300 in the United States and $65 in Mexico. Recently Congress almost passed a bill to allow wholesalers to re-import prescription drugs, but the bill was killed. The Speaker of the House said that if it had passed, it would have dropped prescription drug costs by 30% to 50%.

I watch gasoline prices closely. Why do they go up 10-15 cents a gallon but only go down a few pennies at a time? How about the oil companies that spill thousands and thousands of gallons of oil in accidents and say it is really nothing to worry about? What really makes me want to vomit is the commercial on TV about what good the tobacco companies are doing to help people by pouring millions and millions of dollars into good causes – but they still manufacture a product that kills people! Another good one is the TV advertisement for antacid. Just pop those pills in your mouth and everything will be fine. Why not tell the people to avoid the food that causes the problem and they won't need the antacid pills?

How about man?

If you trust them, they will fail you because they are sinners. An example of this is the divorce rate which is soaring even among saved people. They took a pledge "till death do us part". That was a trust.

How about wealth?

You could lose all your money in a minute. When the depression hit, people lost fortunes and jumped out of windows or shot themselves. You might say, "Now we have the F.D.I.C. – it's federally insured and nothing could go wrong." If it all collapses, that guarantee means nothing.

How about youth?

More young people die and are sick than ever before. I've been teaching for 40 years and I've never had so many young people with sickness problems – asthma, allergies, hemophilia, and other diseases with hard-to-pronounce names. It wasn't like that years ago.
What then can you really have trust in?

God's Love.

Think about this – nothing you can ever do can stop God from loving you. No matter what sin you have committed, God still loves you.

The Word of God.

Romans 10:13 says, "Whosoever shall call upon the name of the Lord shall be saved." If you call upon Him, you will be saved. Do you remember what it was like when you were a kid and someone gave you something and then later took it back? Aren't you glad God isn't like that? When He gives us eternal life, it is forever.

First Thessalonians 5:24 states, "Faithful is he that calleth you who also will do it." Whatever God called you to do, He will give you the ability to do it. Some time ago I was asked by the pastor to teach a 13-week Sunday school class to adults. I was extremely nervous. I have worked with young people all my life, not adults. I thought there is no way that I can do it, but then I realized I couldn't do it—but He could. He did do it and He received the glory, not me.

Some of you want to go to a Christian college, but you don't have the money. If God calls you to go to college, He will provide. But you can't just sit there. You have to do your part.

Let's tie all of this in with volleyball. The more you do something over and over and over again, the better you get. The better you get, the more confident you become. Let me share a personal experience. When I was a volleyball player, we were going to be playing in a national A.A.U. tournament in Elkhart, Indiana. Some months before that tournament, I spent about 15-20 minutes of my lunch hour everyday working on my ball skills. My confidence level was so high that I played my very best at that tournament and our team finished second in the national A.A.U.

Galatians 6:7 states, "Be not deceived God is not mocked; for whatsoever a man soweth, that shall he also reap." How many of you say you're really working hard at volleyball. Are you really?

Jeremiah 17:9 says, "The heart is deceitful above all things and desperately wicked: who can know it?" Sometimes we deceive ourselves. If you had told me when I was a player that I could have worked harder, I would have said you were crazy. Now, years later looking back, I realize that I could have worked harder.

You have to have confidence in your teammates. Spikers must have confidence in their setters and vice versa. When I was in college and later in open ball, I had a teammate who would call a special play and it worked every time. It was a short set just above my head. The confidence level between the two of us was so great that it was always successful. In another tournament, a spiker and I had an automatic shoot set every play when the pass was good to me. It worked every single time. Again, the confidence level was the reason for the success. You must have confidence that you can do something or else you will fail. You should also have confidence in your coach – that he or she wants the best for you and for your team.

Be Confident but Watch Out!

There is one thing you must guard against and that is overconfidence. I had a friend that was a champion table tennis player. He had an 18-2 lead in a game. He got overconfident and let the other player get a few easy points and, before he realized it, he lost the momentum and eventually lost the game.

Here is something I came across called, "A Creed to Live By". I did research about the author of this piece and found it either to be by a lady named Nancy Sims or the CEO of Coke, Brian Dyson.

If you take these words to heart, then you will have confidence in your God-given abilities to play ball and honor Him through your life.

Don't undermine your worth by comparing yourself with others.

It is because we are different that each of us is special.

Don't set your goals by what other people deem important.

Only you know what is best for you.

Don't take for granted the things closest to your heart.

Cling to them as they would your life, for without them,

life is meaningless.

Don't let your life slip through your fingers

by living in the past or for the future.

By living your life one day at a time, you live all the days of your life.

Don't give up when you still have something to give.

Nothing is really over until the moment you stop trying.

Don't be afraid to admit that you are less than perfect.

It is this fragile thread that binds us each together.

Don't be afraid to encounter risks.

It is by taking chances that we learn how to be brave.

Don't shut love out of your life by saying it's impossible to find time.

The quickest way to receive love is to give;

the fastest way to lose love is to hold it too tightly;

and the best way to keep love is to give it wings.

Don't run through life so fast that you forget not only where you've been, but also where you are going.

Don't forget, a person's greatest emotional need is to feel appreciated.

Don't be afraid to learn. Knowledge is weightless,

A treasure you can always carry easily.

Don't use time or words carelessly. Neither can be retrieved.

Life is not a race, but a journey to be savored each step of the way.

Yesterday is History, Tomorrow is a Mystery and Today is a Gift:

That's why we call it The Present.

Chapter 25

Thoughts, Words, and Deeds

The following is a quotation from Phillip's book on Genesis.

"God's judgment is not arbitrary. Records are kept, not because he needs them, but so that those about to be condemned might face the record of their own actions and words. There is not an incident, however small, however seemingly insignificant, in all the long history of mankind's tenure on this planet that has escaped the all-seeing eye of God. It is all written down.

"Historians often miss significant facts or deliberately or unwittingly distort the facts. God misses nothing. The crime against humanity and the highhanded sins against God of which all this world's Alexanders and Caesars, Genghis Khans and Napoleans, Hitlers and Stalins, are guilty, are all part of the record. The miscarriage of justice by every unscrupulous magistrate, the untold sufferings caused by crime lords, dope kings, vice peddlers – all are written down. And the books are to be opened. Their records are detailed and complete; the places where, the time when, the manner how, the motives for, the consequences of. The books contain it all. Every thought, word, and deed of every man, woman, boy, and girl – and all written down."[4]

Your Thoughts

Everything starts with the thought life. People just don't sin or do evil deeds. They think about themselves first. There have been many school shootings, but the one in Colorado we remember best. Those two students just didn't wake up that morning and say, I think we'll go to school today and kill as many people as we can.

They thought about it for a long time and planned it, and then they did it. Someone has said that what the hand does is because of what the heart thought. Jesus said, out of the heart proceeds evil thoughts. Jeremiah 17:9 explains, "The heart is deceitful above all things, and desperately wicked: who can know it?"

A few years back, I was talking with a close friend in the hallway just outside our gym. He was saying that he had to guard himself because his heart was deceitful. God spoke to my heart at that time and said, "Don, your heart is deceitful also." I think I always knew that, but this time I really knew it more certainly.

Someone has said you become what you think about. If you think something is possible, it may well be but if you think something is impossible, it definitely will be impossible. One of the biggest mistakes you can make in sports is to underestimate your opponent. I remember playing in a county softball tournament where the semi-final games were played in the morning, and the winners of the semi-finals would meet that evening for the championship. We were so confident that we would beat the team that some of our best players weren't there. But they were going to be there for the final game that evening. Needless to say, we lost the game 2-1 and had to play for third place instead of the championship.

Another example was when I was coaching volleyball at Oak Forest Christian. We were playing Calumet Baptist from Indiana in our tournament. It was a double elimination tournament, and we beat them fairly easily in the first game. In the second game, I took out two regulars and put two substitutes in. We played poorly and fell behind. I remember one of our seniors foot-faulting on the serve. I put the two regulars back in but we couldn't come back and we lost the second game. I started the regular line-up in game three, but we did not play well and lost the game and the match. We did come back through the losers' bracket to beat them four straight games to win the tournament, but the loss cost us an undefeated season.

Another mistake is to think the team you are going to play is far better than your team, and you think you can't beat them. If you think that way, you will lose. The strange thing is, I've coached teams that were better than the opponent and yet we lost. On the other hand, I've coached teams that were not as good as the opponent and yet we won. How do you explain that? I think a lot has to do with the mind and what people think. You watch the other team and the mind says, they are so tall, they spike so hard, they jump so high, they pick up everything. Those thoughts affect your play negatively. There were times when I was a player when I thought that there was no way that I could reach that ball, but I always gave total effort and sometimes I forced myself and saved some balls that I thought I couldn't. The right way to think is, "I can play or reach any ball, and nothing is out of my range."

Your Words

I have a card on the board above my desk that reads "Psalm 141:3 Set a watch, O Lord, before my mouth; keep the door of my lips." Some fancy places have people called bouncers. They keep people out that shouldn't be let in and let others in that should be in. God should be like that bouncer: not letting things come out of our mouths that shouldn't and letting only the good things out. Words can cause great pain. Someone has said that I would rather that person had hit me than said what they did.

There are two categories here: intentional and unintentional. You may have said something or someone has said something to you and you know it was intentional and meant to hurt. But I think most of the time it's done unintentionally without thinking.

An evangelist came to our church and told the story about a rebellious teenage girl who told her mother that she hated her and wished she was dead. A few weeks later she got her wish – her mother was killed in an accident. He said that it took three grown men to pull the girl from her mother's casket with her sobbing, "Mother, I didn't mean it." She has to live with that for the rest of her life. I sat as a deacon in a pastor's office for a meeting where there were two businessmen from our church. One man had been dishonest and had defrauded the other man out of a huge sum of money. The man who committed the offense said that he was sorry. The man who was defrauded said that being sorry was not enough and that the man had to make restitution. That was years ago, and to this day the man has never made any attempt to repay. The person offended became bitter and left the church and now doesn't go to church and doesn't serve God.

Words mean nothing if your actions do not back them up. I've had girls tell me they were going to work hard over the summer to become much better players and have a much better team. My pet saying I've used over the years is, "Don't tell me, show me."

Your Deeds

At times I have heard people say "I don't want to do this task." "I don't like it." "It may be time consuming." "It may be difficult." I've always answered, "There are a lot of things I don't want to do, but I do them anyway. Why? Because it's the right thing to do." First Corinthians 10:31 states, "Whether therefore ye eat, or drink, or whatsoever ye do, do all to the glory of God." Colossians 3:23 shares, "And whatsoever ye do, do it heartily, as to the Lord, and not unto men."

Ecclesiastes 9:10 says, "Whatsoever thy hand findeth to do, do it with thy might." We should examine our actions: What we do, how we do it, when we do it, and most importantly why we do it.

Remember every thought, word, and deed of every man, woman, boy, and girl are written down.

Chapter 26

How to enjoy volleyball and your Christian life more

Who enjoys the game of volleyball the most? The highest skilled people do. How did those people get to be so good? Some are born with a greater amount of natural talent or ability and so it doesn't seem to take as much work for them to get to the top of their game. However, many of the players I've coached through the years would not be in the category of having much natural ability. Some people might have even called these players "klutzy" without the ability to perform even the most rudimentary skill. Yet, these players have often turned out to be the very best. What they lacked in ability, they made up for in desire. They ran those extra laps and practiced faithfully on their own. Those players end up enjoying the game of volleyball the most.

Volleyball works like a circle. As you work hard at the skills and drills, you get better at it. The better you get at it, the more you like it. The more you like it, the harder you work. The circle continues until you decide to stop it by not working harder.

When I was a player, when we were playing well, it was really fun. But when we started to play poorly it wasn't. When we didn't play up to our normal standard, it was usually because of several reasons.

Rest

While coaching a junior high match at a nearby town one year, my best spiker had a terrible match. We lost and I knew that if she had played up to her potential we would have won. Later, I talked to her parents. They told me she had stayed up very late the night before doing a school assignment. While I'm not saying that sometimes your players won't have to stay up late completing assignments, there is no question that staying up late will affect your performance negatively. Sometimes the reasons for staying up late aren't quite so reasonable. Perhaps your team has a slumber party before a big game or tournament and stay up late talking. Maybe a good book keeps a player awake. Whatever the case, a player won't be able to show the same effort tired as when she isn't. You will enjoy the game more and play better too if you get the proper rest.

Now to take the concept to the Christian life, it is not only important in volleyball to get enough rest. I believe some people actually run themselves down and get sick because they don't rest.

Years ago, my wife taught in a Christian school. She worked with first graders. She began the day with the children early in the morning, ate lunch with them and taught them all day with no breaks. Expected to go on church visitation and teach Sunday school, she had many other responsibilities which together affected her health negatively.

God designed us so we need rest. Didn't Jesus say, "Come apart and rest for awhile"? If you don't come apart from your responsibilities at times and rest, you'll fall apart.

Proper Physical Condition

The majority of players at the high school level are not in good enough shape. Maybe you are okay in short games, but in longer games and matches your skill level decreases as you play. If you are in good physical condition, the skill level stays up longer and you have a greater chance for success.

Michael Jordan said, "I approached practice the same way I approached games. You can't turn it on and off like a faucet. I couldn't dog it in practice and then when I needed that extra push late in the game, expect it to be there. But that's how a lot of people approach things, and that's why a lot of people fail."

In the Christian life, you must have the proper spiritual conditioning. You must read your Bible daily if you expect to be a mighty witness for Christ. You must cultivate a strong prayer life if you expect answers to your prayers. If you neglect spiritual conditioning, you will not be a strong believer.

Diligent Practice

When you practice with your team, don't waste time with poor effort. I had a close friend when I was a boy, and we grew up at a playground in Chicago. Mike and I spent hours and hours practicing for sports contests. He was a super athlete. Recently I got a letter from him. He's living in Florida now. He mentioned in the letter that he and I had some great successes, and that the practices at the playground were really challenging. I thought about what he said, but I didn't consider what we were doing as practices because we had so much fun pushing ourselves to the limit.

How many of you have the attitude "Oh boy, we get to go to volleyball practice!" Or do you have the attitude "We have to go to volleyball practice again."? The secret in life is to thoroughly enjoy what you're doing while you are doing it. Don't let the enjoyment of the game of life be spoiled by looking ahead to the next game, high school graduation, college graduation, marriage, kids, home, car, etc. Enjoy the present.

God's time frame is always now. No one is guaranteed tomorrow. Second Corinthians 6:2 explains, ". . . now is the accepted time. Behold now is the day of salvation." Satan's time is always later. He will tell you that you can live your Christian life tomorrow. Enjoy your salvation right now. Don't forget to let its perfect joy transform your life.

Your major questions should not be "Why?" as in, "Why do I have to wear certain clothes?", "Why can't I listen to pop music?", "Why can't I go to certain places?", "Why do I have to follow all those rules?" Instead of the "Why?" questions, the question should be "What?" as in "What can I do to please God more?"

Here are some practical things to prepare you for volleyball.

- Focus—don't let your mind wander.
- Listen—and keep eye contact with coach.
- Act—don't react. Get to the proper place on the court so you can act.
- Drink plenty of water all day, not just when you are thirsty.
- Eliminate soda pop.
- Have the mind set that every ball is playable – "I can get any ball."
- Improve eating habits. Stay away from fried foods; eat more fruits and vegetables. Avoid partially-hydrogenated products.
- Be an encourager to your team – "What can I do to help?"
- In all situations, think positive thoughts – "I can do this", not "I can't do this."
- Be persistent - keep at it, don't quit. Remember Michael Jordan was cut from his high school basketball team. He didn't quit - he worked harder. The rest is history.
- Give God the glory for all that you achieve (First Corinthians 10:31).

When you apply these principles to your life, you will enjoy volleyball and the Christian life more.

Chapter 27

Thankfulness

Raise your hand if you thanked God for something today. Now raise your hand if you thanked someone else for something today. Usually more hands are raised on the first point than the second. As Christians, we should show our gratitude by saying thank you to others as well as to God.

A little more than a year ago, I began to think about ways in which I could become a more thankful person.

Remembering Past Influences

I received an invitation last summer to a special dinner honoring our 1960 National Collegiate Volleyball Championship Team into the University's Athletic Hall of Fame. I enjoyed reminiscing with those team members who were able to come. They hadn't been able to locate our coach, and after 40 years, I wondered if he was still living. I spoke for a few minutes to the large audience composed of many teams being honored from other eras. I said I was thankful to the University for the honor and wished that I had the opportunity to thank our coach. I encouraged them to become more thankful in the future.

When I returned home, I asked someone with a computer to check and find our coach, Marvin D. Veronee. The information came back that he lived near Charleston, South Carolina. On a Sunday afternoon I called and asked if this was the Marv Veronee who coached volleyball at George Williams College in the 1960s. Sure enough, it was. We had a wonderful time of fellowship on the phone. We relived so many fun times. Towards the end of our conversation, I told Marv that one of the reasons I had called was to thank him for what he had done for me and for the team. He responded by saying that my thanks meant a lot to him because he knew it came from my heart.

This summer I needed some books on past performances at national tournaments for research for this book. I stopped in Des Plaines, Illinois, to pick them up from a man named Dick Caplan.

Dick is 88 years old and is in the Volleyball Hall of Fame. Manager and coach of our open volleyball team after college, Dick was valuable to our team. I got the chance to personally thank him for all he did. I was thankful I was able to thank him for what he had done for me.

My wife likes to shop a lot; so I spend a lot of time in and out of stores because she doesn't drive. Many times I'll open doors for other ladies to walk through and some will say thank you. Others will walk by and say nothing. I'll softly and quietly say "you're welcome".

I marvel when I read the account in Luke 17 concerning the ten lepers. Leprosy was a terrible disease like cancer is in our day. Jesus healed ten lepers, and only one was thankful. Could you imagine being healed from cancer and not thanking the Lord? How ungrateful!

Wholly Thankful

I don't think we are partially thankful. We are either thankful or unthankful. Thankfulness must come from the heart. We tell kids, "Johnny, say thank you" and he does, but does he really mean it? Don't get me wrong, we should train children to be thankful; but are we training them just to recite meaningless words?

I'm thankful that God gives more than one chance to be saved. When I was in my teens, we were competing in a city horseshoe championship in Lincoln Park in Chicago. While walking through the park, a lady stopped me. I think she was from the Moody Bible Institute. She witnessed to me and at the time I didn't know what she was doing. I was trusting in my church and my good works to get me to heaven. I rejected what she said. I'm so thankful that God didn't say, "That's it, Don, you're now doomed for hell. There are no more chances for you." God gave me the chance later in life to receive His Son as my personal Savior and I did.

Testimony of Thankfulness

Some thank you's bring tears. During one high school graduation ceremony I was setting up extra chairs for late comers when one of my players gave a testimony. From a broken home, she lived with her physically handicapped mom. She didn't have much of the world's possessions, but she had a sweet Christian spirit and a wonderful testimony. She started out by saying that she wanted to thank someone who had been like a father to her. She started to say nice things about me. I started to cry because I was so moved. This same girl graduated from college and became a volleyball coach at a Christian school. She brought her team to one of our tournaments. After the tournament, her husband, now a pastor in Minnesota, talked to me and thanked me for the tremendous influence I had been in his wife's life. I felt so thankful for his kind comments.

A young man who officiated our volleyball tournaments for many years eventually married one of my players. I was accused of being a matchmaker. At their wedding service, they came to each pew and greeted the guests. They came to our pew and he looked me in the eye and said, "Thank you, thank you, thank you."

I answered that "if you can thank me twenty years from now, it will be even more special."

My mom and dad are both gone now. My sister was digging through my mom's possessions after she passed away and came across a letter that she returned to me. It's dated February 8, 1980.

Dear Mom and Dad,
    I was thinking in church tonight while our pastor was preaching, and I realized that I had never really thanked both of you for all the things that you've done for me throughout

my life. Some of these are respect for authority, kindness, paying all the money to put me through school—buying me cars, clothes, food, etc. - for taking care of me when I was sick - for putting up with me when I was wrong - for loving me - for providing a home for me. I just wanted to write this note and say thank you and to tell you that I love you both!
Your son,
Don

I'm so thankful that I was able to tell them while they were still alive.

While I was growing up in Chicago, a playground teacher named Mr. Kipp greatly influenced my life. Without his gentle prodding I never would have gone to college. I never would have taught for 40 years, coached volleyball for over 27 years, or worked in so many camps and clinics over the years. He died about a month before I graduated from college. I owe him so much.

As the years went by, I often wondered if he was saved or not. Just this summer, I was cleaning out our garage and came across some old letters that I didn't remember having. I found something that I thanked God for. It's dated May 26, 1960.

Dear Donald,

We acknowledge with grateful appreciation your contribution given in memory of Mr. Lammon Kipp. We have placed this money in our general memorial fund and it will remain there until Mrs. Kipp designates what she would like done with it. On behalf of Mrs. Kipp and the church, I extend our sincere appreciation for this gift. May God richly bless you for your thoughtfulness at this time.

William Meyers,
Pastor of the Irving Park Baptist Church

I know that not everyone that goes to a Baptist church is saved, but the chances of him being in heaven have greatly increased. I was so excited when I read that letter. If he's in heaven when I get there, I want to give him a bear hug and tell him I love him and thank him for all he did for me.

Thankful for Much

We should thank God for what He's done in the past and what He will do in the future. We should thank Him for forgiveness - when we sin and then ask His forgiveness. I'm thankful for the Biblical example we have to pattern our lives after. My two favorites are Joseph and Daniel. What tremendous character they had!

I'm thankful for close friends. I have four very special friends, Larry, Wally, Nick, and Max. You should thank God for your special friends. I'm thankful for the girls He's allowed me to coach over these many years. Many have written testimonies back to me thanking me. I've shared many of those testimonies in Part 5 of this book.

I'd like to share three verses on this subject: Ephesians 5:20 says, "Giving thanks always." The first part of Philippians 4:6 says, "In everything by prayer and supplication with thanksgiving let your requests be made known unto God." Lastly, Colossians 3:15 says, "And let the peace of God rule in your hearts to the which also ye are called in one body, and be ye thankful."

Jesus is the ultimate example of thankfulness. When He was here on earth, He always thanked His Heavenly Father. We should do the same and more. We should thank others also. You should thank Him for your health and strength that enables you the opportunity to play volleyball.

Thanksgiving Every Day

The third Thursday in November we celebrate Thanksgiving Day, yet often the remaining 364 days we put no emphasis on Thanksgiving. I think it should be the other way around. We should celebrate Thanksgiving all the days of the years, not just one.

I encourage you to take Thanksgiving one step further - write a note to someone. Besides saying thank you, it is an even greater encouragement when someone takes the time to write it down.

Lastly, when someone corrects you in volleyball or in your Christian walk, don't get angry at them, but thank them for their concern.

I pray that those words will always stay with you. "Be ye thankful."

Chapter 28

Love

If I asked those of you who loved the Lord to raise your hands, how many hands would be raised? Some people love money, power, pleasure, sports, cars, homes, music, and food. If you are around me for any length of time, you will know that I really love the game of volleyball. I must make sure that loving volleyball isn't more important than loving God.

One of my players was looking for a club team to play for. Her mother related this story. She talked to one man who was in charge of a club team. He listened to her as she told him that her daughter would have to miss any games on Sunday morning because she would be going to church. He couldn't quite understand this and actually said, "I guess then volleyball is my god." It's probably easy for a lost person to say this, but I wonder how many Christians do love volleyball more than God.

When the Chicago Bulls were winning NBA championships, a lot of their playoff games were on Wednesdays and Sundays. It seemed to me that the attendance at church during those times was less than usual. Could some people have loved the Bulls or basketball more than God? How much do you love the Lord?

Deuteronomy 11:14 shares to "love the Lord your God with all your heart and with all your soul." Matthew 22:37 explains, "Jesus said unto him, thou shalt love the Lord thy God with all thy heart, soul, and mind."

Mark 12:30 says, "And thou shall love the Lord with all thy heart, soul, mind, and strength." These verses start out with the same two parts, the heart and soul. Then mind and strength.

Loving With Strength

Strength infers action or doing something. John 15:13 says, "Greater love hath no man than this: that a man lay down his life for his friends." There is a huge water filtration plant in Chicago named after Milton Olive, a soldier who was in a fox hole with other soldiers. The enemy threw in a hand grenade, and Milton Olive fell on the grenade with his body and shielded the other soldiers. He was killed and the other soldiers were spared. This is a supreme example of love, and this leads me to think about the Lord Jesus and how He could love us so much that He would willingly lay down His life for me and for you.

John 14:15 says, "Jesus said, 'If ye love me, keep my commandments'." If we say we love Him and keep breaking His commandments, we have to wonder if we really love Him or not.

Love Is Honor

Exodus 20:12 says, "Honor thy father and mother: That thy days may be long upon the land which the Lord thy God giveth thee." How many Christian young people obey their moms and dads but do not honor them? What is your attitude when you obey? Is your action done immediately and not grudgingly? The sitcoms on television are such a bad influence with kids smarting off to their parents. Maybe some of you need to write a note to your parents thanking them for what they have done for you. As I mentioned before, I am so thankful I was able to do that with my parents before they died. Maybe some of you need to write that kind of note, or better yet, tell them in person. I know that they would be thrilled to hear that. What a great way to honor your parents.

If we say we love the Lord, and then consider how much time do we spend watching television versus how much time reading our Bibles?

The Lord Jesus is the greatest example of love in the Bible. It wasn't the Roman soldiers that put Him on that cross; it was my sins and yours.

John 15:17 says, "These things I command you that ye love one another." I think our churches and schools are lacking in love. It's easy to love someone that thinks like you, dresses like you, has the same interests as you and loves you. But what about the others? The hardest thing is to love the unlovely – someone who doesn't show love to you, someone who doesn't have nice clothes, someone who doesn't have a good attitude. Do you immediately stick to your own clique and exclude and ignore that person? Jesus would have time for that man or woman, boy or girl.

Proverbs 17:17 states, "A friend loveth at all times." First Corinthians 13 says, "Love never seeks its own . . ." – it's always doing something for others. John 14:21 says, "He that hath my commandments and keepeth them, he it is that loved me."

Love is Being Separated from the World

I John 2:15 tells us, "Love not the world, neither the things that are in the world. If any man love the world, the love of the Father is not in him." We are to be separated from the world and not act, dress, and talk just like the world. People should be able to see we are different. If you love God, you'll want to please Him. One way is to live a holy life and be a good testimony for God.

You should show love to your teammates and coach. You shouldn't give half-hearted efforts, goof off and not be serious during practice, be late or miss practices unnecessarily, nor backbite and gossip. One of the great ways to show love is to be faithful.

People like Joseph and David were faithful in small jobs, and God gave them bigger things to do. Being faithful in little things like volleyball will help you be faithful in bigger things. Our goal is to some day stand before God and hear Him say, "Well done, thou good and faithful servant." I worked in a public elementary school, and on the wall of the gym was a big banner which read "Love Can Change the World". As Christians, we know His love did change the world. Go back to your schools and show love. It will make your school a special place.

Chapter 29

Team

A team is a group of people working together for a common goal. Our major goal should be First Corinthians 10:31: (a) to glorify God, and (b) to try to achieve victory. The dictionary defines a team player as one who subordinates personal aspirations and works in a coordinated effort with other members of a group in striving for a common goal. The word subordinate means: (1) under the power or authority of another; (2) inferior to or placed below another in importance. This goes contrary to our sinful nature of "Me First" and "I'm the most important one."

When you were born, you were placed under the authority of your parents. Ephesians 6:1-3 tells us, "Children, obey your parents in the Lord, for this is right. Honor thy father and mother which is the first commandment with promise: that it may be well with thee, and thou mayest live long on the earth." This is a clear command from God. When you were saved, you were placed under the authority of God. We have a different standard than the unsaved.

Not Your Own

First Corinthians 6: 19-20 says, "What? Know you not that your body is the temple of the Holy Ghost which is in you, which ye have of God and ye are not your own? For ye are bought with a price; therefore glorify God in your body and in your spirit which are God's."

When you became a student at your Christian school, you were placed under the authority of the leaders of that school. When you became a member of your volleyball team, you were placed under the authority of your coach. Hebrews 13: 17 states, "Obey them that have the rule over you . . ."

You became a part of that team, a valuable part, but not the most important part. Since you become part of a team, you must sacrifice some of your individuality. You really give up a part of yourself. Team becomes more important than you or your desires. Your thinking should be, "What can I do to make this team a success?" Maybe this means playing a position you would not prefer or maybe sitting on the bench some or maybe a lot of the time. The true team player not only does what the coach asks but goes beyond that. When a coach gets a group of players with this kind of attitude, they have something special together. It's a real joy to be a part of that kind of team.

The Righteous Life

When you become a Christian, God desires you to live a righteous life - doing the right thing. Remember, right is right even if no one is doing it, and wrong is still wrong even if everyone is doing it. I was listening to the radio just this past week, and a person said that her father gave her the same advice.

Coach Vince Lombardi of the champion Green Bay Packers of the 1960s said that you don't do the right thing some of the time, but you do the right thing all the time. In your volleyball practices, work hard all the time, not just when you feel like it. Practice hard all the time because it is the right thing to do.

Will your team be a success this season or not? You could be undefeated this year and win the state championship and still be a failure in God's eyes. It is possible to lose many games and not win the state championship and still be a success in God's eyes. I'm firmly convinced that the success or failure of your team this season is determined by only two things: (1) how much you love God and want to please Him; and (2) how much are you willing to sacrifice to be the player you should be.

In the early 1990s, our major opponent was a small school from southern Illinois named Arthur Mennonite. When our two teams played, they were classic battles. Sometimes we won, and sometimes they won. One game stands out in my mind. We hosted a winter tournament in 1992 called the Icicle Invitational. We played Arthur in the finals. It was a best of five match. They beat us in the first game and again in the second game. The third game they had us match point, and we fought back and won the serve. They had us the second match point, and we fought back and won the serve. They had us match point for the third time, and again we fought back and won the serve. We eventually won the third game. Then, we won the fourth and fifth games to win the match. It was the greatest comeback I had ever seen as a player, coach, or spectator.

The first contact with Arthur was when Julie Scudder Dearyan, the coach of Quentin Road's team, suggested I invite them to our tournament. After watching them for the first time, I thought they were an average team. They came back the next year and they had improved greatly. By the third year, they were outstanding. I had never seen a team improve at such a rapid pace. I was talking to their coach, Mrs. Yoder, and I asked her what she did with her girls for conditioning. She said she did nothing. The girls did it all on their own. I was really envious because getting my girls to work on conditioning was one of the most difficult things about coaching. Here her girls did it all on their own. Another time I was talking to her, I told her that we had 16 teams at this tournament and I bet there were probably 10-12 girls who were doing all they could to be the best players they could be. She said, "I've got five of them." Again, I was envious. How could she have so many dedicated players? I talked to a lady in our church that was from a Mennonite background. She told me that the Mennonite children are taught from a very young age to be hard workers. That made a lot of sense. No team could have improved as fast and achieved what they did without dedicated, hard workers.

Practical Pointers

A few things you can do to have a better team this year:

1. Start praying for your teammates and coach every day.

It's hard to have bad feelings toward someone when you are praying for them. The Holy Spirit will bring conviction and cause you to make any wrongs right.

2. Be a real encourager to your teammates.

It might be a kind word, a smile, or a short note. Make your teammates feel that they are important to you and the team. Years and years ago someone suggested praying for our players. I took the suggestion, and I pray by name every day for the players I have coached - not only the current ones but those from the past. I was walking in a mall recently and I heard someone say, "Coach Casey". It was one of my players that I hadn't seen in many years. We talked for a few minutes, and it was time to go. I told her that I'd been praying for her every day. She got teary-eyed and gave me a hug as we said goodbye. I pray that that was an encouragement for her - to know that someone cares enough about her to pray for her everyday. Another player told me that her mom and dad don't even pray for her every day.

I am thrilled that some players have chosen to do the same for me. It is an encouragement to me. The Bible says that fervent, effectual prayer availeth much.

3. Make sure that you are in the right relationship with God and with your teammates.

A classic example occurred one struggling season. I wasn't sure where the problem was. One of my girls called me at home and told me that we had a problem. She had been talking to a girl on another team and this girl asked her if all of our players were saved or not. I thought, "Oh no, our testimony must really be bad." We had a tournament the following Saturday so when the girls came to practice, I sat them down and said that there must be some unconfessed sin on our team that is holding back God's blessing. I told them to go into the locker room, talk to one another, share their feelings, and when they felt things were resolved to come on out. I took the young JV girls and started working with them, fully expecting any minute the varsity team would come out of the locker room. Time passed and no one came out. It must have been about an hour and a half before that door opened and the girls came out. I could see the mascara had been running because of shed tears. That Saturday we were a different team, and we won the tournament even though the team we beat in the finals was the better team. I believe the girls got things right with each other and with God and then He blessed us. The really neat thing about this is that the girls got to see and understand that for themselves.

Remember, to make it in the Christian life and on the volleyball court, the team must always come before you.

Chapter 30

Obedience

In 1 Samuel 15:3, God told Saul, through Samuel, "Now go and smite Amalek, and utterly destroy all that they have, and spare them not; but slay both man and woman, infant and suckling, ox and sheep, camel and ass." This was a clear command to follow. Starting in verse seven, we see how Saul responded to that order, "And Saul smote the Amalekites from Havilah until thou comest to Shur….. And he took Agag this King of the Amalekites alive, and utterly destroyed all the people with the edge of the sword. But Saul and the people spared Agag, and the best of the sheep, and of the oxen, and of the fatlings, and the lambs, and all that was good, and would not utterly destroy them: but everything that was vile and refuse, that they destroyed utterly."

In verse 13, the Bible says, "And Samuel came to Saul: and Saul said unto him, Blessed be thou of the Lord: I have performed the commandment of the Lord." What a big fat lie! Samuel responded by saying, "What meaneth this bleating of the sheep in mine ears." In verse 20, Saul lies a second time by saying, "And Saul said unto Samuel, 'Yea, I have obeyed the voice of the Lord, and have gone the way which the Lord sent me, and have brought Agag the King of Amalek, and have utterly destroyed the Amalekites'." In verse 23, it states that "the Lord...hath... rejected thee from being king." Saul lost the privilege of being king because of his disobedience.

Partial Obedience is Not Obedience

Obedience must be total. There is no such thing as part obedience or some obedience. Anything less than total obedience is disobedience.

Do you remember what God told Moses in Numbers 20? God told him to speak to the rock. What did he do? He struck the rock. There was a punishment for his disobedience. He could not enter into the Promised Land. Do you remember Lot's wife in Genesis 19? She was told not to look back. There was a punishment for her disobedience. She turned into a pillar of salt. Do you remember Jonah in Jonah 1? He was told to go to Nineveh and preach. He tried to go to Tarshish away from the presence of the Lord. He spent three days and three nights in the belly of a fish. Do you remember what happened to rebellious and disobedient children in Deuteronomy 21? The men of the city stoned them with stones. Do you remember Achan in Joshua 7? In chapter 6 they were warned not to take of the accursed thing. Achan took the gold, silver and the garment. Thirty-six men died in the battle of Ai, and Achan, his sons and daughter, and cattle were stoned and burned with fire. Do you remember Adam and Eve in Genesis 2 and 3? They were told not to eat of the tree. The punishment for their sin was "pain and sorrow in childbirth and the husband ruling over thee" for the woman and the "ground cursed, brining thorns and thistles in the sweat of thy face shall thou eat bread" for the man.

Practical Examples of Disobedience

I once had a player transfer to our school as a senior. She made a statement to one of our girls that she wasn't going to buy another wardrobe to meet our school's standards. My wife heard another player speak to her mother and say in a rebellious tone, "I am going to that party." She showed great disrespect for her mom. Our school dress code was culottes to the knee. Your standard may be shorts to a certain length. You might think what's the big deal if my short or culotte is one inch, two inches, or three inches above the knee? Your parents might not have a certain standard, or even your church. The big deal is the principle of obedience. If it is partial obedience, it is not obedience.

Obedience always brings blessings, and disobedience always brings punishment. Mark it down: if you have trouble with obeying your parents, pastors, teachers and coaches, you will have trouble in your marriage in being submissive to your husband. The Bible teaches that we are to obey those that have the rule over us.

When it comes to volleyball, this same principle of obedience is true. It doesn't matter who starts or who plays, just that God gets the glory. My life verse which I've mentioned several times so far is First Corinthians 10:31: "Whether therefore ye eat, or drink, or whatsoever ye do, do all to the glory of God."

You've all been taught not to date an unsaved guy. Take it a step further. Don't date a guy who claims to be saved, but has no evidence in his life that he loves God and wants to serve Him. I had a player that told me she was getting married. I asked if she had talked to him about where they would go to church, tithing, and service to the Lord. She couldn't say that she had. I had two other players who left the protection of the church and the Christian school and later became pregnant without being married.

Different from the World

Second Corinthians 6:17 says that we are to be separate. We should be different from the world. You may have heard this or used it yourself, "But everybody's doing it." Right is right even if no one is doing it, and wrong is still wrong even if everybody is doing it. This world always tries to make things sound better. Consider the following terms and how they have changed throughout the years.

Swearing - Inappropriate language
Gambling - Gaming
Drug abuse - Substance abuse
Race track - Race course
Taverns - Lounges
Drunks - Sickness
Sexual sins - Alternate lifestyles
Pornography - Adult entertainment
Rock music - Christian rock
Used car - Pre-driven

Smaller - Downsized
Prisons - Correctional institutions
Deaf - Hearing impaired
Report cards - Progress reports
Abortion - Pro choice

Our Example

The greatest example of obedience in the Bible is Jesus. John 4:34 says, "I do the will of Him who sent me." He was totally obedient to His Father.

Why do we disobey as believers? Because we want our own way and we think we can get away with it. Number 32:23 says, "But if ye will not do so, behold, ye have sinned against the Lord: and be sure your sin will find you out." John 14:15 says, "If he love me, keep my commandments."

As you continue to play volleyball and then go on to eventually get married and have children, remember this: obedience is the key to a happy life. If you live in disobedience to our Lord, then you will reap pain, frustration, and chastisement.

Chapter 31

Trees

As I was reading the Bible one day, I thought about the many instances that trees are mentioned. I checked with Strong's Concordance, and "tree" or "trees" is used 348 times in the Bible. There are over 100 different kinds of trees mentioned.

Let's take a short quiz: When we read about Zaccheus, we know he climbed a tree to see Jesus. What kind of tree was it? A sycamore. When we read about Elijah, what kind of tree was he under? A juniper. Remember Absalom was caught up in an oak tree; and lastly Nathaniel was seen by Jesus under a fig tree. Some were up in the tree and others were under the tree. When I think of this fact, it reminds me of some Christians who are always up in their attitudes regardless of circumstances, while others are always down when things go wrong.

Why was God so specific in regard to what kind of tree was involved in those four instances? Why didn't He just say a tree rather than a specific type?

The only thing I can figure out why He was so specific is because He is a God of order, organization and detail. First Corinthians 14:40 says, "Let all things be done decently and in order."

When I think about trees, I think of all they are good for.

Shade in the Summer

In the summer when it is in the 90s with bright sunlight, what do we search for? A tree and some shade from the sun. I've taken some gym classes outside in the late spring when it has been very hot. If it's an activity where we spread out on the field, you can be sure that in a few minutes the kids will start to head for the row of trees on the side of the field.

Food for All

Everyone has their favorite fruit tree. When I was a boy in Chicago, we had a plum tree in our backyard. Whenever I was hungry I would shake the tree and would hear the sound of ripe plums dropping on the ground. I would pick them off the ground and eat sweet and delicious fruit.

Fuel for the World

Everyone has had the experience of sitting by a fireplace or a campfire and enjoyed the warmth.

Beauty in Greenery

Many people have read the poem by Joyce Kilmer which says, "I think that I have never seen a poem as lovely as a tree". My favorite tree is a silver maple - the wind blowing through the leaves creates a beautiful glistening color.

Shelter in Storm

Everyone has had the experience of getting out of a storm into a house or shed or some form of wood shelter.

Uses for the World

Books, magazines, newspapers and writing paper. Think about tables, chairs, beds, bookcases, cabinets, hutches, staircases, floors. The list could go on and on.

Trees and the Christian Life

God made the parts of trees to look differently - leaves, bark, and root structure. Some trees have different kinds of fruit, and some are different in color. Trees reproduce themselves when a seed falls to the ground. As Christians, we are to do the same. We are to lead others to the Lord. As trees are different, so are people. Stacy is short while Heidi is tall. Some of you wish you had different hair - another color, curly or straight. Some of you may wish you were more attractive.

When God made you, He didn't make a mistake. He made you specifically the way He wanted you to be. Because He made you that way, you should be content and satisfied. God made you for His own pleasure. Revelation 4:15, "For thou hast created all things. For thy pleasure they are and were created." He made you to glorify Him.

Each of you has been given a special talent by God. It could be singing, playing a musical instrument, working with children, helping with people, cooking, having a sharp mind to solve problems, or peacemaking. Use that specific talent to glorify your Savior.

Different but Similar

Although trees are different in some ways, they are also similar. They all have bark, leaves, root structure and need light and moisture. As Christians, we may be different in specific practices or standards, but unless those differences are contradictory to God's Word, we should get along with one another. We've all seen pictures of trees blown over in a storm while others close by just bend but don't break. That's just like some Christians. Some stand strong when the storms come, and others fall away.

I have a tree in my parkway that was hit by a car many years ago. We came home from church one evening and saw flashing lights down our street. As we got closer we could see they were right in front of our house. There was a car smashed against that tree. It took a big cut out of the tree but it stood strong, and the car was in worse shape than the tree. I coated the cut with a protective coating and everything seemed okay.

Some years passed and I happened to look closely at the tree. I could see a trail of ants coming from the tree carrying little particles.

If I hadn't done something about them, they would have destroyed the tree a little at a time. When I think about this, I think of the little sins in our lives that we think don't matter very much. But in reality they could destroy our testimony for the Lord.

Growing Trees, Growing Believers

One thing is the same about all living trees – they are all growing – some taller, some sideways. As Christians, can we say that we are growing? I planted some evergreen trees many years ago. They were about 2 feet high. Now they are over 50 feet high. What happened? They grew, just like some Christians who pray, read their Bibles, tithe, memorize God's Word, visit the sick, witness to the lost, and go to church.

Yet other believers show little or no growth. Which kind of Christian are you? Are you closer to the Lord today than you were a year ago at this time? If the answer is no, why is that? Take a moment to pray to the Lord and ask Him to help you grow closer to Him.

Let's get specific to volleyball now. You have a specific talent for your team. Some of you may be saying, "Who me?" Yes, you. Maybe it's spiking, passing, blocking, digging, setting or serving. Maybe it's to go in and play back row or front row. Maybe it's just to go in and serve or just to be an encourager while on the bench. Your responsibility is to be ready to do whatever the coach asks to help your team. You've got to accept your specific role no matter how large or small that might be.

When I was coaching the All-Star Team at camp this past summer, one girl told me more than once that she could spike, but I asked her to set because that was where the team needed her. To be a team player you've got to accept what the coach wants you to do – even if it's not what you prefer. You have to accept what God wants you to do.

Finally, when you pray, be specific. Don't pray in generalities such as "I pray for all the sick of the church" or "for all the people with problems in the church." Be specific.

Whenever you see a tree, I pray that you will remember that God is a God of order, organization, and detail. Your life should show those same characteristics. You and everything you do are important to Him. No part of your life is small or insignificant to Him. Live today in the light of His glorious presence and peace.

Chapter 32

Success

The majority of you are reading this book to become more successful— to develop into better volleyball players. The dictionary defines success as the gaining of wealth, fame or rank. Success is measured by two standards - God's and man's. The two are worlds apart, totally opposite. The world measures by the number of wins. If you don't win the championship, you're considered a failure.

Think about it. There are 31 National Football League teams. If you win the Super Bowl you are a success; if not, a failure. There are 30 National Hockey League teams. Win the Stanley Cup, that team is a success; all the others are failures. There are 30 Major League Baseball teams. Win the World Series, you are a success; all the others a failure. There are 29 National Basketball Association teams. Win the NBA Finals, one is a success; others a failure.

Everything hinges on the result of that last game. Some volleyball coaches and players think that if they don't win the state championship or get a certain number of wins, they are failures. We have to be careful as Christians not to fall into the world's philosophy of success.

True Success

Think of missionaries all around the world. Some struggle financially, live in primitive conditions, have poor health facilities, or are oceans away from families. The world says they are fools wasting their lives when they could just live in the United States. God thinks differently. I believe that missionaries will receive some of the greatest rewards in heaven. Think of Christian school teachers dedicating their lives and talents at small wages. The world says they are fools wasting their lives when they could be working in the public school sector and getting more money. God thinks differently. God will reward their dedication and faithfulness. Think of Christian school parents who sacrifice financially to put their kids in Christian schools. The world says they are fools: they should put them in the public schools and save all that money. God thinks differently. Their sacrifice will bring huge dividends in the future. Think of Christian school volleyball coaches. Many receive small stipends while others volunteer their time. They could go to the public sector for more money but they don't because they consider it a ministry. The world can't understand this, but God thinks differently.

Joshua 1:8 says, "This book of the law shall not depart out of thy mouth, but thou shalt meditate therein day and night that thou mayest observe to do according to all that is written therein for then thou shalt make thy way prosperous and then thou shalt have good success." The most important words in this verse are "meditate on God's Word" and to do according to that Word.

The Downward Spiral of Compromise

Psalm 1:1-3 says, "Blessed is the man that walketh not in the counsel of the ungodly, nor standeth in the way of sinner, nor sitteth in the seat of the scornful. But his delight is in the law of the Lord and in his law doth he meditate day and night. And he shall be like a tree planted by the rivers of water, that bringeth forth his fruit in his season. His leaf also shall not wither and whatsoever he doeth shall prosper."

In verse one we see what the blessed man doesn't do. The downward slide begins with walking with the ungodly. He is there with them. Next he stands with them. He is closer to them. Lastly, he sits with them. He actually takes part or joins with them. We should not seek counsel with ungodly people, but we should seek it from those who love the Lord. When we get to verse two, we see what the blessed man does. His delight is in the Law of the Lord.

God's laws are not a burden to him. He meditates on them day and night. He thinks about them again and again and again. He lives his life by God's principles.

The next part of the Psalm speaks of a tree planted by the river that brings fruit. As a Christian we give out God's Word, and then He does the saving. Part of the fruit of a Christian is winning others to the Lord. The next part speaks of its leaf not withering. Someone has said that God's trees should be like evergreens. They should never lose their testimony.

We have a sycamore tree in our parkway. When the builder of our home supplied that tree, it was delivered without a piece of soil attached to its roots. It looked like someone plucked it up out of the ground and put it on a truck. In the middle of the summer, this tree will start to lose some of its leaves and large pieces of bark. Then after about two weeks, it stops. In the fall it then loses all of the rest of its leaves. When I think about this tree, I think about some Christians who seem to have a good testimony and then lose it. Then, they do good for a while, and again they lose it. This person doesn't understand the importance of testimony.

The last part of the verse says "whatsoever he doeth shall prosper", or another way of putting it is: "shall succeed."

Pat Riley, an NBA coach who has had great success, says that "winning demands commitment, moral principles, hard work, sacrifice, and unselfish teamwork."

Think about you and your team. Do you exhibit these characteristics? Do players on your team complain they don't get enough sets or playing time? Are they lazy and taking it easy all the time? Do they consider themselves more important than the team? Are they really committed to the team and think that it is important?

Personal Success

Success depends upon individual responsibility. If you expect to be successful, you must decide to do what is necessary. The more you do, the greater the chance of success. Little things are important. It is hard to be 100% better than another team in every area, but you can be a little better in many different areas. Your chance for success will then increase.

Problems should be viewed as a challenge. Is your passing or serving, or spiking, or blocking, or digging, or setting not quite up to par? Work hard on these specific weak areas to make them strengths. Don't be like the basketball player who is a good shooter spending all his spare time on shooting, or the good dribbler working always on dribbling. How about the good hitter in baseball or softball always wanting to hit, or the good fielder always wanting to stay in the field and not work on hitting? You should never be satisfied with your skill level or your team's skill level.

Keep striving for higher goals. You should dedicate yourself to excellence. Vince Lombardi was a great football coach. The winner of the Super Bowl receives a trophy named in his honor. Vince said that "you strive for perfection and somewhere along the way you reach excellence." His team, the Green Bay Packers, reached excellence. The choice to succeed is really up to you.

Danny Ainge, a professional baseball and basketball player, said, "There is a huge difference between showing up, playing, having fun and doing well, and really playing to win. It's an entirely different mindset. It's not a physical thing. It has nothing to do with athletics. It has to do with attitude."

Ivan Lendl, the number one ranked men's tennis player in the world for many years, said, "If you want something bad enough, nothing anyone can do can stop you from achieving that goal, and if you don't want something bad enough nothing anyone can do can help you get that goal."

When I was a very young boy, I started to play table tennis. In the beginning I was not very good. I worked hard on improving my game, and little by little I did improve. I started to win consistently until I was the best player in my playground. It led to city championships and a state championship. There was something inside of me that wanted to be the best I could be. No one pushed me or forced me, although some did encourage me. Achieving the goal was worth all the effort and time. I don't know when this desire to excel became a goal or how it got there, but it was there. I've coached some players with that same desire, and they were a real blessing to me.

Second Corinthians 9:6 says, "He which soweth sparingly shall reap also sparingly, and he which soweth bountifully shall reap also bountifully." In simple terms, what you put in, you are going to get out. My wife and I were in our car after work one day, and we saw that the car in front of us had a vanity license plate. The car was a Mercedes Benz and the plate said "I'm Successful". My immediate thoughts were: "in your eyes and the eyes of the world you are successful, but what about in God's eyes?"

My next thought was what a prideful statement that was, and we know that God hates pride. You must always guard that success doesn't lead to pride. Our pastor, Milton Jones, says that "success is being where God wants you to be and doing what God wants you to do".

I've been around the game of volleyball for over 44 years, and I've seen a lot of players not willing to pay the price for success. Are you willing to pay the price to achieve success? I ask you to take a moment right now and ask God to give you the strength to become a success in His eyes.

Chapter 33

Little Things Mean A Lot

When I was a very young man there was a popular song by a recording artist, Kitty Kalen, titled "Little Things Mean A Lot." It talked about a relationship between a husband and wife - a smile, a shoulder to lean on, a touch, a line a day when you're far away. The message was that little things are very important.

Life is made up of a lot of little things. Sometimes it gets boring - get up, clean up, eat, go to school, study, eat lunch, more school, volleyball practice, home, eat supper, do homework, watch a little TV, go to sleep, start all over again. It's the big things that are exciting - getting a good job, going on vacation, winning a championship, making an All-Star Team, getting engaged, getting married, having children, leading someone to Christ. Many times we slough off on the little things and neglect to have the right attitude or to give the right effort; and so we don't get to experience the big things the way God would want us to.

Volleyball is a game made up of a lot of little things. These things make the difference between winning and losing. Here are some little things that are really important:

Failure to be in the Right Place on the Floor

If you are in the wrong place on the floor, one of two things will happen. The ball will either land where you should be, or you will get in someone else's way. Remember when King David committed adultery with Bathsheba and then later murdered her husband? David was not in the place he was supposed to be. He should have been in the battle. First Samuel 11: 1 explains, "And it came to pass, after the year was expired, at the time when kings go forth to battle, that David sent Joab and his servants with him, and all Israel; and they destroyed the children of Ammon, and besieged Rabbah. But David tarried still at Jerusalem."

If you pay attention to the lines on the floor and your teammates, you will be a much better volleyball player. There is nothing worse than a player who keeps forgetting where she is supposed to cover. Many points have been lost just because a player wasn't in the right place on the court.

Lack of preparation

You can't play well if you are not prepared - conditioning, doing skill drills, resting, being in the right mindset, eating healthy foods, taking vitamins, and drinking water. Just wishing you could play well without preparing will not work. Someone has said that performance is determined by the five P's: Proper Practice Prevents Poor Performance.

Controlling Your Emotions on the Court

Why is it some players fall apart in pressure situations and others remain seemingly calm and relaxed? Players that haven't learned to control their emotions are players always on the verge of losing it. Ask God to help you stay calm during a game, even when the pressure is on and you have to perform well or your team will lose.

No "Step-Hop Movement" toward the Ball

Some players stand there and swing the arms out at the ball. They make no effort to go toward the ball with the proper motion. Remember, good passing begins with the body getting in line for the ball. One coach often said, "Remember if you move your body, your arms will follow you."

Lack of Focus

The mind starts to wander and becomes easily distracted. It could be someone in the stands or a problem that robs you of your focus. Don't allow yourself to think of anything except the game and how God can help you play your best.

Lack of Thinking Positively

It should be "I can do this," not "I'll probably mess up". "I can and will get this serve in," or "I will spike this ball into the court" is better than, "I hope the ball goes to someone else." It should be "I hope they hit it to me."

Not Visualizing what the Perfect Performance of a Skill Would Be

You must visualize yourself making the perfect set, or spike, or serve, or block, or dig, or pass. Think of yourself as successful before the game. Ask God to help you play your best.

Setters Not Facing the Target

Sets will drift in the direction that you are facing. If you don't turn your body toward your target, your sets will go to the wrong person or the wrong position on the net. Practice running to get behind the ball, then face your target as you release the ball. You will be a much more successful setter if you get in the habit of doing this.

Dropping the Elbow When Spiking

When you drop the elbow, you rob yourself of full extension and the ball will probably go into the net. Watch great spikers and notice what happens to their elbows as they spike. Getting in the habit of fully extending the elbow while spiking will greatly increase your power and accuracy.

Spikers Failing to Pull Back and Take a Good Approach

When the spiker fails to pull back from the net and take a full approach when going to spike after she has blocked the ball, she is robbing herself of power. Make it a practice to go to the net to block and then go back to get ready to spike.

Missing Key Serves

During games, it is always important that you make your serves, but this is especially important after time outs, for game point, and the first serve of the game. Don't just shrug off a missed serve and say to yourself, "It was just a serve". Determine that during your next practice, you will give it your all during serving practice, and never make that mistake again.

Sometimes there is a missed serve because of fear of making a mistake and dwelling on that thought. Don't let yourself dwell on your mistakes. Instead, concentrate on asking God to give you the strength to serve true.

Getting Angry on the Court

Many great players shortchange themselves from becoming all they can be because they can't control their anger on the floor either at themselves, their teammates, opponents, coaches, fans, or a ref's call. This anger will lead to more mistakes by affecting concentration. Ask God to help you control your anger and be aware that an inappropriate display of your feelings might destroy your career. Ask Him for strength when even the smallest feeling of anger comes, and cling to His promise that He will provide a way out of your temptation.

Failure to Pray for Everything

I think sometimes we pray over big things in life but not for the seemingly small things. Nothing is too little to pray about. Have you ever jammed a finger or thumb playing volleyball or hurt your toe? How could something so little as a finger hurt so badly? Think about anthrax or e-coli which are so little they can't be seen with the naked eye, but can kill. There have been plane crashes because of a failure of a very little part. Tires have fallen off cars and caused crashes because of lug nuts not being tight enough.

Many years ago, I had just gotten a new brake job. Driving on the Eisenhower Expressway toward Chicago, I noticed that when I touched my brakes the pedal got lower and lower. Through God's grace, I found an exit ramp that was uphill, not downhill like most. This helped to slow down the car by the top of the ramp so I could stop safely. I found out that the mechanic that did the new brake job did not connect it properly and there was a leak. His mistake could have been a deadly one.

It's Just A Little Sin (Not!)

A little spark creates a giant explosion, and it is the small sins in our lives that act like that spark. With God there is no such thing as a little sin; sins are all big. Satan might not ask you to rob a bank or kill someone. He's too smart for that. He will try to get you to compromise something that seems small, like listening to garbage music or dressing immodestly under the guise that it is fashionable and everybody does it. Sometimes we justify bad scenes or swear words in movies because we say the rest of the plot is okay.

Even thinking that church services or chapel services aren't all that important is a way for Satan to get into your mind and get you to do even more sin. Maybe that one service you decide to miss is the one that God wanted to speak to your heart. If you start at point A and compromise a little, someday you'll wake up at point B and wonder how you got there. You didn't jump there; you moved a little at a time.

I know that you desire to do something for God, that you want your life to be a bright light shining for all the world to see. The key is never letting yourself believe that lie that there is such a thing as a little sin.

Go out and conquer that difficult spike or frustrating serve and then open yourself up to God and allow Him to control every aspect of your life, even the areas you once considered little.

Chapter 34
Promises, Promises, Promises

Raise your hand if you have ever broken a promise in your life. Did you know that there are over 7000 promises in the Bible? God hasn't broken a single one yet, and He never will.

There are two kinds of promises in the Bible - conditional and unconditional. A conditional promise is one in which you must do something, and then God will do something. Some examples of these are I John 1:9, "If we confess our sins, He is faithful and just to forgive us our sins and to cleanse us from all unrighteousness." We must first confess, and then He will forgive. Romans 10:13 states, "For whosoever shall call upon the name of the Lord shall be saved." We must first call on Him, and then He will save.

Malachi 3:10 tells us, "Bring ye all the tithes into the storehouse, that there may be meat in mine house, and prove me now herewith, saith the Lord of Hosts, if I will not open you the windows of heaven, and pour you out a blessing, that there shall not be room enough to receive it."

An unconditional promise is one which we don't have to do something for God to do something. He is just going to do it. Examples of this are Genesis 8:22, "While the earth remaineth, seedtime and harvest, and cold and heat, and summer and winter, and day and night shall not cease." Hebrews 13:5b shares, "I will never leave thee nor forsake thee." He won't leave us even if we attempt to leave Him.

Your Word

What really is a promise? It's your word. It's one of the most important things you have. Once you break a promise, it makes it that much easier to do it again.

Statistics tell us that more than one out of two marriages end in divorce. Each marriage began with a promise before God and witnesses to stay together for better or worse, till death do them part. You would expect the world to break promises, but not God's people. Yet, divorce is rampant in God's church. When the world sees this, it brings shame to the cause of Christ. Why should the world listen to a witness for our Lord when we act just like unbelievers?

One of my saddest visits was to a Christian man who was leaving his wife for another woman. This man had at one time a very strong testimony for God. When we had talked years earlier about spiritual things, tears would come to his eyes. He was a faithful, dedicated Christian who witnessed to the lost. When we visited him, he admitted what he was doing was wrong and cried and cried. No matter what we said, he was going to do what he wanted to do. I remember saying that I would be fearful that God would punish my wife or son if I were to do what he was doing. He said that the men he worked with and used to witness to would now laugh and say he is just like them.

I asked this man what it would take to get him to do what he knew was right. He responded with these sad words, "What if I don't want to do the right thing?" I left that home feeling helpless.

Keep Your Promises

When you make a promise to God, be sure to keep it. Ecclesiastes 5:4-5 explains, "When thou vowest a vow unto God, defer not to pay it; for He hath no pleasure in fools: pay that which thou hast vowed. Better is it that thou shouldest not vow, than that thou shouldest vow and not pay." We've all heard of the stories of soldiers in combat with death all around them saying, "Lord, get me out of here safely and I'll serve you." That same soldier gets back home and forgets his promise and lives just as sinful as before.

At the store, I noticed a father who had his two-year old son on his shoulders. The father said, "If I put you down, do you promise to stay right here?" The boy said, "I promise, I promise." The father put him down, but he didn't stay where he was supposed to. The young boy didn't realize what a promise really was. He must be trained.

When I was a young man, I remember a phrase used about a woman's prerogative to change her mind. It was sort of a license to take a certain position now, and then change it later.

My state's past governor made some election promises. One was not to support expansion of the airport and another was not to raise taxes. He broke both of those promises. He was asked about it on a news interview and his answer was, "I changed my mind." He didn't change his mind; he broke his promises.

Then we had the example of a President who said, "Read my lips", meaning no new taxes. He broke that promise, and the next election we had a new President.

I've known of some people who had low paying jobs. Many times they would not work diligently, and their answer was that they were paid too little. They knew up front the salary and the responsibilities. There was no excuse for that kind of attitude. I've been in church when a request was made to make cakes for a church fellowship. The number of cake volunteers never matched the actual number of cakes that were brought.

When you came to your Christian school, you promised to abide by the school rules listed in the handbook. Yet, you may not think that is important. When you break those rules, you might have had the excuse that that rule was not your personal conviction. It doesn't matter if you had a personal conviction regarding a rule or not. You made a promise to keep those rules.

When you become a part of your team, you should have promised your coach to do whatever possible to help your team. Are you doing all you can to make your team a success, or are you always questioning your coach's leadership? If you haven't already made this kind of promise, maybe you should do that right now. If everyone on your team did that, I'm sure you would have a better season.

Have You Kept Your Promises to Yourself?

We've talked about promises to God and promises to others, but we have neglected to mention another important area. How about promises to yourself? Some of us break promises in this area. We have lost the realization of the seriousness of a promise. It is a matter of your integrity. You may have promised to lose some weight, start eating healthier, do better in school, read your Bible more, faithfully pray for others, use your talents for God's glory, or make a greater effort to live a holy life. A promise to yourself is just as important as a promise to others. Make sure you keep those promises.

Ask God to help you keep your promises. Ask Him for wisdom and strength to not make promises you can't keep. God keeps His promises to us; we can do nothing less than keep our promises to Him.

Chapter 35

Faithfulness

Faithfulness is defined as steadfast adherence to a person or thing, unwavering determination, and maintaining allegiance to someone or something.

In Proverbs 20:6 God says, "Most men will proclaim everyone his own goodness: but a faithful man who can find?" Most people think they are pretty good, and some even say they are good—but a faithful person is hard to find.

God is looking for faithfulness in a day when this character trait is almost gone. His desire is that we would be faithful people for His service. In First Corinthians 4:2, we find, "Moreover it is required in stewards, that a man be found faithful."

God gives different gifts or talents to different people. We are to use these talents to glorify Him. God did not give us all the talent to sing beautifully, to skillfully play a musical instrument, to pastor a church, to be a brain surgeon, or to be a rocket scientist. He did give each of us some talents. You might be saying to yourself, "I don't have any talents; God forgot me when He was giving them out." That's not true. There is something you can do for God. Everyone can be faithful to Him.

If you start a new program in the church, many will join and start strong. As the weeks go by, the numbers will shrink. At the end of any program, you will usually have many fewer people than when you started out. Most people are sprinters, not marathoners.

Old Faithful

In Yellowstone National Park, there is a famous geyser named Old Faithful. The geyser erupts on the average of every 75 minutes for up to five minutes at a time. It shoots a column of steam and hot water as high as 184 feet with about 10,000 to 12,000 gallons of water at each eruption.

Many years ago I saw a story of a man on television who was retiring after a long time with one company. The remarkable thing about this man was his faithfulness. He never missed a day of work. Can you imagine not taking one sick day or even a personal day in 30-plus years?

At the opposite end of the spectrum is the newspaper article that reports 20% of employees acknowledged that they try to take more vacation days than they are entitled to. The same study shows that the cost to employers for unscheduled absences rose 30% in the last two years.

Dick Caplan, an old teammate of mine, played in 52 consecutive United States National Open Volleyball championships.

Many couples in our church are wonderful examples of faithfulness as they have been married over 50 years.

I think there are six major areas of faithfulness for a Christian. Let's look at each of them now.

Prayer

Most people do not pray for any length of time unless there is a real pressing problem. There is a song in our hymnal titled "Sweet Hour of Prayer." I wonder how many of you pray for an hour a day. A half-hour? Fifteen minutes? Or even ten minutes? You might say, "You don't know my schedule; I don't have time to pray for very long." You are too busy if you don't have time to pray. Every Christian could be faithful in prayer.

Confession of Sin

The second area of faithfulness is in confession of sin. Psalm 66:18 states, "If I regard iniquity in my heart, the Lord will not hear me". During a television interview, a former pastor whose son had committed immorality with a teenage girl said his son was a good boy and had just made a mistake. That boy didn't make a mistake; he sinned. We must constantly confess our sins, forsake them, and ask the Holy Spirit to help us not to repeat them again.

Bible Reading

The third area of faithfulness is Bible reading. We talk to God in prayer; He speaks to us through His Word. It is amazing how many people have time to read the newspaper or watch television, but do not have time to read their Bibles. How about those who say they are too tired to read the Bible today but they will double their reading tomorrow? Tomorrow comes and they have the same excuse. Before long, many days have passed and they haven't read the Bible at all. To stay close to God, we must be faithful in reading the Bible every day.

Church Attendance

The fourth area is church attendance. Many churches have three services each week. Sunday morning has the highest attendance, with fewer people on Sunday evening and the least amount of people on Wednesday evenings. I wonder how many people stay at home to watch sports or their favorite television program. Some of you young ladies might say, "I go to chapel services at school and most of the church services, but I miss some here and there. What difference is it if I miss one or two services?" It makes a huge difference. We need all of the Word that we can get and if we aren't there, then we won't know what God wants us to do. At church your attitude should be, "God, speak to me and help me to be more Christ-like."

Giving

The fifth area is faithful giving. Money is only one part of giving. Most people know the term *tithe* meaning "a tenth." It's easy to give a tithe if you have a dime: that's only a penny. It's harder for some to give a tithe if they have one thousand dollars because that's a hundred dollars. God makes the 90% go farther than the 100%. Don't ask me how He does it, I personally know He does.

Luke 6:38 tells us "Give, and it shall be given unto you; good measure, pressed down, and shaken together, and running over, shall men give into your bosom. For with the same measure that ye mete withal, it shall be measured to you again." In Malachi 3:10 it says, "Bring ye all the tithes into the storehouse, that there may be meat in Mine house, and prove me now herewith, saith the LORD of Hosts, if I will not open you the windows of heaven, and pour you out a blessing, that there shall not be room enough to receive it."

Before I knew Christ, my wife and I were friends with another couple. The man was a graduate student at the University of Chicago. The wife supported them by teaching in a public school. My wife told me that Evie gave 10% of their income to the church. I remember telling my wife what fools they were. They could have used that money. Years later, I got saved and started to tithe, and the Lord reminded me that they were not fools. They were just being obedient.

Maybe some of you have part-time jobs and are saving for college or a car. If you are faithful about giving and have the right attitude, God will bless you. The tithe is the beginning point in giving. Many give above their tithe, and that's called an offering. Giving can be summed up in two points.

1. God owns it all.
2. You can't out-give God.

Giving also involves your talents and your time. Do you faithfully give your time and talents to God? Do you do it cheerfully or grudgingly?

Witnessing

The sixth area of faithfulness is in regards to sharing your testimony of faith with the unsaved. This is the one area where the majority of Christians break down. We use many excuses.

1. I am shy.
2. I don't know the Bible well enough.
3. I am afraid.
4. I will be laughed at.
5. They will think I am weird.
6. People won't like me.
7. Witnessing is the pastor's job.
8. I am too busy.

Mark 16:15 states, "And He said unto them, Go ye into all the world, and preach the gospel to every creature." You notice it is not an option to witness; it is a command. Faithful Christians share their faith. Think about different Bible characters such as Moses, David, and Joseph. Each one proved faithful in his job and because of that, God trusted them with much bigger positions. Luke 16:10 tells us: "He that is faithful in that which is least is faithful also in much: and he that is unjust in the least is unjust also in much."

Do you want to do a great work for God? It starts with being faithful in the little jobs. When you prove that you can handle the small jobs, He will give you bigger things to do.

Let's apply that to volleyball for a while. Have you ever thought, "Am I being faithful to my team and my coach?" When everyone else is working hard, are you loafing? When everyone else has a positive attitude, are you negative? Is there some sin in your life that's holding God's blessings from your team? Are you praying for your teammates and coaches? Are you jealous of your fellow athletes? Are you seeking your own glory, not the team's best interests? It takes a conscious effort to say, "I'm going to be faithful in every area of my life—God, family, job, church, school, team, and friends." Why don't you take a moment right now and ask God to make you a faithful servant in every area of your life.

Chapter 36

Encouragement

The dictionary defines encouragement: to give courage, to give support, to help. Deuteronomy 1:38 explains, "But Joshua the son of Nun, which standeth before thee, he shall go in thither; encourage him for he shall cause Israel to inherit it." Deuteronomy 3:28 says, "But charge Joshua, and encourage him, and strengthen him; for he shall go over before this people, and he shall cause them to inherit the land which thou shalt see."

If God says something in His Word once, it is important—but saying it twice emphasizes how imperative it is. Second Samuel 11:25 shares, "Then David said unto the messenger, Thus shalt thou say unto Joab, 'Let not this thing displease thee, for the sword devoureth one as well as another: make thy battle more strong against the city, and overthrow it: and encourage though him.'" Isaiah 41:6-7 says, "They helped everyone his neighbor; and every one said to his brother, 'Be of good courage.' So the carpenter encouraged the goldsmith, and he that smootheth with the hammer him that smote the anvil, saying, 'It is ready for the soldering': and he fastened it with nails, that it should not be moved."

Encouragement is something we all need both on the giving side and on the receiving side. I've already mentioned how a playground teacher, Mr. Kipp, greatly influenced and encouraged me. The older I get, the more I appreciate what he did for me.

Once when I was in college, I complained to him about a poor teacher I had. He told me that I could still learn something even if it wasn't from the best teacher. I asked him what I could learn from him, and Mr. Kipp told me I could learn not to be like that teacher. This advice has helped me throughout the years.

When I think of Mr. Kipp, I think about a quote from another of my college professors who was a great teacher, Arthur H. Steinhaus. He said, "A pupil wants to be like the teacher he admires — and before he knows it, he is like him. This is often not what the teacher was [saying with his mouth] — it is more often what the teacher was living [with his life]. The grandchildren of the pupil who has been inspired by a good teacher will be different because of his teaching. Though they may never identify him to sing his praise, their changed life is, in truth, the immortality of the teacher. Thus in his pupils, the teacher is extended even as in himself he finds the likeness of the one who taught him."[1]

Practical Encouragement

I've always tried to be an encouragement to the volleyball players on my team. One way I tried to do that was by praying for them every day. When a former player comes back after some years, I look her in the eye and tell her I've been praying for her every day. If that fact doesn't encourage her, I don't know what will.

A fellow church member, Jim White, has been an encouragement to me. In spite of numerous back operations, and always being in pain, he showed the love of God through his life.

A Christian car dealer in Ottawa, Illinois, Terry Bentz, shared a story with me that fits perfectly. He said he felt burdened to spend some time with a man he knew who was not a close friend. He said they went out to dinner and spent time talking together that evening. A day or so later, the man called and thanked Terry for spending the time with him. Terry acknowledged the thank you. The man said, "You don't understand. I had a loaded gun under my car seat and I was contemplating suicide."

I shudder to think what would have happened if Terry didn't obey the prompting of the Holy Spirit to encourage this man.

Our church supports Bill Smith, a missionary to Papua, New Guinea. Some years ago while he was teaching in our Christian school, he sat in front of me at an evening service at church. The Holy Spirit prompted me to give him some money. He later related this story to me. That same morning he had taken his brother to the airport to leave for Pensacola Christian College. He knew that his brother needed some money for books; so he gave him some money. My giving to him that evening was God's way of blessing him for what he had done that morning. I know that action encouraged him, and when he told me the whole story, I was encouraged also.

God's Encouragement

We can get encouraged by reading God's Word. Think of the examples of Joseph and Daniel. Think of the encouragement between Elijah and Elisha, Jonathan and David.

Former players have been an encouragement to me. One of our young Christian school coaches passed away suddenly; he was in his mid-20s. I went to the funeral home to be an encouragement to the father who was a close friend. At the casket I broke down, and the father, showing great composure, consoled me. He turned out to be the encourager.

Practical Encouragement

How can we be an encouragement to others?
1. Taking a genuine interest in other people and what they are doing.
2. Showing a Christ-like example through our lives.
3. Praying for others
4. A smile.
5. A touch.
6. A hug.
7. A few words.
8. Just listening.
9. Just being there when needed.

How can we be encouragers through volleyball?

Say things to your teammates like, "That was a great spike, nice dig, or a beautiful set." "You're really improving." "You've become

a very hard worker." "It's okay you missed; you'll get the next one."
"Great effort." "I'm praying for you both on and off the court." If
you get in the habit of saying these things, you will have a great,
encouraging effect on your teammates.

I ask you to go to the Lord and ask Him to help you become an
encourager to others.

Chapter 37

Discouragement

Isn't it so easy to become discouraged? You've got everything planned out and something unexpected happens that throws everything out of whack. The first thing we usually say is "Why me?" Probably the best discourager is reading the news in the paper or watching the news on television.

I remember reading about a girl who went to her prom and during that evening delivered her baby and discarded it in the bathroom. She then went back to the prom with no more thought or regard for the baby. How could someone be so heartless?

A man in our church had a brother that was a Chicago policeman killed in a gun battle with a criminal. After some years, the man was paroled from prison and is now walking the streets of Chicago. Think of how discouraged the victim's family is now.

I saw another incident on TV that really discouraged me. A drunk driver crashed his car in a road construction zone resulting in the death of his friend. Two different juries could not find agreement to find him guilty and wound up in hung juries. The juries said they couldn't find him guilty, even though he was legally drunk, because one or two of the jurors said the construction zone was not marked clearly enough. The guy was drunk. If he wasn't, his friend would not have been killed.

How about all the scams to steal people's money? One of our custodians at my school told me that he received a letter telling him that he had won a new car. He was excited! He was supposed to send some money before he could claim the car. It turned out to be a scam. Someone has said that if it sounds too good to be true, it probably is.

Road Rage

There are so many situations in life that cause discouragement. Some situations are just so discouraging that people snap. An example is road rage, which is on the increase. Some people start shooting others because they lose their job, or family, or girlfriend, or house. This is depicted on the news with increasing regularity.

One year we had a player transfer in as a senior from the public school. She was one of the best players I ever coached. She helped us win all six tournaments that year, plus finish undefeated; and she was MVP in every tournament. When she came to our school, not everyone was as happy as I was. Someone else had to sit on the bench because she took her spot. It was discouraging to know that someone's playing time was more important than having a great team.

Here are some discouraging things that you might be experiencing. You think you're working hard, but you don't seem to be improving. You study for a test and you bomb out. Your best friend lets you down. You sit on the bench and don't get any playing time. You get sick and have pain. I had a case of arthritis some years ago. I was so discouraged because I was focusing on my pain. It's so hard to think of helping someone else when you are hurting yourself.

All of the situations I've just described are discouraging, and if you let them take over your life, then you won't learn to be an effective Christian. Life is full of discouragement, and the sooner we use God's power in our lives, the sooner we learn how to overcome it.

Sometimes it's the little things that discourage us. Recently our telephone broke, and right after that, the oven broke. Or you might wind up waiting in a long line at the store. A big discouragement is when that special guy who thought you were very nice starts to show attention to another girl. Probably one of the biggest discouragements is when another brother or sister in Christ says something to us that really hurts, or someone doesn't say something to us that they should have.

How to Discourage Your Coach

Do coaches get discouraged? I say a loud "Amen" to that. We tell the front line girls when they're not involved in the block to pull back and then step in. We say that over and over again, and they keep pulling back but not stepping in—and the ball continues to hit the floor right in front of them.

We tell the setters to overhead pass the second ball and what do they do? They start too slowly and then forearm pass it instead.

We tell the setters to square off and face their target when setting. What do they do? They don't follow directions, and the sets drift away from where they should be.

We tell the defense to move the feet and what do they do? They look like they put glue on the bottom of their shoes.

We tell the diggers to stay low. What do they do? They look like soldiers standing at attention.

We tell the spikers to pull back and take an approach. What do they do? They get stuck at the net and have to try to spike without the benefit of an approach.

We tell the servers to hit the ball softly, with less force, because they are constantly hitting it past the end line. What do they do? The same thing they did before we told them.

We tell the blockers to focus on the hitter instead of the ball. What do they do? The eyes stay glued on the ball.

We tell the server to really concentrate to keep the serve in the court after the other team has called a timeout. What do they do? They lose their concentration and miss the serve. The same thing often happens on game point.

One year we had a match at a nearby Christian school where the ceiling is lower than what my team was used to having. We kept on receiving serves and spiking and passing in such a way that the volleyball kept hitting the ceiling. It happened time and again. I was so frustrated that I called a timeout and said to our team, "Stop hitting the ball so hard. Hit the ball softer and keep it off the ceiling." I turned and sat down on the bench. The very next serve was hit to us and guess what happened? You guessed right. We hit it off the ceiling. All I could do was sit and shake my head.

Another time we had a very important match at one of our home tournaments. I told the girls to be there at a certain time. That time passed and we were warming up when two of my starters strolled in. Needless to say, I didn't play them. God did bless us with the victory in that match.

Another time we were going to Sterling, Illinois, for a tournament. I told the girls to be at our gym at a certain time. The time came, but one girl wasn't there. My captain asked if we could stop at her house on the way out. She lived very close to the school. The captain knocked on the door and awakened her. She came out a few minutes later, and we left for the tournament. After the tournament, one of my players said that the late player asked her if she thought that Coach was angry at her because she was the only one that didn't get to play. I would say that girl guessed correctly.

Some of the girls I've coached have not been outwardly rebellious, but in some stressful situations, their inward spirit has come to the surface.

I think the single most discouraging thing to me as a coach is when former players go out into the world and live in sin. They forget all the chapel services, church services, godly instructions and examples, and wind up being immoral and getting pregnant out of wedlock. Some marry the wrong person and wind up divorced.

I've told my girls to not date an unsaved guy, and they have heard that advice from many others. I go a step further and say to not date a saved guy. They say, "Wait a minute! That means I can't date anybody." Let me explain. I say, "Don't date a saved guy that doesn't show that he really loves God with all his heart." You can tell what's important to people by what they talk about. Does he talk about his love for God and how he intends to serve Him? If you find a guy that really loves God with all his heart, your chances for a happy, successful marriage are much greater. I told my girls that there is something worse than not getting married and that's to marry the wrong guy. I could tell story upon story of girls I've coached who have made this terrible mistake.

Watch Out

We have to be very careful that our discouragement doesn't cause others to be discouraged. If we are not giving the example of holiness, it will discourage others. Our pastor preached a message, and he said that we get discouraged when we take our eyes off God and our goal of pleasing Him and instead look at our own circumstances. We forget all the many past blessings, and we really don't think clearly.

It seems that when I'm really discouraged, God sends someone to encourage me. If we are discouraged, we should try to find someone to encourage. This will help us to be encouraged ourselves. Don't be a discourager by complaining, gossiping, not giving your best, or not obeying your coaches. Be the opposite: be an encourager. Be a person who loves the Lord and desires to serve Him with your whole heart.

Chapter 38

FAB

I formed an acrostic with the word FAB which is short for fabulous:

F - Feelings

A - Attitudes

B - Blessings

When I think about the word FAB, the first thing that comes to my mind is the Fab Five. In the early 90s, the University of Michigan recruited five of the most outstanding high school basketball seniors in the country. They were so highly touted that they were referred to as the Fab Five. The anticipation was running so very high that they thought they would win multiple NCAA National Basketball Championships. They got very close, making it to two national championship games, but each time they lost. They never achieved their great potential.

I wonder if we as Christians are achieving our potential with regards to feelings, attitudes, and blessings—or do we, as the Fab Five, fall short.

Feelings

Let's start with "F" for feelings. One of our pastors gave the example of trying to offend a dead man. It can't be done. No matter what you say or do, you can't hurt his feelings. As Christians, we should be like that dead man. No matter what someone says or does, we should not have fragile feelings. Psalm 119:165 says, "Great peace have they which love thy law and nothing shall offend them."

All of us have at some time or another offended another brother or sister in Christ by saying or doing something they perceived as offensive, or by *not* saying or not doing something they expected from us. We must consider other people's feelings. Sometimes these feelings have built a wall between people that continues for many years.

One time we were warming up for a match at Maranatha Baptist Bible College. One of my spikers hit a spike high and out that hit the bleachers. I said something in jest trying to be funny. I looked at the spiker's face and could tell I had offended her. I stopped the warm up and called the team over to me. I then apologized to her in front of the team. I had hurt her feelings unintentionally, but I still needed to be forgiven. We must always humble ourselves and go to that person and ask for their forgiveness. Sometimes it's not easy, but it has to be done to restore fellowship. .

I thought of a person in our church that had just lost a husband. I wondered how many were praying for her faithfully every day or had called or visited her or were pouring out love to her to get her through this difficult time. You may be thinking about some person in your church or school who is feeling down. It could be illness, lack of finances, family difficulties or a host of other problems. The church that I attended years ago caused many hurt feelings. People left the church and there was a lot of bitterness. Our new pastor asked us to reach out to these people and apologize for the hurts that we caused. We must be so careful from now on to consider other's feelings by our actions and by the church's actions. God's people should desire harmony and not cause deep hurts.

Two of the hardest words to say with meaning are "I'm sorry", because most of the time these words are used insincerely.

Attitude

You've heard it said in life that attitude is everything. In one week, our TV broke and the washing machine died. It would be so easy to have a bad attitude about these things, but when you consider we got the TV for free and the washing machine was purchased in 1968, you then tend to look at it from a different perspective. It's all attitude.

The pressure of competition brings out the best and worst in attitudes. This is the reason you can see so many bad attitudes in sports. Someone has said that sports do not develop character, they reveal it. I agree, but I also think that sports can help to develop good attitudes when this is important to those in leadership.

When I was in college, we were playing a team in a national tournament when two players on the other team had to be separated to avoid a fist fight. This all happened while the match was going on.

I can personally recall attitudes I displayed in sports before I was saved that I wish I could have changed. I wonder how many of you could say the same thing. Have any of you ever been taken out of a match or played very little or not at all? What kind of an attitude did you display with your face or your mouth? I remember a match between two Christian schools where the coach of the other team took out a player and put in a substitute. If looks could kill, the coach would have been dead. The substituted player without saying a word displayed the attitude of "How could you take me out? I'm a starter."

Volleyball Attitudes

Have you ever displayed or seen these attitudes?
1. I missed the ball because someone got in my way.
2. We lost because the referee was unfair.
3. The other team just got lucky.
4. I'm not spiking well because of the poor setting.
5. We lost because they didn't set me enough.
6. Some noise or something in the stands distracted me.
7. I'm not getting enough playing time because the coach doesn't like me.

Athletes who have these attitudes think nothing is their fault. They don't realize that many times their lack of ability is because they weren't focusing or working hard enough to prepare for matches.

God has blessed me with many players who had sweet attitudes and they were a joy to be around whether they were playing or sitting on the bench. During the season, may I encourage you to keep examining your attitude that it may be always pleasing to God? It doesn't matter who starts. It doesn't matter who plays or how long they play. All that matters is that God gets the glory.

I had a soul winning partner for our Thursday evening church visitation program. We knocked on a door and a woman came to the door dressed very immodestly. After talking for a while, the woman said she was a Christian. My partner immediately said, "You call yourself a Christian and you dress like that?" The woman was highly offended and later called the church to complain about our visit. My friend's attitude ruined any chance of getting this person back in church to hear God's Word.

Another deacon in our church was very strict and wouldn't even let his younger daughter play with other girls who wore slacks. This man later divorced his wife and married another woman. One of the girls that he wouldn't let play with his daughter years later told me that she thought he was a hypocrite.

When I think about attitude, I think of Joseph. Remember in Genesis when he told his brothers you meant it for evil but God meant it for good? He said he would nourish and take care of them. He had forgiven them. What a fabulous attitude! Many times our attitudes of pride show through when we compare ourselves with others. We can look pretty good because we can always find someone who is spiritually below where we are.

When we go to church or chapel services, what is our attitude? Is it just another service? Just another song? Just another offering? Or is it another opportunity to worship and give God our best? I don't know about you, but sometimes my attitude leaves something to be desired. Sometimes my attitude is just plain bad. Circumstances get me down. We have to consistently examine our attitudes and see if they need adjusting. The bottom line is do our attitudes glorify our God?

Blessings

We are either getting, giving, a combination of both, or none of the above. I remember hearing a pastor preach a message when he said he thought the biggest room in Heaven would be the "unclaimed blessings room." His point was that God has so many blessings for us, but we don't receive them because of our sinful behavior. When you give blessings, they have a way of coming back so you receive them.

When I was in college I became a friend to a large family with many smaller children. They didn't have very much money. At that time I was working part time at a children's home in Bartlett, Illinois. At Christmastime, large amounts of toys were donated to this home. I secured permission to take some of the toys that were left over to give to the children of this needy family. I had the privilege of wrapping these toys and delivering them. The kids received a blessing by getting the toys, and I received the blessing by watching them receive, open, and play with the toys.

For many years, my church gave out Thanksgiving baskets to needy families. Each year I would help out by delivering these baskets. What a blessing to see how thankful the people were that someone cared about them. We used to have a ministry called "basement blessings." Church people would contribute clothes, shoes, toys and appliances that we stored in the basement. People could come and take whatever they needed for free.

We used to have a man in our church that was an auto mechanic. In the evenings he would work on cars out of his garage. He was honest, reliable, talented and very reasonable. He saved God's people thousands of dollars. He was a great blessing to me and many other Christians.

Our son, daughter-in-law and grandkids live in the state of Washington. My wife's brother and wife live in Florida. Holidays can be lonely. Friends have been a blessing to us by inviting us over for dinner and fellowship. I've been blessed with great Christian friends, and I'm so thankful for them.

The greatest blessing of all is God's love-gift of His Son Jesus and His sacrifice for us for the forgiveness of our sins. I think we should ask God everyday for someone to whom we can be a blessing. If you are going to be that blessing, there is a price to pay. It's going to cost you something. It will take your time, your effort, and maybe even your money. But when you are a blessing to others, you truly will be a fabulous Christian for our Lord.

Chapter 39

Fear

If we are honest with one another, we would have to admit that we have all experienced fear at some time in our lives. When I was young, I was afraid of the Boogie Man, of the dark, and of strangers. Some have a fear of flying, heights, sickness, death, losing a job, not having the money to go to college, failing grades in school, not having a boyfriend, not finding a husband, or of spiders. The list could go on and on. When these fears become persistent, abnormal, and intense, they are referred to as phobias.

One of our presidents, Franklin Roosevelt, gave a famous speech in which he said, "The only thing we have to fear is fear itself." What he was trying to do was to reassure the people that everything would be okay and that there really was nothing to fear.

Many years ago, I was sitting at my desk at work and the thought came into my mind that someday I was going to die, and I remember I actually trembled. There are about 397 verses in the Bible listed under fear and that's not even including those listed under feareth, feared, fearful, fearing, or fears.

The dictionary defines fear as a feeling of alarm caused by awareness or expectation of danger. Fear can actually kill you. It raises stress levels to the point where it can lead to heart attacks. In Genesis chapter three, Adam and Eve were afraid and hid from God. In Genesis chapter 20, Abraham told the king that Sarah, his wife, was his sister because he feared the king would kill him. In Acts chapter five, when Ananias and Sapphira lied to the Holy Spirit and were killed, it says that great fear came upon all the church and upon as many as heard these things. In Genesis chapter 32, Jacob was greatly afraid that his brother Esau was going to kill him.

When I was a little boy my mother took me to a YMCA for swimming lessons. They told us to jump into the water so they could see what ability we had. The water was above chest-high level, and I was frightened. I finally learned how to swim as a college student, but to this day, I don't like the water and do not swim.

In a less serious matter, what about volleyball? How many of you fear you are going to fold in a tight situation, and your mistake will cost your team the game or match? How many of you, in a tight situation, say to yourself, "I hope they don't hit it to me? I hope it's hit to someone else." As a Coach, I've tried to reassure my teams in clutch situations not to fear because when they did, they would tighten up and make more errors.

I had a player some years ago tell me that one of her teammates tried to hide behind her during serve reception so the ball wouldn't go to her. She did this because she feared making a mistake. You can't have that kind of an attitude. You have to develop your confidence by working very hard and dedicating yourself to improve your skills and conditioning so that you can say, "I hope they hit it to me. I want the ball."

I've seen players who were afraid to play a certain team because that team was so good. I've seen spikers that were afraid to spike the ball in tight situations so they would half-speed the ball over the net. I've seen setters afraid to set the ball in tight spots so they would forearm pass it instead. I've even seen servers who normally serve overhand, switch to underhand in pressure situations. These players let negative thoughts affect them.

The right way to approach a tight situation is with positive thoughts. "I have done this well in the past, and I am going to do it again."

Replace Fear with Love

What do we really know about fear? We know that fear does not come from God because II Timothy 1:7 says, "For God has not given us the spirit of fear, but of power and of love and of a sound mind." The power for a Christian comes from the Holy Spirit. The love is the agape love of God. We love God because He first loved us. We, in turn, should show love to others. The sound mind allows us to think clearly, to overcome fear, and to remember Bible verses to help in time of need.

Fears increase as we get older. Ecclesiastes 12:5, speaking of aging, says, "Also when they shall be afraid of that which is high, and fears shall be in the way." When fear starts to bother us, we should quote Bible verses. Psalm 34:4 says, "I sought the Lord and He heard me and delivered me from ALL my fears." Isaiah 41:13 assures, "For I, the Lord thy God, will hold thy right hand saying unto thee, Fear not, I will help thee." Isaiah 41:10 states, "Fear thou not, for I am with thee."

First John 4:18 explains, "Perfect love casteth out fear." Psalm 21:1 tells us, "The Lord is my light and my salvation: whom should I fear? The Lord is the strength of my life, of whom shall I be afraid?"

Good Fear

I've seen those decals on car windows and on t-shirts that say "No Fear." Only a fool would say "no fear" because there are some good fears.

Some of those fears are fear of touching a hot stove for a little child, fear of speeding in your car and either getting a ticket or getting in an accident, and fear of taking drugs or tobacco because you know the destruction they can have on your body.

The best fear to have is the fear of offending a holy God Who loves us even though we don't deserve it. The wisest man who ever lived said in Ecclesiastes chapter 12, "Let us hear the conclusion of the whole matter: fear God and keep His commandments, for this is the whole duty of man."

Do You Fear God?

Just read your newspaper or watch the news on television and you will see that people don't fear God. How about those of us who profess to be Christians? Do we fear God? If we really did, it would change some of our actions. Second Corinthians 5:10 says that Christians will all appear before the judgment seat of Christ. We will be held accountable for what we've done with our lives. The thought of standing before a holy God should cause us to try to live our lives to please Him instead of pleasing ourselves.

One of the reasons people do not fear God is because He doesn't immediately send a lightning bolt down on us when we sin. Because the punishment is not instant, we think we can get away with it. Ecclesiastes 8:11 explains, "Because sentence against an evil work is not executed speedily, therefore the heart of the sons of men is fully set in them to do evil."

The Opposite of Faith

Those who fear God have healthy fear, but those who fear man have unhealthy fear. Fear is the opposite of faith. Isaiah 12:2 says, "Behold God is my salvation; I will trust and not be afraid." Someone has said, "Fear knocked on my door. I sent Faith to answer it. No one was there." God does not want us to be immobilized with fear. He wants us to trust Him. The next time you worry about how you are going to pass the volleyball, ask God to help you step out in faith. When you worry that you are going to blow a test, ask God to give you the strength and the memory you need to study. When you fear God and then give Him your fears, you will be surprised at the depth of your faith.

Chapter 40

Rejoicing In Truth

It is very easy to rejoice when things are going good – everybody is healthy, there's enough money, good grades, good friends, everything seems to be just wonderful. Philippians 4:4 says to rejoice always in the Lord.

Do we rejoice when things are going wrong—someone dies, you have health problems, you experience a loss of popularity, the loss of a job, or you are not good enough to play for your team? It is hard to rejoice in these situations, but we are commanded to rejoice in the Lord always—and it is emphasized twice.

Grant Rice, a church planter, always greets people by telling them he's rejoicing in the Lord.

Throughout this devotional, I will be referring to verses in Philippians chapter four. The first part of Philippians four, verse six says, "Be careful for nothing." This means we are not supposed to worry. The word *careful* there means anxious. How many of us could honestly say that we do not worry?

The next part says, "…in everything by prayer." In other words, we should worry about nothing and pray about everything. I think most of us make the mistake of only praying for the seemingly big or important things and neglecting to pray for the so-called little things. When I was younger, I used to paint the exterior of my house. This meant climbing up ladders to get to the high places. I remember praying every time before going up that ladder. I would use one arm to hang on as tightly as I could to that ladder as I painted. This was one worry that never left me the entire time I painted my house.

One day, I filled my garbage can to get it ready for the truck to pick it up. In our town we have to put a sticker on each can we put out on the curb. The stickers cost about $1.60 each. Being a thrifty person, I was trying to get as much as I could in one can. The can was on a slight incline on my driveway. I put one foot into the can and tried to push everything down to get more room. Since this wasn't working too well, I put my other foot in too.

Suddenly, the can started to tilt. I tried to pull my feet out, but they got caught on the plastic bags in the can. The can fell, and I fell on my seat and hip on the driveway. I'm surprised I wasn't the laughing stock of the neighborhood, but I don't think anyone saw me. It was only by God's mercy that I didn't break a bone. I should have prayed before trying to do this seemingly small job. We should pray about everything. Nothing is too small or insignificant to God. He cares about us and all that we do.

Earnest Supplication

In verse six, the word *supplication* means "to ask for humbly and earnestly". We do not demand nor ask flippantly for our desires. Our pastor defines it as "passionate prayer".

The next words in the verse are "with thanksgiving." We should thank Him for all the things He has done for us in the past, what He is doing in the present, and for what He will do in the future. The words of "Thank you" must be sincere and heartfelt.

The last part of this verse says, "Let your requests be made known unto God." Talk to Him. Share your heart with Him. Don't just think He already knows what you are going through although He does know everything. But He desires to be in a relationship with you and can't be unless you open up to Him. He loves you.

Verse seven says, "And the peace of God which passeth all understanding shall keep your hearts and minds through Christ Jesus." The world can't understand this, but we know that God's peace, through His Son Jesus, will help in all situations.

Thinking on Eight Truths

In verse eight, there are six important things listed that we are told to think on. The first one is "whatsoever things are true."

We know that whatever God says in His Word, He will do. John 17:17 says, "Thy word is truth." Jesus said in John 14:6, "I am the way, the truth, and the life. No man cometh unto the Father, but by me."

The first thing people say when they are confronted about something they have done is "I didn't do it." Many times, they don't tell the truth until the evidence is presented. I've heard people say that they just tell little white lies. That's nonsense. Adding the words white and little to the lie doesn't justify it.

Did O.J. Simpson commit murder? Did he tell the truth? Did the Menendez brothers kill their parents because they were abusing them? Some money was missing at our school, and they questioned a boy who said, "I didn't do it." Later, a witness who saw him do it came forward with this evidence. The boy finally admitted that he did it.

Isn't it amazing how many people "didn't do it"? Prisons are full of people who "didn't do it." I have always wished that there were a machine on which two people could place their hands. The machine would then zap the one that was lying.

The Best Policy

The second important thing listed in verse eight is "whatsoever things are honest." Second Corinthians 8:21 says, "Providing for honest things not only in the sight of the Lord, but also in the sight of men." If you give your word, there should never be a question that you will keep it. Many years ago, businessmen would seal a deal with a handshake. They did not need to sign a contract. That handshake was all that was needed, because in business deals, it was always honesty first.

I heard about a factory that originally paid their workers on Friday mornings. They began to find out that there was very little work production in the afternoon; so they decided to start paying at the end of the day. I have heard people say that they would rather do business with people in the world than with Christians. What a terrible testimony for the Lord! I have personally known of so-called Christian businessmen who were dishonest in their dealings with others. A man in our church loaned a large sum of money to a so-called Christian businessman who was in financial difficulty. The man has made no attempt to repay that loan.

I have loaned money to two different Christian families. One was to pay a mortgage payment on his home when he had an operation and could not work. The other was to help pay to keep his kids in a Christian school. There has never been an attempt to repay these loans.

Justice

The third important thing mentioned in verse eight is "whatsoever things are just." There are not many things that are just in this world. A rapist who goes to jail is let out and rapes again. Someone commits murder, serves a few years in prison, and then is set free. People steal thousands of dollars with scams and seem to get away with it. Wicked people seem to prosper. People lose their jobs, savings, families, and health because of drugs, and the drug dealers wind up rich. Christian teachers and missionaries work for very little wages. However, some day, justice will be given out. People will personally give account to a just God.

Purity

The fourth important thing is "whatsoever things are pure." You cannot go anywhere in this world without the filth of the world bombarding you. Television, magazines, newspapers, and billboards give occasions for sin. When my son married, both he and his wife gave a testimony at the ceremony that they had kept themselves pure with each other.

Young ladies, God wants you to keep yourselves pure and clean for the man that you will marry. When I think about "pure," I immediately think of Daniel 1:8, "But Daniel purposed in this heart that he would not defile himself with the portion of the king's meat, nor with the wine which he drank. Therefore he requested of the prince of the eunuchs that he might not defile himself."

Lovely

The fifth important quality mentioned in verse eight is "whatsoever things are lovely." How do you handle other people? Would someone watching you say your actions with others were lovely? Think of how Jesus was with the woman at the well and the woman taken in adultery. Did He condemn or did He show love? How did Jesus handle the little children or those who came to Him with illnesses? Do you show love to some Christians, but not to others? Do we really show the love of God to the lost people of the world?

Good Report

The sixth and last important thing listed in verse eight is a good report. The current news is usually full of murders, earthquakes, storms, terrorists, and catastrophes around the world. When you think about it, are there any good reports?

How about the people in your church and school who love God and serve Him with all their heart? How about missionaries serving God all around the world in difficult situations? How about pastors who faithfully preach and teach God's Word without compromise? How about those who tithe, teach, clean the church, visit the sick, and witness to the lost? We must always remind ourselves of these good reports. When people think about you or see you, what do they really think? Is it a good report? Does that report show you love God and want to do what's right?

Virtue and Praise

The last part of the verse says, "…if there be any virtue and if there be any praise, think on these things." Virtue is defined as moral excellence and righteousness. Praise is approval or admiration. We should admire moral excellence, which is explained in this verse. All of the traits listed in this verse really speak of the character of the Lord Jesus.

Verse nine states, "Those things which ye have both learned and received and heard and seen in me, do, and the God of peace shall be with you." Before we do anything, we should examine if our actions are and will be true, honest, just, pure, lovely, and will result in a good report. We should examine our thought life and see if we are dwelling on the things of God. Philippians chapter four is sure to change us, but we need to prayerfully and carefully apply each part to our lives.

Chapter 41

Pride

Pride is an overly-high opinion of one's self and an exaggerated self esteem. A pastor preaches on tithing, and some say "Amen." He preaches on church attendance, and some say "Amen."

One Sunday morning, our pastor said, "Some of you have already made up your mind that you are not coming to the evening service." He preaches on soul winning, and some say "Amen." Those that are saying "Amen" are those that are doing those things. However, when I mention pride, you may be thinking, "Amen. That's not my sin."

What really is pride? It is the look-at-me attitude that says "Look what I did." The opposite is to look at God and look what He did.

We vaccinate for some diseases. Some vaccinations are received once for life, and others are received a few times throughout your life.

There is no vaccination against pride. Wouldn't it be nice if there were? You have to be vigilant and guard against it every single day of your life.

Sneaky Pride

Pride is sneaky. Sometimes it is there, and you do not even realize it. You do not just wake up one morning and say, "I'm going to be proud today."

Sports are one of the best examples where pride seems to flourish, but it can be in other areas of your life, too.

You do not even have to say something to be proud. You can just think proud thoughts. Perhaps you are tempted to think, "I am the best spiker, setter, server, or digger on my team."

Proverbs 27:2 states, "Let another man praise thee and not thine own mouth, a stranger and not thine own lips."

Taking this concept out of the realm of sports, you can have false pride in your voice, intelligence, talent, wealth, clothes, music, boyfriend, or your beauty. If you are not careful, some of those items could be a source of pride for you.

In 1985, the Chicago Bears were the best team in football. They had just won the Super Bowl, and someone was interviewing a player. That player said pridefully, "We are the best team in the world." They were a young team. Many thought they would win again and again. The truth is that they did not win it again. Could pride have been the reason for that failure? They let their guard down quite possibly like the boastful hare in his race with the tortoise.

When I started coaching at a Christian school, we did not have a gym. We practiced whenever we could find a gym to rent, which wasn't often. I remember thinking when we got a gym, no one is going to beat us. As I look back on that, I realize those thoughts were full of pride.

Years ago we were in an association that had a state volleyball championship. A strong team had beaten us three different matches that year – once at their place, once at our place, and once in a tournament. We were hosting the state tournament. Our pastor told me he was talking on the phone to the pastor of that church. That pastor said, "Get that first place trophy ready for our girls." You guessed it. They did not win the championship. I believe with all my heart the only reason we won was because God was humbling the man's pride.

Humble but Powerful Contributors

One summer, I had the opportunity to do a volleyball clinic at the same time the soccer coach from Northland Baptist Bible College was doing his. We talked about sports, and he told me about his experiences coaching his college team. He said the players that he looks for are not the ones who tell him about how many goals they scored in high school or how many all-star teams or MVP awards they have won. Instead, it is the quiet humble guys who put the team first that are the real contributors.

A great player for Maranatha Baptist Bible College when they were winning multiple National championships gave a testimony at volleyball camp that was so precious. She, as a high school senior, was so sure she was going to be the MVP of the state volleyball tournament that she had picked out a place to display the award. But she didn't win it. She was devastated. Again, it was pride that caused the fall. She got her attitude right with God, and He rewarded her in her senior year in college by winning the MVP of the National tournament. This was a wonderful testimony of how God blesses when our attitudes are right.

I encourage you to examine your own heart to see if any pride resides there. Confess it to God and ask Him to help you have a humble spirit toward every aspect of your game and life.

Chapter 42

Joy

God placed *joy* second on the list of the fruit of the Spirit listed in Galatians 5:22-23. A common error is to call this list the *fruits* of the Spirit. It is really singular, the *fruit* of the Spirit. This joy comes from deep within, a wellspring that when cultivated, bubbles forth into your life showing others the way to the Savior.

Some of you have recently received your driver's license, and others of you will soon be getting yours. Every car has a fuel gauge which some call a gas gauge. It goes from F to E. F does not stand for finish, and E does not stand for enough. A wise driver always checks the fuel gauge. Traffic jams and extra trips can cause real problems. I ran out of gas once in my life. I said I never would again. It was the middle of winter, early in the morning. I had to walk miles and miles across open fields in biting cold temperature. That was 35 years ago and guess what? I have never run out of gas since then.

God wants us to have our Joy Fuel Tanks on the F, not the E. John 15:11 states, "These things have I spoken unto you, that My joy might remain in you, and that your joy might be full."

John 16:24 explains, "Hitherto have ye asked nothing in My name: ask, and ye shall receive, that your joy may be full."

First John 1:4 shares, "And these things write we unto you, that your joy may be full."

Let me ask you a question. How is your joy gauge? Is it full, half full, or nearly empty? To have a full joy gauge we must love God, spend time with Him, and keep His commandments.

Part of this fullness of joy comes from fellowship with one another as brothers and sisters in Christ. Sharing how God has blessed us will encourage and lift up others. I just want to shout for joy when someone tells me of a special way God has blessed him or her.

Second John 12 tells us, "Having many things to write unto you, I would not write with paper and ink: but I trust to come unto you, and speak face to face, that our joy may be full."

Third John 4 says, "I have no greater joy than to hear that my children walk in truth."

What brings me great joy is how some of the girls I've coached love God and serve Him faithfully. Their lives are a testimony to all they come in contact with. I love it when they come back and share with me how God is blessing them. I'm sad when I think of former players who have disregarded the warnings of their coach.

Just three years ago, I talked to two girls and warned them about how Satan would attack them and how they should keep themselves pure. They ignored that warning and wound up pregnant without being married. It starts innocently with holding hands and eventually leads to sin. Our former pastor, Dr. Bill Schroeder, used to say skin on skin leads to sin, sin, and sin! You don't need to be going steady at your age. Some of you are sitting there thinking, "It won't happen to me." Those girls didn't think it was going to happen to them either, but it did. You can't trust the flesh. When you play with fire, you are going to get burned. This is one definite way for your Joy Fuel Gauge to be on E.

Manufacturing Joy

You cannot manufacture joy. It comes from within, overflowing into every aspect of your life. People will see it in your countenance. The Holy Spirit does not make people depressed. Do you want to be joyful? Then take the following, familiar acronym to heart.

J---Jesus first

O---Others second

Y---Yourself third

This is the exact opposite of the world's philosophy. The world says take care of yourself because you are the most important.

However, true joy depends on Jesus. Happiness depends upon circumstances such as a new car, winning the tournament, earning an MVP award, getting an A on a test, or buying a new outfit.

Joy is much deeper than mere happiness. Joy is something that should always be there in good times as well as bad times. The last part of Nehemiah 8:10 says the "joy of the Lord is your strength." Can you say that? Again I ask you how your joy gauge reads. If it's not full, you need to spend more time with God.

When you're driving your car, and you look at your fuel gauge, I pray that God will bring to your mind your spiritual joy level. I encourage you to spend time in God's presence that you might find lasting joy and peace.

Chapter 43

Pleasing

When we become Christians by receiving Jesus as our personal Savior, we are faced with an all-important decision: Are we going to live our lives to please God or please ourselves? God's Word says we were put on this earth to please Him.

Revelation 4:11 states, "Thou art worthy, O Lord, to receive glory and honor and power: for Thou hast created all things, and for Thy pleasure they are and were created."

Romans 15:1 says, "We then that are strong ought to bear the infirmities of the weak, and not to please ourselves." Psalm 19:14 explains, "Let the words of my mouth, and the meditation of my heart, be acceptable in Thy sight, O LORD, my Strength, and my Redeemer."

The words that come from our lips and the things we think about—are they pleasing to God? Matthew 15:18-20 explains, "But those things which proceed out of the mouth come forth from the heart; and they defile the man. For out of the heart proceed evil thoughts, murders, adulteries, fornications, thefts, false witness, blasphemies: These are the things which defile a man: but to eat with unwashen hands defileth not a man."

Pleasing Yourself, Not God

There are many examples of people in the Bible who chose to please themselves instead of God. Here are just a few:

King David in 2 Samuel 11 committed adultery with Bathsheba to please himself.

King Solomon in I Kings 11 had 700 wives and 300 concubines, and his wives turned his heart after other gods. He did this even though Deuteronomy 11 forbids kings to have multiple wives.

Adam and Eve in Genesis 3 ate of the forbidden fruit. Verse six says, "And when the woman saw that the tree was good for food, and that it was pleasant to the eyes, and a tree to be desired to make one wise, she took of the fruit thereof, and did eat, and gave also unto her husband with her; and he did eat."

Samson in Judges 14 chose a wife of the Philistines instead of one of the daughters of his brethren. He said in verse four, "She pleaseth me well."

Achan in Joshua 7 took the garment, the gold, and the silver for his own pleasure, and because of it, 36 men died in the battle at Ai.

Gehazi in II Kings 5 took two talents of silver and two garments and wound up with leprosy.

God's Honor Roll

There are also many examples of people in the Bible who chose to please God and not self.

Noah in Genesis 6:8.9 "...But Noah found grace in the eyes of the Lord. These are the generations of Noah: Noah was a just man and perfect in his generations, and Noah walked with God."

Enoch in Genesis 5:22, "...And Enoch walked with God: and he was not; for God took him."

When Potiphar's wife wanted to be immoral with Joseph in Genesis 39:9, "... There is none greater in this house than I; neither hath he kept back any thing from me but thee, because thou are his wife: how then can I do this great wickedness, and sin against God?" Joseph desired to please God and not himself.

Abraham in Genesis 22 was willing to sacrifice his son to please God.

Moses in Hebrews 11:24.25, "By faith Moses, when he was come to years, refused to be called the son of Pharaoh's daughter;

Choosing rather to suffer affliction with the people of God, than to enjoy the pleasures of sin for a season."

Daniel in Daniel 6:4b, "...but they could find none occasion nor fault; forasmuch as he was faithful, neither was there any error or fault found in him." His life was such a great testimony for God that the unsaved could find no fault in him.

Are You Pleasing?

Our goal as Christians should be as Titus 2:8, "Sound speech, that cannot be condemned; that he that is of the contrary part may be ashamed, having no evil thing to say of you." All Christians want to succeed and want to have their prayers answered, but it takes constant effort on your part toward God.

There are two verses that we should dwell on: I Thessalonians 4:1, "Furthermore then we beseech you, brethren, and exhort you by the Lord Jesus, that as ye have received of us how ye ought to walk and to please God, so ye would abound more and more."

First John 3:22, "And whatsoever we ask, we receive of Him, because we keep His commandments, and do those things that are pleasing in His sight."

We should ask ourselves this question about everything we do: "Is this pleasing to God?" Titus 2:12 states, "Teaching us that, denying ungodliness and worldly lusts, we should live soberly, righteously, and godly, in this present world."

Teaching is training. God wants us to live for Him and please Him. He wants us to help teach or train others to do the same. Ungodliness is sinful behavior. By denying it, we refuse to take part in it. Worldly lust means an inordinate desire for something in this world. This self-gratification means more to us than pleasing God.

Soberly means without excess by showing self-control in all matters. *Righteously* means doing what is right and just. *Godly* means devotion to God, loyal and faithful. In regard to volleyball, do we please God when we fail to give our best, when we are selfish, late or miss practices, gossip about teammates and coaches, or fail to be obedient? There are some things we do during games that displease coaches. Here are some examples:

1. Missing serves to start a match or after a timeout, or on game point, or after a teammate misses one.
2. Balls dropping on the floor between two players with no effort by either player.
3. Players out of position.
4. Players not focusing - being distracted.
5. Players not expecting the ball to come to them.
6. Players not moving to the sidelines on every ball that's hit near there.
7. Players not calling for the ball on every play.
8. Players showing discouragement or frustration on their faces.
9. Players quitting on a ball that is playable.
10. Players not thinking clearly but acting only on emotion.
11. Setters not squaring off and facing the target.
12. Spiking getting caught at net and not taking an approach before spiking.
13. Blockers watching the ball instead of the spiker.
14. Players making mistakes because they are focusing on previous mistakes they have made.
15. Players thinking negative thoughts while playing.
16. Players not giving 100% of their attention when coaches are speaking or instructing.
17. Players stepping on the court and not being completely ready to play.
18. Players who are prideful and don't give God the glory.
19. Players who discourage teammates with words or facial expressions.
20. Players who make excuses for their mistakes.

I read an obituary about a woman, and it said that she loved playing bingo. What a sad ending to a life! Wouldn't it be great if our obituary read like Enoch's? He had a testimony that he pleased God. Girls, I pray that your decision will be that you will live your lives to please God and not yourselves.

The idea for this devotional came to me from the Lord this summer when I would walk for exercise in the early morning before the heat of the day.

The sun was just rising, and I was walking westward. The sun was very low in the sky behind me. I looked down and saw my shadow. It was huge—at least forty feet long! I turned at the corner going north, and the shadow was to the side of me. I turned again heading east, and now the shadow was behind me.

Scripture Shadows

Job 8:9 says our days upon the earth are as a shadow. Psalm 102:11 states, "My days are like a shadow that declineth; and I am withered like grass." Psalm 144:4 explains, "Man is like to vanity: his days are like a shadow that passeth away."

Psalm 23 states, "Yea, though I walk through the valley of the shadow of death, I will fear no evil: for thou art with me; thy rod and thy staff, they comfort me."

Shadow Uses

One of the dictionary's definitions of "shadow" is a feeling of gloom or depression. Another definition of shadow is an area of shade upon a surface by a body intercepting the light rays.

I remember as a boy before television. Yes, there was a time before TV! I listened to the radio to a show called "The Shadow." The main character had the Houdini-ability for escaping. He was a crime fighter, and the show ran for twenty-five years, making it the longest running mystery series on the radio. Each week the announcer in a deep voice would say, "Who knows what evil lurks in the heart of man?" The answer would come, "The Shadow knows."

As kids, we would use a flashlight to make shadow pictures on the wall with our hands and fingers.

We all know about the groundhog. Will it see its shadow? Will that mean six more weeks of winter?

We've seen a boxer shadow-box. They swing and punch, but only hit the air and not an opponent. When I think of boxers doing that, I think of First Corinthians 9:26, "I therefore so run, not as uncertainly; so fight I, not as one that beateth the air."

Shadow boxes are usually small open boxes framed and hung on a wall to display small objects.

X-rays use shadows as the rays make shadows of our bones on the film.

We have eclipses when the moon gets between the sun and the earth. The earth is then in the moon's shadow. The moon also has a shadow. The side away from the sun is dark. Some call it the shadow side of the moon.

When I was a young boy, I played second base in softball. Our field at Davis Playground was laid out so the east was to my back. As the game progressed, the sun started to go down. We didn't wear sunglasses back then, and we had to squint to try to see the ball hit by the batter. After a short time, the sun would drop down behind a tall building across the street. The shade or shadow made fielding so much easier.

As young boys, we would play volleyball at night against the girls. Boys always seem to like to play against the girls probably because they want to show off. There were two light towers on top of the field house. The lights back then were not as bright as we have today. We would hit sky ball serves. We would hit the ball as hard as we could so the serve would go high over the light towers. It would come down out of the shadows and was difficult to return. If we got it in the court, it was a sure ace. The problem was we missed hitting them in the court the majority of the time!

I played four years of volleyball in college. We played at Ball State University one year. Their field house had a narrow window area high on a wall near the ceiling. The volleyball court was laid out so the window area was to your back for one team and toward you for the other team. I remember being on the court facing the windows. At a certain time, the sun was directly in our eyes. It was so hard to pick up the flight of the ball on a serve receive. After a little while the shadow or shade was a welcome relief.

As young boys we would meet at night at a friend's house. He lived next to an alley. Across the street, there was a small street light and a long alley. There were shadows along with some darkness. My friend would tell ghost stories and after would dare someone to walk down that long, dark alley. No one would take that dare. At night we played hide and go seek. I found a place down a few steps near a basement apartment where the shadows hid me. I waited and waited and waited. I finally got tired of waiting and came out of the shadows to find out everyone had gone home. The game was over. They had forgotten me!

Shadow of Success

Are you content to be in the shadow of some person when they are successful? They get the glory, and yet you have contributed to their success—but no one recognizes you. How do you handle that?

I remember as a setter putting up the perfect set and watching the hitter bury the ball. The crowd would "ooh" and "ahhh" over the spike, but not think at all about the set that made it possible.

The easiest persons to set to were the ones who never complained when I put up a poor set. The hardest athletes to set to were the ones who always complained about the sets. Most of the time their complaints were verbal, but sometimes it was in the form of a glare. Their complaints made the next sets to them more difficult.

Shadow behind Me

The example of seeing my shadow behind me when I was walking could represent all the people in whose shadow I had walked: my mom and dad; my pastors; my teachers; my coaches; and especially my playground teacher, Mr. Kipp. These were all people who had a positive influence on my life.

Shadow to the Side

The shadow to the side could represent those people who are now under our shadow. How are we influencing them? Is it godly? Everyone is influencing someone. For you girls, it could be a fifth or sixth grade girl that thinks you are the greatest. The speaker at my last church's service said his five year old daughter looks up to all of you. They want to be just like you. What a tremendous responsibility this places on you!

Shadow that Trails Another

When I played in college, a guy named Chuck Osborn was my backup setter. He followed me around and copied everything I did. When I graduated, he took my place. I had influenced him. He was an example of another definition of "shadow", a person who trails another closely.

Shadow in Front

Finally, the shadow in front of you could represent those people in the future that have or will be influenced by our lives. Some of these people will be after we have passed from this earth.

Many of you have had a great teacher. I had a professor in college name Dr. Arthur H. Steinhaus. He was a world renowned physiologist. He was a great teacher and wrote a book entitled *Toward an Understanding of Health and Physical Education.*

What Kind of Shadow Do You Have?

Is your shadow very large or is it very short? You either have a large positive influence on others or a very small influence. Have you thought about the shadows you have followed? Are these people still living? Have you really thanked them? God's Word says, "...be ye thankful".

Are you doing all you can to be godly and live a holy life to influence those walking in your shadow? We are all teachers in some ways. We are teaching someone whether we like it or not.

When you travel to games and stop afterwards to eat, how do you act? Do you pray over the food? Do you clean up after you eat? Do you act like a lady the entire time you are there? Others are watching you. What are you teaching?

One of the great thrills about coaching is teaching and training someone and then seeing her go out and perform well. It's really exciting to see the enjoyment they get just as I did many years earlier.

Many girls who have walked in my shadow are now coaching Christian school volleyball teams. Some of them I expected to do this, but many of them I never thought that God would specifically use them in this way.

The concordance lists the words "shadow" and "shadowing" as appearing 79 times in God's Word. Our main goal as a Christian is to someday stand before a holy God and hear Him say, "Well done, thou good and faithful servant."

I retired a year ago from teaching. My school district used to publish the notes of their open meetings. When teachers retired, they listed either one of three responses: 1. Mrs. X submitted her resignation. We accept her resignation. 2. Miss Y submitted her resignation. We accept her resignation with regret. 3. Mr. Z. submitted his resignation. We accept his resignation with deep regret.

If the administration thought you were an okay teacher, they would use the number one response. If they thought you were a pretty good teacher, they would use the number two response. Those that were outstanding received number three.

I wonder what people will say when we die. He or she was a pretty good Christian. He or she was a very good Christian. Or he or she was an outstanding Christian who loved God with all his or her heart, mind, and soul.

A fourth definition of shadow is "without reality or substance." Does your life have reality and substance for God? I don't mean comparing ourselves with others. We can always find someone less spiritual than us that makes us look good. The Bible says we are not wise if we do that. If we compare ourselves to God, we see how we far miss the mark.

When I was a young boy, there was a popular song entitled "Me and My Shadow." The words went like this: "Me and my shadow all alone and feeling blue, and not a soul to tell my troubles to."

As Christians we cannot say that. We always have someone to tell everything to. He loves us. The best place to be is in His shadow.

Psalm 17:8 shares, "Keep me as the apple of the eye; hide me under the shadow of Thy wings," Isaiah 49:2 states, "And He hath made my mouth like a sharp sword; in the shadow of His hand hath He hid me." And Psalm 63:7 says, "Because Thou hast been my help, therefore in the shadow of Thy wings will I rejoice."

The next time you see a shadow, I pray God will call to remembrance the shadow behind us that represents those that who have influenced our lives. The shadow to the side represents those that you are now influencing. The shadow in the front represents all those that you will influence in the future even after you are gone.

And finally, rejoice in the shadow of His wings! He is with you and will never forsake you. There is great joy in this wonderful truth.

Part 6

Letters

These letters are a compilation from many of the girls whom I've had the privilege to coach. I felt that their personal testimonies would help bring home to you the wonderful joy of Christian athletics. My purpose is not to bring praise to myself but rather to only bring glory to God. While many of the players personally thanked me in these letters, the sincere truth of their experience on the volleyball team tells more about what Christian athletics are, better than I could ever express. These letters are personal and enriching and just might change your life.

Chapter 45

My Wonderful Players

Encouragement in Action

Dear Coach,

I will always remember, "If you practice more, you will play better, and if you play better, you will love volleyball more." The many things you have taught me through the years have made me work harder to become the best player I can be. Your words of encouragement and jokes have meant so much to me.

Through volleyball instructions and devotionals, I have been influenced by your life. One of my most memorable moments in all the years of volleyball was last year when we left an important tournament. I sat on the bench and cried. I remember you came up to me and put your arm around me. You told me that I had played well, but that you knew it was still disappointing to lose. We just sat there watching the other teams play. After we sat there a while, you told me that I still had two more years to play. Then you told me something that I remembered throughout the whole season whenever I played. You said, "You had a good year." It was just a simple sentence, but it meant the world to me. It meant all my hard work had gone for something.

All the days working out at the YMCA—all the practices, camps, hard tournaments—everything had paid off in a simple sentence from one of my favorite people. "You have had a good year." Thank you for being a part of my memories and teaching me so much. Thank you from the bottom of my heart.

Sincerely,
Alli Carr

Routine Faithfulness

Dear Coach,

You know it's funny that with all the excitement and events of Saturday, one thing now stands out in my mind more than the rest — routine faithfulness.

When the girls were taking pictures and celebrating, you started to take down the nets like you've done a thousand times and will keep on doing until you're no longer able. Why do you do this? Because deep in your heart you're committed to serving the Lord, and in this ministry you're influencing, whether seen or unseen, girls who you would never be in contact with otherwise.

Sometimes I wonder what lessons I have learned from volleyball. Then I try to think which lessons I did not learn from volleyball. One or two of them I am still learning, simply because of my stubbornness. One of the most important lessons was teamwork. In every area of life, we work with a TEAM: our families, our classes, our co-workers, and our friends. As the saying goes, "There is no 'I' in TEAM." There cannot be just one person out there to cover the whole court or make everything right. We all have to work together to accomplish our goal - whether to win a game or finish something or just have fun. However, as Christians, our main goal and only joy should be to honor and glorify God.

Another lesson I learned was that in anything I do, I can be a testimony and example of Christ. I know that people are always watching me, now as a coach and teacher more than before. They see my every face and action, and hear every word.

Volleyball has been used to teach me a great many things. Thanks for your encouragement to me through the years.

Yours in Christ,
Brenda Bayless

Behind the Scenes

Dear Coach Casey,

A few weeks ago I had the opportunity to sit in the bleachers and watch the girls and boys volleyball teams play at my children's school. The excitement and the memories came back as I watched the teams work through their strategies of bumping the first hit and getting it to the setter, the setter getting the second hit no matter what, and the spiker getting the best hit that he or she could; also the blocking strategies and calling the ball for another player, etc.

Some of the rules have changed over the years, but the thing that struck me the most was the sense of pride and team membership that the kids possessed.

Later I was going through some boxes in my basement in an attempt to work on some scrapbooks for my kids and for my own childhood memories, when I came across all of my volleyball pictures and memorabilia. That same day your letter came, and I knew I needed to write to you and let you know that my experience on the volleyball team was truly a positive experience in my life.

From a purely athletic point of view, I benefited from the sense of knowing that we were doing the best job that we could, that we were involving our individual skills, and that we were working as a well-oiled machine.

I often think back to the determination and perseverance we had with lots of practices throughout the year and the church league games to keep our skills up. I don't recall ever objecting to going to volleyball practice. I even remember spending summer days outside with Brenda Koning practicing our digging skills. I guess that means we really loved what we were doing. That's the part that I learned and that I try to pass on to my own children — love what you're doing.

My teammates hold very special places in my memories even if I don't have regular contact with them as adults. I was very blessed to be part of a Christian team where Christian ethics and morals took precedence over competitiveness. I hear a lot of parents talk about how competitive school sports have become, and I can appreciate how we always prayed and thanked God for His blessings on our team. For that I owe you thanks. You always kept us mindful of our responsibility to give God the credit.

I have two favorite memories about our volleyball season. I remember being the "team from the little Christian school" that came in and beat Chicago Christian. It was so fun to be the underdog and win. My other favorite memory was our trip to Tennessee Temple's tournament. I remember the feeling of our being a team that was very strong on that trip (on and off the court). Winning the championship was pretty great, too.

Volleyball at our school was a year-round sport. This taught me hard work, dedication, and faithfulness. It also taught me to love the game and the coach who invested so much time in me. My coach taught me to be faithful not only to the game, but also to church and the other areas of my life.

My teammates and I were taught the importance of teamwork and the need to pray for one another. It was difficult to be upset with or hold a grudge against a teammate if you were praying for her daily. It is such an encouragement to hear him say still to this day that he is praying for me. My coach taught me that the team was more important than any one individual player. He treated us fairly and always tried to build us up. A corny joke during a timeout was a regular occurrence.

My coach taught me so many lessons that it is hard to mention them all. He was a great role model. My parents were divorced; so it was good for me to have a strong male influence in my life.

My dad and I had a good relationship, but Coach was there for me on a daily basis. He was always caring and giving. After he realized that my sister and I were taking the city bus and then having to walk more than a mile to get to practice, he just happened to start showing up to pick us up. He was quite a welcome sight, especially when it was raining.

Our season always ended up with a tournament at Tennessee Temple University. After my sister's last game, she did not want to give up her jersey. She wore it around her shoulders all the way home.

When I made varsity the next year, Coach made sure that I got her uniform. He made me feel that he was confident enough in me to fill her shoes. Coach always made you feel like he believed in you. An example of this came one week before the first game of my senior year. I had been a setter for five years starting in junior high. He had four setters; so Coach decided that I should become a spiker. I was devastated. I didn't think that I could learn this new position. I didn't even know how to rotate because I had always been a setter. Coach took me aside and told me that I could do it. He said that he would not put me in that position if he didn't think that I could handle it. After working with me throughout the season, I made an all-tourney team as a spiker. The fact that my coach believed in me made all the difference.

I had one other experience that many of my teammates did not. I was able to coach alongside my role model for one year. I had a behind-the-scenes view of my coach. I was able to learn from him as he handled different situations. I was able to see what made him tick. I only hope that I was able to make a fraction of a difference in a player's life that Coach Casey was able to make in mine.

Yours in Christ,
Maaike Koning Taylor

To God be the Glory

Dear Coach,

I don't have any children that are old enough to play volleyball, but if they ever express an interest I certainly will encourage them. If I took one personal thing out of being on a volleyball team, it's that whatever you do you should do it to the best of your ability, and even more importantly, it should be done to the glory of God. That's what you taught us as a coach, and I thank you for that. I also thank you for keeping each of us in your daily prayers.

It's pretty special to know that someone is praying for you every day. I've had a particularly difficult heartbreak in the past (the loss of a child), and as a result of my prayers I was blessed through the assistance of a former teammate who called me out of the clear blue (She told me she didn't know why she was calling me that day; she just found herself dialing my number. I hadn't heard from her in years!).

But she had the exact information I was praying for so hard for that day. So, in a sense my volleyball teammate was used by God to bless my life as an adult also.

I hope this helps as you write your book. I hope it turns out to be a blessing to lots of people. As a parent, I am always thankful when one of my children has an adult that takes an interest in them and affects them in a positive way. These "significant adults" help children feel good about themselves and develop a positive self-image. Thanks for being a "significant adult" in my childhood. I like to think that part of the adult I am today is because of people like you who shared their time and talents and their faith in God with me. God bless you!

Love,
Sherry Bringle Groset

Teamwork is Key

Dear Coach,

What I learned through volleyball was that you cannot do everything yourself. You need to work as a team to get the goal accomplished. Team means "together each achieves more".

While I was playing volleyball, our team verse was Philippians 4:13: "I can do all things through Christ which strengthens me." Throughout that year we changed the verse to say *We* "can do all things through Christ which strengthens me."

We realized that without Christ we would not be able to win any games. Our team had seven members of the team on the court. Whenever we took our seventh Member (Jesus) off the floor, our team would fall apart.

I have noticed in my home, if I don't allow Jesus to work with me in my house, I begin to mess up and fall apart.

Sincerely Yours,
Jill Hon Christian

Attitudes Count

Hi Coach!

I learned lots of things from volleyball. I learned good sportsmanship; I learned that God does not always reward you with a win just because you pray for it. I learned that you have to work as a team to win; I actually learned what the meaning of teamwork is all about. If your attitude toward your teammate off the court is not right, it will affect the entire team during the game. If I had listened and actually *applied* what my coach taught me from the beginning, I could have been twice the player that I was in high school.

I learned everything that I know about volleyball from Coach. I coached and assistant coached my society volleyball team my junior and senior years of college, and we placed second and third.

Coach always said that you never know if you'll be needed as a volleyball coach in some Christian school. For the past three years I have coached the JV and Varsity teams at Bensalem Baptist School and utilized everything my coach taught me. The team's record ranged from 0-1 wins a year and is now up to 10. I owe all this to my coach and everything he taught me.

One thing I wish I had learned was Coach's patience. He is such a godly man, and that has made such an impression on me. I remember as I went through hard times after high school, through college and beyond, it was such a comfort to know that "Coach is praying for me today." Unfortunately, I cannot say that I am the prayer warrior that my Coach is, but I pray for my girls as well.

I know my Coach had the wisdom to sometimes see the end of the path when we came to crossroads in our lives, and he would help steer us in the right direction. I have tried to do the same with my girls. I have several close relationships with some of them, and I hope that I have helped influence lives as I know my Coach has done.

I made many friends through volleyball. Coach taught me a desire to win, not just play for fun. Our team loved volleyball and played to win. It was a big competition. Coach helped us realize that if we didn't do our best, we weren't pleasing the Lord.

Every year we had a verse Coach had us learn. I did the same with my team; we have a team verse the girls memorize to help them become better players (The verse is applicable to sports, whether it be concerning sports competition, attitude, teamwork, or glorifying God.).

I also learned that you can give a good testimony through sports. I remember our "small" Christian school going up against big public schools. Many times we won, and we definitely gave them excellent competition. I also know that if we stunk, Coach would not have let us play public schools because it would be a poor testimony to our Lord to get whipped. This is something I taught my own girls.

I greatly respect and am thankful for my coach. I did in high school and do even more now. I realize now how much time he gave to us. He volunteered his time freely and never got paid. He didn't get anywhere near the recognition he deserves. And I thank you, Coach, for all the time and energy you invested in our lives, including the past, present and future. I know you will be rewarded someday.

Coach was always there for us and always did what was best for us, even if we didn't like it. Coach, I hope you'll put some of this "praise" into your book. It wouldn't be right if people didn't see the entire picture!

It's funny how you buck at the rules as a teenager, have a bad attitude, and push the limit, but once you become an adult in the same position, you are on the opposite side of the coin and understand the need for obedience and good attitudes, and how much it contributes to the team.

I first started playing volleyball in seventh grade. I didn't like the underhand serve, so I started overhand. I would have gotten it too, but some older girls used to come over and chide me, telling me I was too young and that I should serve underhand. So, I quit volleyball (what an influence we can have on younger children, good or bad). I didn't return until my sophomore year. I learned to love volleyball. I never did perfect my underhand serve, even though I require my own team to perfect theirs before going on to overhand!

In our first JV game against Marquette Manor we were winning 14-2. The final score was 14-16. We lost! What a lesson that was.

My sophomore year I was on JV, and I remember the one-man volleyball team coming and playing against the varsity team, and I think he won. That year, Varsity went to an away tournament, and Coach asked me to sit bench. He put me in once. I was so elated! I served four times (I might have aced one), but I missed my last serve.

I remember many things about volleyball, from sad times to joyful, exciting times. Every year we hosted two tournaments, a Classic and an Icicle. Coach always told us that it was easiest to win and go straight to the championship rather than go through the loser's bracket. So of course we lost one our first games, and then went all the way through the loser's bracket. We were tired when we got to the championship game, which was played right after the previous game we played in; and although we wanted to win, we lost

Before one tournament, Coach sent us into the locker room to get right with each other because we were bickering amongst ourselves over things that had nothing to do with volleyball. Our arguments were affecting the team and how we played with each other.

Coach Phelps was our old athletic director who had moved to Iowa where he coached their volleyball team. We played them at one of our tournaments, but my varsity team had never beat them (previously varsity teams had).

We played them in the championship game, and they were winning. The score was (approximately) 14-11. We got the ball, and I was up to serve. I served in the back right corner on the line two to three times for aces. I'm pretty sure the next serve was out, but the other team played it because they couldn't believe that the other serves were in! I served into that back corner the rest of the game, and we won the championship! It was an exhilarating feeling.

Julie DelPriore and I became best friends through volleyball. We would play volleyball all night long when we had overnight activities in the gym at our school and church.

We practiced volleyball all summer long. We would squeeze through the fence at the end of our block where there was a large water reservoir. We used to run up and down the reservoir, even though we both hated running. We would also go biking and play in the sand volleyball court at the park when the net was up. If not, we would salt and pepper in the street to stay in shape for volleyball season.

Julie Del always dove for the ball. In 1990, we had gone to Coach Phelps' tournament in Iowa, and I remember Julie Del diving for a ball and landing right in the wooden chairs at the end of the bench. She hopped right up and got back into the game. My senior year (1991) at one of our tournaments, she dove for a ball but landed on her arm. She had a knot the size of a golf ball on her forearm, up by the elbow, but she kept diving on it.

One tournament at Pillsbury, Julie Del hurt her knee. We were staying on the third floor in the dorm, and I carried her up and down all three flights of stairs. The same tournament, I remember having a tied score with Somonauk going into the elimination phase. We were to play each other in one game, and the winner would be seeded on the higher level. I also remember that we tended to "warm up" in the first game of a match, and win the last two. Well, we weren't warm yet, and we lost.

In one of our tournaments, the other team had game point, and the setter set me up. The ball was close to the net, and I dinked it into a hole. We were ecstatic until the ref called a carry. I was upset. The Coach told me, "Well, if you had the confidence, you would have spiked the ball instead of dinking it." And while I believe it was a clean dink, I also believe my coach was right.

At the same tournament, Julie Del was teetering and almost hit the net, but I held onto her shirt to pull her back. She didn't hit the net, but the ref still called it.

My senior year, my parents took me to Hawaii for two weeks. The only problem was that we had a volleyball tournament scheduled during the time; so I came back a week early to play. My dad always said I would regret that decision, but I can't say that I ever have. I would have regretted missing it. It was a nine hour flight home, and I came back Friday afternoon. Our first game was Friday evening. I remember Coach taking me out; so later I asked him what I had done wrong. He told me that my jump was getting lower and lower each time I spiked. I guess the only thing I regret is jet lag.

I remember Julie Payne diving for the ball every time she bumped. She always dove first and bumped after.

One session at camp, Chris Lawrence, Julie Del and I came late to a session that Coach was teaching. He punished us by making us sit out of the team competition. That was definitely a way to help us remember to be on time.

The summer before my senior year, Julie Hon and I got picked as camp all-stars. I remember playing one of the best games of my life against the college volleyball team. Although we didn't win, it was a blast.

In one game at Schaumburg Christian School, someone bumped the ball out of bounds behind the serving line. Julie Payne and I both ran for it, but neither one of us expected the other to be there (We didn't run and look at the same time!). We would up running into each other, and I jammed my finger. I *think* we saved the ball. Only one time did Schaumburg Christian School beat our varsity team. Mr. Rieman was our Bible teacher, and his baby died that day. I remember that we all felt awful and cried on the way to the game. That was also the only day we ever tried playing a 5-1. We didn't get it, and we lost.

I remember Coach telling us that someday he was going to write a book about all his players he ever had and was going to call it *Flakes I've Known*. I look forward to reading it!

I have also prayed for you over the years. I don't know details, but I know that your health has not always been at its peak. I pray that you are healthy and strong!

Love,
Tracy Martenson Bedford

Thanks for Praying

Dear Coach,

I truly do appreciate that you still pray for me daily. What a blessing and encouragement that is to me! Also, your prayers are a testimony of your true biblical love for the girls that you coached in volleyball all of these years.

I have fond memories of playing volleyball at Oak Forest. Volleyball was really the first team sport that I had participated in and it was such a good time of learning to work together as a team and being willing to share the ball for the good of the team. The emphasis on working together as a team and not as an individual applies to much of life - an excellent lesson to learn in my young teen years.

I believe that probably my most lasting memory of those years was your ability to be calm in tough situations. We never saw you lose your temper, and yet you had the ability to spurn us on to work harder and to improve. When I saw other coaches losing their tempers at their girls, at the refs, there you always sat as cool as a cucumber.

What an example of what life is about! Not losing control, but in all of life's situations being under the control of the Holy Spirit. We also learned that when we lost control that in reality our playing worsened. Playing with intensity is so different than playing with an attitude or a spirit that is out of control. Each team member knew that your love for the Lord was much greater than your love for volleyball, and that it was important to you to keep your testimony in the most pressured of situations. Thank you for that type of coaching.

Yours in Christ,
Bobbie Alexander Schroeder

The Difference

Dear Coach Casey,

I want you to know personally that you made a difference in my life through your coaching and the game of volleyball.

You believed in your girls and showed us how to hold our heads high both in victory and defeat. You taught us endurance and stamina. Personally, you taught me that hard work paid off. I wasn't a "natural athlete" but my desire and your belief in me pushed me to succeed and stay on first string varsity and compete in the state tourneys. I also was recognized as MVP, all tourney and most improved.

As a coach you truly cared for your girls on a personal level. Looking back now I see how you were developing our character through the game of volleyball. You prayed with us and for us and taught us integrity on the court. Your humility spoke volumes.

As an adult I see myself believing in my own kids the way you believed in me. I have learned that perseverance goes a long way and to tough it out. Many times in my personal life I think of different matches and what I learned. Those experiences are priceless.

Thank you, Coach Casey. You will never be forgotten.

Dawn Pazdell Smith

Convinced to Try

Dear Coach,

Volleyball played an important role in my life. As a young child, I was shy, withdrawn, had low self-esteem, and never spoke to anyone except my family and church friends. When I was in sixth grade, I was eligible to participate in interscholastic sports. Volleyball and basketball always looked fun to me, and my older sister Kellie was already a great athlete in softball, volleyball, and basketball. I dreamed of playing, but my fear of people and fear of failing overtook me, and I convinced myself I just couldn't do it.

Kellie, on the other hand, talked to me and tried convincing me to try out for the volleyball team. I told her I was afraid that I didn't know how to play, someone would laugh and I'd be out on the court in front of everyone. She pushed and pushed until tryout day arrived and she said, "You are trying out!" She had a way of influencing me - so I did it. I was petrified! It was the worst day of my life! I just knew I had made a fool of myself.

I made the B team, but still felt I wasn't worthy to play and didn't have the skill. I sat on the bench most of that year, but it was okay with me. I was too afraid to be out on the court during competition and with all those fans watching. I loved practicing, even though I knew I had no skill.

As that season went on, and I played again my seventh grade year, I watched as my friends advanced to the A team. It crushed me. I decided to work harder. By eighth grade, my coach praised my hard work and encouraged me to develop my spiking skills. I was thrilled that my coach even thought I had any skill at all. He wrote me a letter upon my eighth grade graduation, uplifting my talent and encouraging me to pursue high school volleyball. I still have that letter, and that year was a turning point for me - not just my athletic ability, but in my overall self worth.

Lessons Learned

Never give up - always think positive

Work as a team - there is no room for individualism in a team sport

Discipline - work hard, even when you don't want to

Encourage others - we all need a pat on the back

Never criticize your teammate when an error is made - we all make mistakes and criticism crushes one's spirit

Talk to each other on the court - it builds unity and lets others know you are pulling your weight out there

Always stretch before practice and games - a life long injury can be prevented (just ask me!)

Volleyball Memories
Chicago Christian - 1983-84 Season

Best competition ever in high school career; played our heart's out; played our best; won the match.

Mr. Casey's prayers after a terrible match. He was never a yelling-type of coach, but his prayers chewed us out good and made us realize that we had not played our best before God. "And whatsoever ye do, do it heartily, as to the Lord, and not unto men" (Col. 3:23).

On the flip side, he praised us through his prayers when we played to our utmost ability, even if we happened to lose that game.

Senior Year - Maranatha Tournament -
1985-86 Season

Very first game of the tournament - double elimination tournament

Had an 8:30 AM game. That year we could never get our act together early in the morning. I believe we were tired, slow, and psyched ourselves out that we just couldn't pull it off. We lost the match. We were shattered, knowing that in order to win the tourney we had to go through the "Loser's Bracket" and win every single match! We would then have to beat the winner of the "Winner's Bracket" twice!

I played every game and rested very little that day! When Coach Casey was able to give me a break, I sat toward the end of the bench next to my friend Jenny. I remember being so exhausted that I just needed to close my eyes for a minute. I told her to nudge me when Coach wanted me back in the game. I prayed for God to give me the strength and energy to fight my hardest. I played that tourney with every ounce of my heart, soul, and body! I begged my body to work when it had no strength to do it. I remember diving for a ball that day. I was certain I would never get it. I was one step slow, but I made a dive for it and let out a grunt that was simply pure exhaustion.

To my surprise and delight, I popped it up, as pretty as ever. Our setter and hitter made a perfect play out of it. I could barely get back up off the ground. When I did, I remember feeling within myself that if I could push through the pain of fatigue; I had to help my teammates do the same if we were going to win. My desire to give up left me! I jumped up yelling words of encouragement, and we all got back into the desire-to-win-mode.

We won that tournament, and our whole team cried from fatigue and from knowing that we worked harder than ever to win that tournament. I think I slept all the way home. Never had I felt such exhaustion.

The final tournament of my Senior year—Spring Tourney at Oak Forest Christian Academy

We won the tournament, and I was named MVP. As we were dispersing, the coach from Calumet came up to me and said, "Kim, I just want to tell you that I have watched you play for four years, and I have coached for many years. You are the best player I have ever seen not just your athletic ability, but your incredible spirit of team work. So many times you could have taken a kill for your own glory, but you always considered your team. You are not an individual, and I wish there were more players like you. You will be missed." She hugged me, and I cried. No greater athletic award could have been presented to me. Coach Casey taught me that valuable lesson of team work - for that I am grateful!

Sincerely,
Kim Duvall McDaniel

Discovering the Value of Faithfulness

Dear Coach,

It has been over 17 years since I had the privilege of playing Varsity Volleyball at OFCA. To this day, I still make reference to Coach Casey and how we won every single game of the '83-'84 school year. If my memory is correct, it was close to 41 matches. There are some things that I call to remembrance and try to express concerning Coach Casey, but find it difficult not getting a little emotional. How could I overlook the fact that he prays for every player he has ever had every day? He reminds me of this every time I see him, in turn, reinforcing to me this act of love, service, and dedication. One could only wonder the direction of a life without this prayer support. It would be understandable if he prayed for his all-star players or those with unforgettable personalities as they were brought to mind, but to think that he dedicated prayer time for those who sat the bench more than they played and listened more than they spoke makes me appreciate his faithfulness even more.

Personally, the greatest impact the volleyball experience has made on my life is learning the character trait of faithfulness. Coach rewarded the players for their faithfulness. If we were faithful in turning out to practices, it resulted in better performance. Our faithfulness to God results in better life performance and blessings. God rewards us because of our faithfulness, and I believe this is the underlying message Coach wanted us to understand.

The most memorable and emotional times for me were not how the games were played or how many games were won, but it was the times when we huddled together in prayer before, during, and after the games. There was one time we came together for prayer in the auditorium and felt it was impossible for any other team to be closer.

To this day, I can't bring myself to get rid of the boxed-up trophies - not because of any personal accomplishments, but because of the team represented that I had a privilege of being a part.

Laura Skolaski Deets

Dedication

Dear Coach,

As a parent, I understand now more than ever the importance of organized sports. In this day and age, if we don't have our children active beyond belief, whether it is in church, in school, in music, or in sports, the chance of sin creeping into their lives is too big to risk.

The Lord blessed me with a healthy body and with a school that led me in the direction to achieve all that I have. He also blessed me with a coach whose influence carried over from volleyball to every day life. And now, 15 years later, his teachings, whether they be volleyball skills or life's lessons, still radiate in my mind and heart.

The sport of volleyball allows one to exercise and build all areas of one's body. The strength you build in your fingers allows one to set the volleyball from all areas of the court and to various heights. The strength you build in your arms and upper body allows you to serve the volleyball (hopefully consistently) and to spike (hit) the ball at various speeds and with different levels of force. The strength you build in your lower body and legs will allow you to develop a high vertical jump, which is vital to consistent and forceful spikes (hits). That strength will also allow you to move from position to position on the court quickly and accurately.

The bond you form with your teammates and coach allows you to work together on and off the court. It teaches you communication skills, and it also forms relationships that last long after the game is over.

If I had to sum it up, I'd say volleyball taught me to be physically fit and it taught me the art of dedication to what you love. It has also taught me the art of communication. Through all those skills learned, I have been able to live a valuable and rewarding life, marry a wonderful man, give birth to fantastic children, with whom I hope to carry on the volleyball tradition.

But most of all, it helped establish love and respect for my fellow teammates and a coach whose ability to teach a group of girls not only how to play volleyball, but also live every day for the glory of God.

Marcy Locke Durham
Class of 1985

Love for Teammates

Dear Coach,

Volleyball has for a long time been a sport that I have enjoyed. I think back to when I first started playing volleyball; I think I was in the eighth grade. My older sister started to play and I really did not have much interest in it then. I remember her waking me up and dragging me out of bed on Saturday morning to go to practice. I now thank her for that.

For me, volleyball has been a great way to meet people. I guess that goes back to high school. Many of my good friends played on the same volleyball team. I guess going to a Christian school was a great thing, because our team had the opportunity to play other Christian schools as well as public schools. When we did play public schools, the team was always prepared to tell others about Christ. It was a neat thing to go share the gospel with the other players and lead others to Christ. Some of the best times were the bus trips back to our school when we would share with each other the different experiences that we had, and what a time of rejoicing when a soul was won to Christ!

After my senior year of high school, I went on to play for a Christian college in Wisconsin. There I met new people and had a new volleyball team.

Our team was in the Lake Michigan Conference, so we too had the opportunity to play several public colleges. Our team would sing and pray after every game and then go share the gospel with others. I remember that the team would get together before every game; this was the time that we would have team devotions and pray for the opportunity to witness to the other team and the referees.

Our team had two referees that were used by the conference a lot. I remember that our team was so burdened for those ladies to get saved. I also remember our coach taking the time out of her busy schedule to establish a friendship with the referees and be a witness to them that way.

Another person that I met through volleyball was my husband. I married the coach's son, so I guess I can say that volleyball will always be in our family. I go every year and help my mother-in-law with a volleyball camp.

I still meet new people every year and the mission of the volleyball camp is to reach out to other girls and share the gospel with them.

Thanks so much for all you have done for me.

Sincerely,
Julie Hon Jackson

Chapter 46
More Wonderful Players

First Love

Dear Coach,

For a man, often his first love is a car. For a woman, often her first love is her high school sweetheart.

For me, my first love was volleyball. The soft leather, the gentle sting on the forearm, the release of a perfect set...could there be anything that could make me feel more complete? Well, yes, another 5 or 6 inches so I could have been a hitter, but we can't have it all now, can we?

I was a mess my first practice. Not only did I not know how to hit the ball properly, I couldn't even get to the ball fast enough to hit it wrong! I went home and cried with full intentions of never going back.

I was resolved to be a rah-rah for the rest of my long high school years. How depressing.

My dad found me and asked how it went. After explaining my utter defeat, he hugged me, handed me a ball and said, "Binners never quit." (My last name is Binner). Then we went to work. Over the next few weeks, Coach Casey was very patient and I began my lifetime love of the game of volleyball. I was smitten or as Bambi would say "twitter paited," with the little white ball. Slowly Coach Casey began to teach us not only proper ball handling skills, but also snuck in little life lessons along the way.

We learned that anyone can hit a volleyball, but to hit it correctly took practice, control and skill. In a game, if you play with a person who does the "one handed swing," you never know where the ball is going to end up-very little control. Just like in life, many people live the "one handed swingers" life - it works but makes everyone else on the team wonder what happens next. On the other hand, if you practice control, live life aware of others around you, know they are counting on you, how your "play" will affect their lives, you are a team player.

Just one of the many life lessons volleyball teaches us. Thanks to Coach Casey, I'm teaching my little team how to correctly "play volleyball."

My best memories were beating Chicago Christian High School my junior year, hanging out with Kelly, Sherry, and Paula at tourneys (The A Team), and bus trips—best of times.

Yours in Christ,
Becky Binner Hunt
Captain 1984-85

Thrived on Discipline

Dear Coach Casey,

I have never been one for a lot of words, so this won't even come close to two pages. Thank you for your prayers on my behalf. What a wonderful blessing to find out that you have been praying for me all these years!

Volleyball Memories

As a young girl, volleyball was simply a challenge. It was something to set my mind to and determine to do. It was a discipline which I thrived on.

Lessons Learned

The lesson that stands out in my mind through the sport of volleyball is to never quit.

Christian Sportsmanship

We made it a practice to pray before each game as well as at practices, which simply showed that we can bring all things to our Lord. At that time in my life, it was something very important to me and God knew that.

Special Memories

To sum it all up, the coach was the best thing about volleyball. I know you don't want to write about you, but you were the one that made playing volleyball such an awesome opportunity for those participating. I was privileged to be a part of the team that you coached.

Sincerely,
Rhonda Skubnick Swangim

Learned About Teamwork

Dear Coach,

I played competitive volleyball in high school and college in the late 1970's. I still play occasionally with my Sunday School class. It is interesting that the skills that I learned in high school have stayed with me all of my adult life. Once I get warmed up on the court, I usually can play a fairly decent game. My spiritual life is like that, too. Spiritual truths that I applied to my life when I was young can still apply to my life now that I am older. It takes discipline to play a good game of volleyball.

Anyone can get on a court and hit the ball over the net; however, in order to play the game correctly and according to the rules, you have to learn how to hit the ball correctly. When I started playing in high school, I found it easy to hit the ball over the net on my own.

However, the coach reminded me over and over that volleyball is a team sport, and the ball could be controlled and hit most effectively if you used your teammates to help set the ball up and spike it. That didn't come easy for me. I tended to always want to go for the sure thing rather than trust my teammates to return the ball. I had to learn to depend on my teammates in order for the team to be successful.

The same thing holds true for me spiritually; I have learned that it order for me to have a successful Christian life, I must be totally dependent on God. I cannot handle life's problems on my own. I have tried to do things my own way many times, but failure has shown me that God's Way is the only way.

I remember playing volleyball in the ACE (now known as School of Tomorrow) State Championship tournament my senior year of high school. We wore our volleyball jerseys and culottes. I have always been a tall girl, and I had trouble finding skirts and culottes that came to the knees (hemlines to the knees were always the standard). Anyway, as I was warming up to play the first game of the tournament, I was called off the court by one of the women officials. She told me that my culottes were not long enough; therefore, I was disqualified from playing in the tournament. I was devastated and embarrassed. Volleyball meant a great deal to me, and I felt it was unfair that I couldn't play. I was the captain of the team, and now I felt that I was letting my team down.

I left the floor and going back to my sleeping quarters and sobbing. I can't remember now who I spoke with, but someone advised me that since there was nothing I could do to change the situation, the best thing to do was to have a good attitude and to try to encourage my teammates. I will admit that I would have preferred going home. However, I went back to the game, and I spent the next two days at the sidelines cheering the team on. The Lord gave me the grace that I needed to have a good attitude. My team won the championship, and my teammates graciously allowed me to accept the trophy on behalf of the team.

The highlight of this experience was when the woman who banned me from playing came up to me afterwards and said that she really appreciated my attitude and regretted that she chose not to let me play. The Lord taught me a lot from this experience. I realized that my testimony in front of others was more important than my ability to win a championship.

Although I was disappointed that I couldn't play, I will always remember the Lord's goodness in allowing me to accept the disappointment. By the way, my team went on to win the National Championship that year, and I played in all the games (with new longer culottes of course!).

I will always remember my years of playing volleyball in school as a means of showing me how to lead a disciplined life. Now that it has been 25 years since I finished high school, I strive to lead a disciplined life both physically and spiritually. I run regularly and even enter a race now and then. More importantly, I try to read my Bible daily and depend on the Lord to meet my needs.

Sincerely,
Diane Ward Wilson

Worth All the Work

Dear Coach,

Volleyball meant so many things to me at different times in my life. For instance, when I was younger and in grade school just beginning volleyball, it meant that I had a fun activity to do with my friends at school. As time passed and I was getting older, I had to start learning discipline and responsibility. This meant doing things that I didn't always like to do such as Saturday morning practices during the summer where we did skills over and over and over. I noticed less and less of my friends participating once I got to this point.

In high school, volleyball became part of who I was, and it forced me to be a leader in the school and gave me something to be proud of after working so hard. It started to seem like it was worth all of the practices.

One of the most important things that I learned at this point was teamwork. You can't be a good team unless you can count on each other and work together. This ultimately helped me transition into my college life. Teamwork at this time in my life was not only crucial on the court with my teammates, but also with my future roommates and classmates. Teamwork is what volleyball is all about. You cannot play with one player though some have tried. I have never been part of a winning team that did not have it, and I have seen many teams that could have been good go down because their lack of it.

Besides learning a lot of important lessons from it, volleyball also gave me so many opportunities that I would not have otherwise had in my life. It was such a fun way for me to learn life's lessons! To this day, I still miss the sound of plays being called and balls bouncing in a gymnasium. It brings back so many happy memories. With other things around me that weren't as they should be, I could always count on volleyball to be a constant in my life.

Volleyball Memories

Our huddles in high school during the games. We could never get out of the huddle until Coach Casey told one of his corny jokes! I think the crowd knew exactly what was happening when we would all grown in unison before breaking the huddle. This was just one of Coach Casey's consistencies. He is the large part of what made us the team that we were. His coaching is what made our teams what they were. He knew each one of us and took a personal interest in us and what our talents were. He taught us to be better players and a better team because of it. We had a lot of outstanding players, but without our coach, we could not have been the team that we were. He told us that he prayed for each one of us everyday. That is special to me.

Christian Sportsmanship

The answer is "Coach Casey" (Coach, I don't know if this is what you asked for to add to this book, but I hope you will keep it in somewhere). He was always such a good example to us all of what a good Christian sportsman is supposed to be. No ill word was ever muttered from his mouth about another team or a bad call made.

Special People

I have met so many special people by participating in volleyball, and I know that it was all part of God's plan for my life. I know that He gave me talents so that I could be part of something special. Although there were times that I did not give 100%, I desired to use those talents to please Him. That desire carries over into everything that I do today—in my job, in my marriage, in my family and in my daily walk with Him.

Volleyball was part of my overall Christian experience and I am forever grateful for it.

Sincerely,
Shelly Reeves Kurshner

Discovered How to Win in Life

Dear Coach Casey,

Volleyball has been a life changing experience for me. It all began when I was in eighth grade. At the time, our coach and PE teacher was Miss Campbell. She needed another player for the Junior Varsity team, and she asked me to join her group. I was so excited to be elected. Then I played on the varsity team in high school. Because of my involvement with volleyball and my God-given athletic abilities, God directed my life to become a PE teacher.

In 1986, I graduated from Bob Jones University with a B.S. degree in Physical Education. Volleyball has become my favorite sport and pastime. I learned how to give my best and never quit. As the saying goes, "A winner never stops trying and a quitter never keeps trying."

You taught us to be disciplined players. During summer vacation, you would require us to practice and exercise every day.

We had to record our practice time on a 3 x 5 card and bring it with us to the following practice. In order to become a better player, I would do my best to have my card completed. Also, I recall staying after practice a half-hour or more to work on specific elements of the game—mainly spiking.

As you would often say, "One of the hardest skills in volleyball to master is spiking." You would diligently work with me to improve my abilities. You taught us to play with confidence and to anticipate each play as if every ball was directed at us. We would always hear you say, "when in doubt, play it." You taught us more than the fundamentals of volleyball; you showed us how to serve God wholeheartedly.

I remember how you had devotionals and taught us how to do right. Thank you for your godly example. I learned from you the benefits of good sportsmanship. It doesn't matter if you win or lose, but how you play the game. During my high school years, we won many championships and through it all, you maintained a humble and grateful spirit.

When I think of Daniel in the Bible, I am reminded of you. He prayed often with full knowledge of the consequences. After every game, we would come together on our knees and pray thanking God for the victory or the loss. Our school verse was First Corinthians 10:31,"Whether therefore ye eat or drink, do all to the glory of God."

Your goal for our team was to give the right opinion of who God is. You truly honored Him by giving your best for us. Thank you for always praying for me. It is a blessing to know that someone cares.

I just completed my sixth year in coaching volleyball. In February, my team won the conference championship. In past seasons, my team made it to the final four every year with two state championships. Thank you for teaching me the qualities and discipline it takes to be a good coach. My assistant this year was Michell Rogers (Anderson). She was on my team from 1986-1989. She is an excellent athlete and a very hard worker. Michell also followed in my footsteps and majored in PE at BJU. My desire is to influence other players to excel at volleyball as you have influenced me. There will be many stars in your crown.

Thank you for your faithfulness.

Sincerely,
Cheryl Gallowitch Tremper

Seven Years Wasn't Long Enough

Dear Coach,

I played volleyball for seven years in grade school through high school. From there, I went on to play three years in college for a total of ten years of competitive ball.

I was fortunate to have one coach throughout my first seven years. Many of my friends were under different coaches who all had different techniques, different aspirations, and different temperaments. Having one coach that knew the game and knew how to teach it was a wonderful stabilizer for my beginning years. My volleyball career was riddled with injury. In grade school, I broke my arm. In Junior High, I sprained a knee. My Junior year, I sprained an ankle putting me out of play for the first four weeks of the season. Through it all, I would say that volleyball helped me to dedicate myself to a goal. I wanted to play. Little speed bumps and obstacles came along in the form of injuries, but I was determined to play.

Once dedicated to a goal, you have to develop a plan of attack. In volleyball, one person cannot win the game. It takes a team. It takes teamwork. It takes unity. Every player had a part on the court and off the court. Every player had to give the effort: 100% effort. In working together, a team can usually achieve the goal of playing and having fun. Winning the match is a goal and you always want to strive to meet it. Yet losing is not the end of the world. Losing was sometimes more beneficial than winning. Losing helps you to re-evaluate your goal, your effort, your unity, your focus. You learn from the mistakes. You correct things. You improve your skills. You better understand your part on the team.

Special Memories

As a young girl in grade school, I can remember riding in the bus or van to games and tournaments. I could not wait to be old enough to play.

My first game that I played in was in the Midwest Classic at OFCA. I was in fifth grade, and one of the girls on the JV team did not come in time. Coach asked me if I wanted to play. How could I say no? I was so nervous, but I had the best time.

Bus trips were always fun. The ride back was usually loud with talking, laughing and singing.

Then there was volleyball camp at Maranatha Baptist Bible College. Oak Forest players were first in the breakfast line. We were usually the ones up the latest at night. If there was trouble, we were usually in the vicinity.

I can also remember when Coach would say goodbye at the final tournament of a player's career at OFCA. It was usually at the closing ceremony as he passed out awards. He would hand out the award and give a hug. It always made me cry a bit to watch the exchange between coach and player, mentor and student. Then one day, it was my turn. It was the last time I would ever play under Coach's instruction.

Seven years did not seem long enough.

Sincerely,
Bonnie Bayless

All Players Are Necessary

Dear Coach,

I learned many valuable lessons playing volleyball. All of the lessons that I learned are lessons that I have applied to my daily life.

Teamwork

A volleyball team consists of six people on the court. One person can not play alone; a whole team is needed. Volleyball is a sport that requires teamwork. The six people out on the court must work together. These six must help each other, because the game can not be played by just one person. I have learned to become a team player because of the lessons I learned playing volleyball. Teamwork is very important in life, in work, and in relationships. It is not necessarily easy to be a team player. It involves sacrificing your own ideas and agendas for others on the team. It involves giving of yourself to better the team, and not just yourself. Not everyone can be a team player, but I believe that volleyball helps instill this quality into those who play.

Responsibility

Another great lesson that I have learned from volleyball is that of responsibility. If you are a part of a team, I believe that you have a responsibility to that team. You have a responsibility to show up to practices, and a responsibility to do your best to help make your team better. When you commit to something, you must do your best to try to fulfill that commitment. Your teammates are depending on you. Your coach is depending on you. I believe that volleyball helps teach responsibility because you are part of a team, a team that needs you. If you do not fulfill your responsibility, the team will suffer. Responsibility is a very important character trait that is lacking in today's society. We are living in a me-first society. There is no sense of responsibility or obligation to others on the team or those around them. Most people today do not feel a sense of responsibility and do not commit themselves to anything. I believe that playing volleyball taught me to be a more responsible person. I learned how to stick by something and to commit myself to something. I learned how to be accountable for my actions and to take responsibility for my actions, whether good or bad. This is another character trait that I have been able to apply to my life outside of volleyball.

Faithfulness

One of the most important lessons that I learned through volleyball was displayed greatly by my coach. He taught us the importance of faithfulness. When playing volleyball you need to be faithful to the team, to your coach, and to practices. If you are not faithful to something, it not only affects you, but it affects all others around you. This is true not only with volleyball, but with all other areas of your life, too. If you are not faithful to your job, it not only affects you, it affects the others you work with. If you are not faithful to your family, it does not just affect you, it affects your whole family, and many others. If you are not faithful in your relationship to God, you are not the only one who is affected. It affects many others. Coach taught us the importance of faithfulness to God and other areas of our life by being an example of faithfulness himself. I am so thankful that my coach portrayed such Godly character to be able to instill in us this important trait.

Hard Work

Volleyball has also taught me how to work hard and push myself toward a goal. Not all of the conditioning that you need for volleyball can be acquired through the practices. You must also do some work on your own. This takes some discipline. I remember Coach giving us little monthly calendars and requiring that we keep track of what we did to enhance our skill on our own. Those made me realize that I needed to give my all, not just at practice, but outside of practice as well. If I am committed to becoming the best volleyball player that I can, I need to put in some hard work, not just at practice, but on my own, as well. It is easy to give yourself to something and do it half-heartedly, but to be able to push yourself to do something takes work, hard work. Playing and learning volleyball definitely takes work. Practices take hard work, the games take hard work, conditioning before the game takes hard work, and blending with your teammates takes hard work. Life itself can be hard work, and being able to push yourself toward something without giving up is commendable. I learned how to do this through my years of playing volleyball.

Application to my Life Now

These traits are not just things that I learned to do on the volleyball court and have left on the court. They are things that I am continually trying to apply to my life. They affect my life as a Christian, as an employee, and eventually as a spouse and a parent. I am very thankful that the Lord gave me the opportunity to play volleyball under a wonderful coach and on some terrific teams, and I am eternally grateful for the many lessons that I learned while playing volleyball. These lessons not only affect my life in the present, and in the future, but also in eternity to come.

Thank you, Coach!

Sincerely,
Cathy Trask

More Than Just a Game

Hi Coach,

Thanks for giving me this opportunity to share my experiences. I think that your writing a book is long overdue! Here is what you asked for; I hope you can use some of it.

Let me just say now that I am so thankful for you and your ministry to so many through volleyball. I was just at a tournament this fall when I ran into a woman who knew you through Maranatha camps and such; we had a good time just reminiscing about you and the impact that you have had. Thank you for following God.

Volleyball Lessons

I have never had an activity impact so many areas of my life as volleyball has. There are very few precious things in life. Who could imagine that I would count a game as one of them? But volleyball has meant more than just a game for me; it has reached into my life physically, mentally, emotionally, socially, and, yes, spiritually. To me, volleyball means making good friends, playing in tough games, suffering through tougher practices, focusing on a goal, reaching that goal, keeping my poise to that goal, and giving God the glory for everything that happens.

I have learned how to work hard, not only at what I am good at, but what I am not. It taught me that I can always go one step farther and do the good things a little better. It has taught me commitment. I could have quit any time—whenever I felt frustrated or in a losing season—but my commitment to my team was a bond I could not break. Along with commitment comes dedication.

These two are different, because you can be committed without involving your heart. But, when you are dedicated, you are involved heart and soul—anything can happen. It has taught me leadership. I can remember being a senior in high school and helping a freshman girl in her first varsity game. She was so nervous! But she looked to me and my good friend (who was a senior on the other team) for strength. I was a captain on my university squad for two years. No one on the team knew how hard it was for me to play, work, plan a wedding, and then get married.

A leader does more than play well; a leader inspires others to play better and be better because a leader is watched on and off the playing court. Leadership has its roots in servanthood. How great it was to see a freshman shocked that I would fill her water bottle! I would never have known leadership in its entirety if it had not been for the outlet of volleyball.

I also learned about friendship—how to be a friend in good and bad times. I learned how to maintain a team, or family, through diversity and at times disagreements. I learned how to trust people, even when they ended up failing me. I learned how to trust them again. I learned how to win, and I learned how to lose. But most importantly, I learned how to play. And through it all, I learned that God is present even in the small stuff.

Christian Sportsmanship

I had the privilege of playing solely with Christian teams throughout my volleyball years, so I have seen many acts of sportsmanship that have gone above and beyond what people would expect. I remember playing in high school and touching a ball that went out of bounds on a block. I told the referee that I had touched the ball, even though he had not seen me. We lost that point, but I will never forget when he told me how honorable I had been. That story never left me because I faced the same situation again in college. And again, I did the same. No recognition followed me the second time, but I knew I made an impact on someone; and if not, I had the satisfaction of knowing that I did the right thing and win or lose I could hold my head high. I have played against many teams, some of them of secular faith.

One college in particular was very skilled in volleyball and beat us every time we played them, except once. I remember the last time we played them. After we shook everyone's hands, the coach came up to me and told me that he was glad he would not have to face me again because his team had a hard time defending me, but that he had not seen a player with such great personal qualities as I had. What he saw as personal qualities was the relationship I have with Jesus Christ. I am thankful that through these situations I could show Jesus without having to say anything.

Special Memories

I remember watching the volleyball games from the bench as a seventh grader. I remember starting in my first game as an eighth grader. I remember my first high school practice where all of these girls were spiking, setting, and serving overhand. I have never been more intimidated in my life.

I remember a game in high school when stoic Coach Casey cheered after one big block I had. I remember making posters for high school games. I remember playing in front of our high school hometown crowd, hearing them cheer, and watching my parents act like crazies!

I remember hearing people cheer for me in college, some people who weren't even from our school! I remember coming back home, and watching my sister play in the same uniform I wore in high school. I remember my last game ever where my college came in second for a regional championship. I remember crying when I realized it would never be like this again. I remember every award and every broken school record. I remember being the first person ever in the history of my college to be First Team All-American for four years straight. Although my memories span over ten years of playing, there is one constant that I found. It was the times I spent with my team praying and singing praise to God that I remember, and miss, the most. I remember being on a court, losing by a lot, and praying, "God, thank you for the opportunity to play this game." There were many times when I sang songs of praise, like "Victory in Jesus," on the court to myself just to remind me why I was there and who I was playing. It was those times that I cherish above all else.

Encouragement to Players

I would just like to say to any player out there that one day, this will all be over. There will be no more games and no more practices. Life as you know it will change. I didn't think that day would come, but it did. I sit here now five months pregnant with my first child. My husband and I are in youth ministry. School is over. I am an assistant coach myself now, and although I am involved with the game, it is still not the same. It was not just volleyball that I played. My coaches didn't just teach me how to spike hard. I learned about life. My coaches are still mother and father figures in my life. My teammates will always be my sisters. And God, He will forever be the Captain of my life. Don't worry so much about how much you win or how often you lose. Make sure you are learning lessons on how to live. These are the lessons that you will be able to pass on to your children someday. Whether therefore I eat or drink, or whatsoever I will do, I will do it all to the glory of God.

Sincerely,
Eydie Clark Reiser

A Consistent Example

Dear Coach,
I can't tell you enough what an impact you were and are on my life. What a blessing volleyball was in my life, and I'm so glad I played on your team.

Volleyball Memories

I remember our team rolling out to our positions from the huddle.

I remember hearing all kinds of jokes even during timeouts. I tried that with my team; it works.

I remember a coach who taught us how to live a consistent Christian life. I am amazed that he prays for us daily. Even today when I talk to him he says "I'm praying for you." I need that and covet his prayers.

I was never very interested in volleyball until I didn't make the cheerleading squad in the spring of my freshman year. I knew I wanted to do something so I gave volleyball a try. I thank the Lord that he opened that door for me.

Volleyball became a way for me to learn a lot of Biblical traits and grow in my walk with God. I had a coach who made it very important to not only teach me the game of volleyball, but also to teach me the Bible. I was from a divorced home so my coach became a very important person to me, much like a father. I learned that whatever I do, "do all to the glory of God." Our team verse, Psalm 115:1-3, "not unto us . . . but unto thy name give glory. . ." stressed that again. It's easy to give glory to yourself when your team is doing so well, but I believe it was God's blessing on us.

Our coach stressed faithfulness. If we could learn to be faithful in volleyball and other smaller things in life, we would be faithful in big things. God is looking for faithful people in His service. We had a great example in our coach who faithfully served our Lord for many years.

My sophomore year, I was brand new to volleyball and to the team. I can remember working all the time so I could make the team.

I learned two lessons that year.
1. The importance of encouragement.
2. The importance of having a right relationship with God and others on your team.

I was very inexperienced and made mistakes. On one occasion I can remember another teammate becoming angry at me and others because of mistakes made. Her anger did not help the situation at all but only made us more nervous. Volleyball teaches you to work with others; that's for sure. I think your better teams can work together because they get along off the court.

We were in a volleyball tournament and lost a game where we were ahead and should have won. I can remember our coach sitting us down and asking the reasons why. Did we have problems with each other or with the Lord? Our coach saw the importance of spending that day of practice making things right. We ended that year winning the state tournament in our gym. What an exciting day! We even carried our coach around the gym on our shoulders.

I played volleyball for three years and was blessed to be part of a great team. My senior year we had a perfect 41-0 record. I have played volleyball and had the opportunity to be on the other side and coach. I remembered things I had learned and tried to be a coach like I had - one who loved us and prays for us daily.

Volleyball can teach you many things:
Faithfulness
Teamwork
Encouragement
Hard work
Perseverance (never give up)

Patience
How to lose
Consistency
I have two daughters. I hope that someday they will love the game I love, and that they will learn the lessons I have, and love their Lord more.

Sincerely,
Brenda Koning Verway

Understood Need for Encouragement

Dear Coach,
Volleyball was so much more than a sport to me. I loved the sport and the physical challenges, but for me, that was just the beginning. Had I been on any other team with any other coach, it wouldn't have meant so much to me. I looked forward to practices as well as games. I loved having a sensitive coach who noticed my talents and needs. Not just my physical needs, but my need for praise when I did something right. A kind word of encouragement when I did something wrong.

When a guy is coached, he can be like a duck and let the water (or harsh words) roll off his back. A girl is more sensitive and needs encouragement. You were that kind of coach.

During volleyball, I was encouraged to be the best I could be. During the game is when I actually got to see my progress.

Volleyball Lessons
Never underestimate your opponent. There were games that were easy to win. Next time we played that same team, if we thought it would be an easy win—we were always wrong.

Never underestimate your own ability. There were games when we would rise above and beyond what we dreamed we could do when we thought that "with God, anything is possible."

Practice makes permanent. Make sure that when you practice, you are doing things the right way because if you aren't, then it will be harder to learn the right way. My biggest problem was getting to the ball in the quickest and most efficient way. Unfortunately, I would always have my weight shifted the wrong way when getting to the ball. I basically had to relearn how to stand. Once I worked on that, my game was so much better.

Being on time for a game is crucial. Some girls lived close to school who could never make it on time. I lived a half hour away and was always able to make it on time. Coach put me in. That was a nice reward for me! Dedication and faithfulness are the heart of sports.

Christian Sportsmanship

I always appreciated some of the older and more experienced students working with me—and not laughing in the process. Becky and Ruth Nazuruk come to mind.

One game while still on the Junior Varsity team, I sat on the bench for varsity. At a home tournament, you put me in Varsity to serve. I aced serve after serve and was doing so well that my teammates neglected to tell me my zipper was broken for fear I would lose my concentration!

After games, the teams would congratulate each other. We would get close to some of the girls on the other teams and would all be genuinely happy for the team that won.

Special Memories

I loved singing "Victory In Jesus" after every away game on the bus ride home. Volleyball Camp was a turning point in my game. I remember hurting in places I didn't know had muscles!

We once played a joke on our camp counselor, taking all of her snacks out of her room and everything else, including the bed! We put it all in the basement of the dorm. Later, you had given us those snacks to show your appreciation for our hard work and accomplishments. You were always good for that.

My biggest memory was winning the home Winter tournament my junior year. All the "big names" in volleyball had graduated, and it was up to us peons to keep up the winning streak. I remember the utter shock of winning the tournament with the win coming when I blocked a spike from Amazon Woman on the other team. We were both shocked. At that tournament, I received my first all tourney award. I never thought I would get one. I enjoyed seeing you throw your clipboard because of your excitement. What a sight!

Thank you, Coach!

Love,
Shari Zwier Roat

Discovered How to Love the Game and More

Dear Coach,

The one thing I enjoyed most during my junior high and high school years was volleyball. It took much of my time and energy, and I loved every minute of it. It is no surprise that I love volleyball, when I was coached by Don Casey, who loves the game with a passion. He always said that there are those players who play the game. Then, there are those who like the game. But, he always encouraged us to be those players who love the game. Under his coaching, I grew to be one of those players.

Some of my best memories of volleyball come from being at volleyball camp at Maranatha Baptist Bible College in Watertown, Wisconsin. My sister and I raised money and looked forward to going each summer. Even when we were tired after playing volleyball all day; we just kept playing, because we couldn't get enough of the game. We wanted to get better and better to become the best we could be. This is just one of the many things I learned through volleyball - giving your all to be your best with the talents God has given you.

Now a Coach

Because the memories I have of my years playing volleyball are so wonderful, now as a coach myself, I want my players to have the same wonderful experiences. For this reason, I try and do much of the same things my coach did. I try to instill the same principles of hard work and giving 100% as Coach Casey taught me.

Coach always reminded us that there was always a higher level of skill that we needed to work hard to achieve. He encouraged us to work to get to get to the highest level through personal fitness in addition to team practice. He expected us to keep a calendar each summer of what we did to stay in shape. And, not wanting to disappoint him, I worked hard to have something to fill in each day. This developed in me a lifelong desire to exercise.

Although playing a sport is an excellent character building activity, it is through the coach that certain character qualities are learned. Because of Coach Casey's great example of always being early to practices and games, I developed an inner desire to be on time, which I have even to this day.

Another important principle that I developed in my life under Coach Casey's direction was remembering to whom the glory belongs for even the slightest accomplishment. I still remember standing on the volleyball court praying, "God, help me to do my best for you and not to impress the people in the bleachers." This principle of giving the glory to God reminds me that all my abilities come from God and that no matter what I do, it needs to be for Him. It was not until my later high school years that I really was able to pray this prayer. I try to apply this principle to life situations even as an adult.

Faithfulness

The greatest character quality that I believe a player can develop through playing volleyball is faithfulness. Your coach and teammates are counting on you to be at all practices and games and to stay physically fit and mentally strong. Making the commitment to play carries the weight of being faithful to the task. Faithfulness is possibly the most important character quality that is necessary for life and can be developed in part through developing a faithfulness to the team in volleyball.

One way Coach Casey has demonstrated faithfulness is through prayer. Prayer was always an important part of each practice and game. And, in his personal life, Coach still prays for me daily. This has been a tremendous encouragement to me.

There is no way to overemphasize the incredible impact playing volleyball has had on my life. In addition to giving me many wonderful memories, it has taught me dedication, teamwork, good sportsmanship, punctuality, fitness, focus, giving 100% effort, the importance of prayer in every area of life, and faithfulness. I thank God for the opportunity He gave me to play volleyball and trust that the positive impact it had in my life may in some small way be imparted to others.

Thank you, Coach.

Sincerely,
Becky Nazaruk

Remembers Team Devotions

Dear Coach,

Growing up, I had the opportunity to participate in various activities that helped teach me many important values. One of those activities was volleyball. A sport can be played just for fun or for the thrill of competition, but I am thankful that my coach taught me many values through the sport of volleyball.

Through volleyball I learned the value of hard work and endurance. I had to continue to play hard even when I didn't feel like it. Giving 100% was always stressed. Doing your best for the glory of God was the goal. It was wonderful to be on a team with a Christian coach, because volleyball was never idolized; God was always first. Glorifying Him was the main objective.

Team Devotions

I remember team devotions, led by various members of the team. We tried to encourage one another to "do all to the glory of

God". Coach also had something special to share from the Bible and we would pray at every practice and game. I learned to be an encouragement to my team members, rather than tearing them down. On the court, we were taught to be positive and uplifting, whether someone made a good play or a poor one.

Teamwork was also a valuable lesson I learned from volleyball. Learning to get along with others and work together was absolutely necessary. These are "people skills" that have been a help to me ever since those days of volleyball.

Time Management

I also had to learn how to budget my time. Volleyball games and practices required a lot of time, and so I had to learn to organize and plan so that I would have enough time for church, homework, and family activities.

I also had opportunities to learn the value of servanthood. With volleyball came times to help in putting up and taking down the nets, setting up for tournaments, etc. Also, since the church held their services in the gym, after practices we had to set up chairs or sometimes take down chairs. Coach never complained about this, but always showed us how to have a servant spirit and worked right along side us in these tasks.

Special Memories

One of the things I really enjoyed about volleyball was actually the bus rides home after the games. We would spend most of the trip singing choruses and hymns together. After a busy, action-filled day, it was great to end the day focusing on the Lord. It was a special meditative time that I still remember.

I have many fond memories of volleyball. Those days are very special to me, for through the medium of volleyball, I had the opportunity to learn many valuable lessons that have helped me in my life. This was only because I had a coach who loves God and serves Him, and he wanted his players to do the same.

Thanks so much.

Sincerely,
Ruth Nazaruk Hornbrook

Chapter 47

And More Wonderful Players

Learned to Trust God

Dear Coach,

Trust God, trust your Coach, and trust your God-given talent. The benefits of High School volleyball abound: Here are some of them:

1. Physical exercise and release of excess energy;
2. Opportunity to build self-esteem (very important for a teen)
3. Good, clean fun
4. Learning to get along with others
5. Exercising Biblical principals; faithfulness, consistency, responsibility, learning to take defeat and victory in stride, and exhibiting good sportsmanship.

But there is so much more. I discovered how to work toward a goal, growing up and moving from self-centeredness to selflessness. Giving up your will to God and then trusting in God and others.

Special Memories

May, 1976 - Lynchburg, VA, Nationals: I missed the first two days of volleyball competition (I was competing in an individual contest at Nationals). Coach Casey kept me on the bench 70 percent of the games I was able to attend. The team was winning without me. We had a lot of good players (yet I had been used to playing all the games, rarely subbing out).

As the semifinals began, I sat on the bench praying. I prayed that God's will be done (but please help us win). I prayed that if it was best for me to be on the sidelines, I'd be the loudest cheerleader (but please let us win).

I played at least one game of the semifinals which turned out to be the most exciting game of the tournament. We were down (in a 3 of 5 games format) two games to Santa Fe. I hadn't played, and we were losing the third game. Coach Casey put me in. When I started to serve, I served 11 aces in a row to win game three. The team pulled together, I served more aces, we trusted God, Coach Casey, and our God-given ability, and we won games 3-5 to retain the National title! Even Coach agrees that it was one of the greatest comebacks and emotional matches he has ever coached.

High school volleyball yields physical, emotional and spiritual benefits to those willing to learn.

Thank you so much.
Denise Phillips

Discovered God's Strength

Dear Coach Casey,
I did coach a J.V. team two years ago while at Tri-City and helped with the fourth-fifth grades intramural volleyball which I really enjoyed.

Coach, thank you for giving me and others the privilege to be a part of your book. Many things that you taught me and lived by your life's example motivate me to better love and serve the Lord.

Volleyball Lessons

One important lesson I learned was the lesson of discipline. Coach did not have to say a word but by his life he exemplified discipline. We were asked to record our outside workout for volleyball monthly and hand it in. This took discipline (Coach directed). Practice started at a certain time; Coach was always early and ready to go. Coach taught discipline by his coaching. I do not ever remember him getting too loud or upset over a player or ref; instead, he respected the players and refs. Thank you Coach for teaching me this important lesson not only in volleyball, but in life.

Biblical Training

I believe that Coach based all of his volleyball training on Biblical principles. I remember short devotions, song time, and singing was a special part of pre-warm-up before our games and tournament matches. This brought a special love for one another, unity and selflessness toward a teammate. Because of the oneness and unity, we played as a team and not as six individuals on the court. A great treasure and memory which I'd like to share was seeing God honored and glorified because of His strength to win games. Always, whether we won or lost, we got in a quick huddle and thanked the Lord for the victory or loss after each game. After matches, we'd sing a song to the Lord. I learned from volleyball training never to give up but to keep working at skills. Coach encouraged this in me. To some who may think, I'll never be able to play varsity, I say, "Don't think that! Keep practicing hard, be dedicated to extra work outside of practice, and heed to the challenges your coach puts before you," and I promise you that you will be happy with the results.

Leadership

It was a great honor to be a part of a varsity team coached by Coach Casey that did very well. I do not take any credit or remember our exact records, but I do know that it was possible only because first of all we had a leader (Coach) who believed we could do it and prepared us for this. Secondly, we had a group of girls who all decided that their contribution was important. Self was not important, but others were all important. Lastly, practice was time to work and improve skills, preparing for game time. We should practice like we wanted to play. Coach used to always say to us, don't tell me but show me. That statement drove me with a relentless determination and still does today.

Love for Each Other

Our team prayed together, shared together, played together, sang together, and to God's glory victoriously won many exciting games and matches together. As a player, I have had the privilege to share with other young girls what Coach taught me about volleyball. It is not all about winning but about disciplining oneself to learn and master the basic skills of volleyball and I believe this, in turn, will bring about the result of winning.

Coach, I know I went long - but can I share one more. You, Coach, helped me to overcome fear and a lack of confidence by letting me play and learn from my mistakes as a youngster, and you many times spent extra time before and after practice individually helping me with the skill of setting. Thank you for caring.

Thanks so much for everything.

Love,
Sara Aulgur

Found My Focus

Dear Coach,

Volleyball was a motivation and an escape for me. It was motivation to get good grades - it was like a reward for me because I loved playing and being a part of the team. It was an escape for me because I went through a lot of things, and when I played I had to focus on what I was doing so all the bad things would fade to the back of my mind. Volleyball was a little light in my life that helped me get through the tough times.

Volleyball Lessons

Teamwork. Hard work. Kind of like life now - but with a family. Teamwork because just one player can't win the game. You have to do your part and be ready to cover your teammates should something happen. Same with a family. It's hard to be the one to have to carry the team, but it happens and if someone either messes up or isn't doing their part, you have to do it. Hard work comes in right about there. You have to be dedicated to your team (family) and that takes hard work.

Christian Sportsmanship

I was pretty sick in high school and there were a few tournaments that I couldn't play in, but because I was a teammate, I still got a trophy. At first I felt bad because I didn't have to work for the prize, but then I just felt blessed because no one ever made me feel that way (like I didn't deserve it).

Special Memories

Any special memories? Well, I thought it was kind of neat when the Zwiers, Nazureks and Hons were all on the court at the same time. Most of my special memories were off the court - like when you gave my mom money to buy us volleyball shoes, when I was so sick and you gave me a gift (pink and green turtlenecks) and bought me a huge bottle of vitamin C. Coach, you've done so much for me. It's too numerous to list - but always know that I haven't forgotten and I will always be thankful.

My coach was more to me than a volleyball coach. He coached me through his life. He was an example of faithfulness and humility. And no matter where I go in life or what I do, I will always know that my coach is still praying for me everyday. . . everyday. . . everyday.

Someday, when I see you in heaven, I hope my words are more eloquent so that I can express exactly how much you meant to me and I can thank you all over again. I thank God that you were put into my life.

May God bless you,
Kristi Zwier Holland

Daily Patience

Dear Coach,

I started practicing volleyball in seventh grade. It was hard to do drills over and over again. Of course, everyone just wanted to get to the fun part—the game. I believe that all the days and hours of hard work taught me about a hard work ethic. To this day, I know that I have to put hard work in before I can go to the game. You can't go to the game without putting in the hard work and practice.

I also saw daily patience in you, Coach. No matter how many mistakes we made, or didn't listen to instructions, you never yelled at your players. You did let us know calmly that you weren't pleased but you never raised your voice at us. A lot of lessons we don't appreciate or fully understand until we are adults ourselves.

One memory that I have was a volleyball tournament at Tennessee Temple University. I was not on the varsity team yet, but there was an opening to go, so I was asked. I was able to bond with some of the older girls, and I even received an opportunity to play in the end. Because of volleyball, I was also able to visit a Christian university and see the possibilities out there.

Volleyball was a goal to keep my eyes on to help me get through. I love the game just because it is fun to play. I would never change those years because I found a lot of Christian friendship that I still have today. I also saw a godly, Christian man dedicate his life to giving to others. And I believe that it had more to do than just volleyball- your love for Christ shone through everything you did.

I personally want to thank you for all of the time, concern and prayers that you have done for me and every single girl that was ever on your team.

Sincerely,
Kathy Baker Kuikman

Impacted Whole Life

Dear Coach,

The sport of volleyball has been such a big part of my life that I probably still don't know the impact it has had on my life. I met some of my closest friends, learned to love athletics, and was able to experience collegiate sports. I started playing in fourth grade and haven't stopped since.

My fondest memories revolve around volleyball. Our team was always laughing and having a good time together. My favorite thing about it all was traveling together either to tournaments or our annual summer volleyball camp. I still wish I could go back to those times. My teammates were all so special to me. One of the traditions we had was singing together whether on the van, in the locker room, or after a match. I loved the feeling of working together to reach a common goal.

However, it was not all fun. Practices could be tough and it was very time demanding. Both of these factors only made me love the sport more. It taught me that everything worth anything in life requires hard work, determination and commitment. One of the many things that I remember you emphasizing was the similarity between being faithful in volleyball and your Christian walk. Going to a Christian school and playing under a Christian Coach was one of the biggest blessings in my life. I learned how to be humble in victory and gracious in defeat.

You always took an interest in me as an individual, not just as one of his players. I always took pride in calling you my Coach. The lessons I took from my experiences in volleyball and by simply watching your life are priceless.

Sincerely,
Amanda Hunter

More Than an Activity

Dear Coach,

The high school years are considered to be one of the major learning periods in an individual's life. As such, the teachers, what they teach, and how they teach it affect the individual in many ways.

Many people view sports as just an activity, yet sports can have a huge effect on an individual. Sports teach sportsmanship, working with others as a team, and physical skills.

A good coach can shape his team in more than just the physical aspects of the sport. Of all of the things that I learned in my high school career, I think I learned the most from my volleyball coach.

I had a good Christian coach who knew how to combine the physical aspects of the sport with spiritual life applications that have stayed with me throughout the years. Of all the things that were taught me I learned the most from seeing them lived out in the life of my coach. Through his example I learned how to work at something and be consistent in things such as daily practice. He taught his girls to be healthier in their eating habits; he gave us things to look for. Most importantly, he taught his girls how to practically apply what they had been taught.

Thank you so much.

Sincerely
Elisabeth Pluth

Still Received Benefit

Dear Coach Casey,

I greatly enjoyed being part of a Christian volleyball team. I still enjoy playing and I'm encouraging my children to love the sport as I do.

Many thoughts come to mind when I think of what I benefited from in being part of a volleyball team. I greatly enjoyed the developing of friendships and teamwork. I know that volleyball offered me a positive diversion, which took up some of my time and helped me stay focused on positive influences.

Another important thing I learned through volleyball is that brownnosing doesn't work! Let me explain. My coach ate healthy. So, I would bring an apple for my coach to many practices. The best apple I could find at the market, I should add. The apple had to be perfect, shiny, and without a single bruise. I would hand him my perfect brownnosing tool (the apple) before practice, but to my surprise, the next game I still sat the bench. Go figure!

Volleyball Lessons

Seriously, what stands out most in my mind is how volleyball helped me develop strong qualities of thoughtfulness, consistency, faithfulness and responsibility. I greatly appreciate the leadership of a loving coach who always demonstrated godly character and used every opportunity to teach me to strive to serve my Lord and Savior.

When I look back at some of the trials I have endured and see that I pulled through or made the right decision, I realize what helped me through many of those tough times is what I learned from my dear Coach Casey's example and wise words, "Perfect practice makes perfect," and the two he always seemed to say when my serve hit the net, "Never give up" and "Keep trying, keep working." I can't forget his all-time favorite, which always seemed to be directed toward me, "Move your feet."

When times get tough, I can picture him standing there and hear him saying those words often. The same smile, the same warmth and the same clarity from not only what he said but also how he said it overcomes me.

I am thankful I had an opportunity to see a man and his family make sacrifices to help young people develop not only in a sport, but, more importantly, develop strong qualities which will help them overcome life's hardships.

Volleyball Memories

Volleyball was a fun and addictive sport. What did having Coach Casey as my volleyball coach mean to me? My answer is one that acknowledges sacrifice and consistency. He not only provided me with the opportunity to develop a skill, but, more importantly, through his consistency, volleyball meant character development. He helped me focus on something worthwhile; he helped me develop stronger character. He offered me an opportunity to become a better person. So, when my life's volleyball hits the net, I am quickly reminded to "Never give up! Keep trying, keep working!!" and, for crying out loud, "Move your feet, Browning, move your feet!"

I greatly appreciate the sacrifices you, your wife and your son, Paul, made in order for you to be used by Him. Your sacrifices go beyond your awareness. I thank you.

Sincerely,
Sue Browning Pujdak

Close Friendships

Dear Coach,

I have been blessed to have been born into a Christian family where I was brought to church and sent to a Christian school where I was exposed to the gospel and became a Christian at a young age. At that same time, I was first introduced to the game of volleyball. It was the only sport offered to females at the school, and every little girl looked forward to the year that she could join the team. In fifth grade I began playing on the junior high team and have been playing ever since. Volleyball has consumed an enormous portion of my time, and as a result, I have spent a lot of time with my teammates.

Close Friendships

Most of the closest friendships I have ever had have been formed as a result of volleyball. I believe the reason that these relationships are so strong is the doubly shared bond of a love for God and the game. Many of these friendships will last me a lifetime. They provide me with encouragement. Playing with non-Christians is not the same. Even if the level of play is higher, the common bond is not there, but in its place is intensified rivalry and jealousy. Another aspect missing in the secular world of volleyball is godly coaches who are genuinely concerned with their players' spiritual and physical well being. Volleyball has come to mean so much to me over the years. It has helped me transition schools easily in high school and in college. It is also an awesome ministry opportunity.

Now a Coach

I recently had the opportunity to help coach a junior high volleyball camp at a local church, and it turned out to be a truly fun and rewarding experience. In the future I'd love to teach accounting and coach volleyball at a Christian school so I can attempt to pass on the blessing that was given to me eleven years ago.

Thank you so much,
Beth Rudnick

The Power of Prayer

Dear Coach,
First let me start by saying how much I enjoyed playing volleyball! The first time I ever went to practice, I had no idea what was ahead. At the time I remember wanting to be a cheerleader - what was I thinking? Well, I guess I caught on pretty fast. I really do not remember much between the first practice I ever went to and the first game. I do know that I had the time of my life. I made my best friends on the team. Although I don't keep in touch

with many anymore, I think of them often and keep them in my prayers.

Teamwork

I learned what teamwork meant playing volleyball. I had never experienced how to work as a team until I played, but teamwork did not mean those six girls on the court. It was the girls who sat on the bench and Coach. We were all the team. All sweating together, crying together, and praying together. I truly believe our prayers, our faith in God helped us win those games. One of the most vivid memories I have is Coach's circle at the back of the court. When a game or match was over, before we shook hands or celebrated a victory - praying. Sometimes we played so bad we did not want to be there for those prayers, but what a testimony Coach has! Every game without fail, on bended knee, thanking the Lord.

Special Memory

Although at the time I did not see how meaningful it was, I now know how special it was for me to play the game with my sister, Julie. All those great memories I will never forget, especially at volleyball camp — what fun!

Thank you Coach Casey for your faithfulness to us and the opportunity to play the greatest game ever - volleyball!

Sincerely,
Amy Hon Hunt

Focus on the Lord

Dear Coach,

I began playing volleyball in the sixth grade and had seven years of training under you. I don't know whether I've learned more about the sport of volleyball or about how to live and walk the Christian life - I think they work together.

Coach constantly reminded us to do our best. Whenever we began to get lazy in practice, he would tell us that Quentin Road and Arthur Mennonite (our rivals) were working hard to beat us in the next tournament. Although these little reminders did help us to push harder, I realize now that it was up to me how I wanted to perform. It was the attitude and determination inside of me that made me jump an inch higher or move a second quicker. "Perfect practice makes perfect" was another slogan Coach used. And it was true. I noticed that when I didn't give 100% in practice, then I couldn't give 100% in the game. When I didn't give 100%, I wasn't improving my game.

No Jealousy Allowed

I also learned that it is important to play as a team. It is so easy to become jealous of the other players if you focus on yourself rather than on the team. There may be a strong player on the team, but without everyone's participation and best effort, you will always fail. Every time that I tried to be number one, either I messed up or the play was unsuccessful. The best feeling is when you get a perfect pass, a beautiful set and a winning hit - but that only happens when you work together.

Trusting God

The most important lesson that I learned through volleyball under Coach Casey is that God is more important than winning or losing a match. After every practice, the team gathered around him and shared prayer requests and praises. After every game we formed a huddle and prayed right there on the court before we got boastful or discouraged. If we won, we sang "Victory in Jesus" first thing. Although Coach wanted us to win, he kept us focused on Christ.

Thank you for the lessons that you taught me about volleyball and about living the Christian life. Thank you so much.

Sincerely,
Shannon Hunter

Surprise Beginning

Dear Coach,

If there is one skill that I have learned from my time with you, it has been how to receive a serve simply because he kept serving up opportunities to me.

I first came under his volleyball coaching as a senior coming from a very small Christian high school. On my team I had been the captain, the MVP, the star.

After just one of those two hour summer workouts, it was pretty apparent that I could maybe start on the Junior Varsity team.

Wow. That was a shock.

Not only was I behind the curve of Oak Forest Varsity Volleyball, I had also come the year the team went on to be undefeated in an amazing record breaking year. So after the jerseys were distributed and my hands were empty, Coach asked if I would be the team statistician. I had no idea of the opportunity he was serving to me.

For that year, I sat a lot and actually did get to play a little - to this day Coach still tells me that I'm on the five year plan... So I sat next to you and absorbed some volleyball skills and strategies, yes: a godly example, definitely.

Dedication

As an adult I am amazed at how dedicated someone must be to spend hours and weekends away from home, driving a bunch of classically silly girls to tournaments and dealing with all the details and "flakiness" that comes with it: people coming late, forgetting of kneepads and jerseys, jammed fingers and poor grades making them illegible, waiting until that very last girl is finally picked up and of course the many years of setting up chairs for church in the gym after practice was over.

Why do all of this? Simply because of a love for volleyball and faithfulness to this ministry God had given you, not to preach sermons to crowds but to give devotions to sweaty tired players, to lead and redirect in prayer after each game be it a loss or as an opportunity to give the glory to God if it were a victory.

Waxing the Car

After high school Coach served up another opportunity to me—to wax his car. Being that I was 17 and yet to even own a vehicle I, of course, would be an expert at car waxing...but no, it was a chance for him to get a fair wax job and for him to give me money for college. Every summer I was asked to wax his car.

You were also a great long distance server through the mail, sending notes of encouragement to me at college and always closing with "I am praying for you every day."

After I graduated, I was all ready to begin teaching in another small Christian school when Coach actually served to me a volleyball, some playground balls, hula hoops, a donut on a string and a folder with a lot of the games and activities he used for his PE classes: his way of helping again to equip me to do the work of the Lord.

He offered another opportunity as well, to be his assistant coach. Most of it is a blur of memory, but I do remember lots of trips to games, hundreds of corny jokes (is there any other kind?) and his continual amazement on how when you told the girls to split up for serving drills, there would be fifteen on one side and four on the other. As I coached with you, another opportunity came my way in the form of a very handsome referee who had actually done his physical education student teaching under you and had been called to referee a tournament.

Serving Still

A few years later, I was still at Oak Forest Tourneys, now as part of a husband/wife referee team. You encouraged me to get my patch, although I'm not so sure if it was for my own advancement or as to have someone available to do all those games!

Has the serving of opportunities to me stopped?

Faithfulness has marked your life and ministry for the years I have known you. As a child, faith in God is an easier thing than living a life of faith as an adult. And as I now have made the transition from a protected innocent child to one now seeking to protect my own children from the evil of this world, the testimony of Don Casey, his humble witness, shines as consistently, however trite this may sound, as a back porch light: dependable, stable, always leading one home to a loving God.

A Friend in Need

When I was at college my junior year, I was talking to my mom about bills and my sister Debbie's tuition and my tuition and I left the conversation trying to figure out what I could do to get more money. I was already carrying a full academic load and working 20 hours or more on work scholarships. I walked out of my room wondering if I could get another job on campus working the really early morning shift in the kitchen to make a few more hours of $1.85 an hour or maybe an off-campus job so I could send something home. That morning there was a letter in my mailbox from you and a check for $20, no, I looked again - it was $200 and the voice of God saying, "Don't worry, I am going to take care of you." A lesson that 20 years later I still cling to as one of those times God really manifested himself to me. So, how many days previous to that must it have been that God laid me on your heart and you faithfully obeyed?

Our God is an awesome God who works great wonders and has amazing timing - all because you have remained faithful - praise the Lord. And thank you.

A couple months ago, I received a flyer about an open house at a local Christian school with the kindergarten times circled. There was no note, just my address in very familiar and beloved handwriting. Why? Because you still pray for me and let your hands be the very hands of God Himself in whatever type of service that may be.

Thank you so much,

Sincerely,
Becky Fisher Eppley

Thanks from a Coach

Dear Coach,

I just wanted to write you a note and say that it has been a privilege to know you over the last years. We have had so many rich and enjoyable times together at tournaments and especially at volleyball camp. I have learned many things from you in our conversations: things about volleyball skills, about coaching, about witnessing, and about God's Word.

I really don't think I could recount it all. I also learned much from your actions. You have such a sense of dignity, humility, and genuine kindness about you. These are the traits I admire most about you. The consistency of your Christian walk has also impressed me greatly. Some of your devotionals at volleyball camp were as good as any sermon I've heard.

You have been a good friend, and I value the many hours we have spent together. They have been rich. God has blessed me with your friendship. I appreciate all the knowledge you have shared, all the mentoring and support. I have thought many times while coaching, what would Coach Casey do?

I know that as you retire from teaching, God has a continuing plan for your life. There are so many more people to influence for Christ. You have had such a positive Christian influence on my life and my players' lives. We will only know the real results in eternity.

Your Friend,
Bruce Brim
Volleyball Coach, Sturgis Christian School

Once a Struggling Coach

Dear Coach,

Many years ago, I was a struggling coach with a small Christian school team. The girls were so small, in fact, they could as a group walk under the net. At the time we played small Christian schools like our own and we did fairly well against them. But one day, we played your team and I knew I was seeing a whole new level of volleyball. Your girls were such good players! They passed the ball consistently, set lovely, high balls and spiked harder than any players I'd ever seen. I knew I wanted to learn from you and so from that day forward, started following you around, gleaning tidbits whenever I could.

I had you for a clinic, then attended another one at a nearby Christian school, and I saw something amazing taking place. I had recently had a practice where I had the girls do five push ups every time they missed a serve, but the serving had been getting worse until I left the gym in total discouragement. At that clinic, I saw a whole new way of coaching as you gave out points every time the girls did something good, no matter how small that thing was. I started doing that in my own practices, and my team started to improve.

I remember that I would compile notebooks full of questions to ask you when I would see you at games or tournaments. I'm surprised that you didn't go the other way when you saw me coming! Although I read every book and watched every video I could about volleyball, nothing could compare with the advice you gave me.

You taught me everything about volleyball and you taught me, just as you have taught so many people, to love the game. Our team started winning against the bigger schools and won second place at our state convention seven years in a row. Then on the eighth year, we won the tournament. I remember telling you about it later and how happy you were for us. I have met many coaches since then who didn't have your ability to be happy for others, and it has made me appreciate your gentle spirit more than ever.

The year I had to stop coaching due to increasing demands from other areas of our ministry, you encouraged me. You must have sensed that I was down and wishing I could still coach. A few days later, I received a letter from you that I will treasure forever. You wrote in the letter that you appreciated all my hard work and that you knew that many girls' lives have been changed forever. Thanks to your letter, I was able to let go of the sport I loved so much, but I will always remember those years and thank God for the privilege of knowing you.

Thank you, Don. I know you are having a hard time publishing everyone's heartfelt praise in this book, but I hope you publish this letter.

Yours in His Great Love,
Julie Scudder Dearyan
Former Volleyball Coach of Quentin Road Christian School

Chapter 48

Closing Thoughts

I would like to thank you for taking the time to read this book. My prayer is that you have received a blessing. I have never grown tired of the game.

I have often joked that if I had a dime for every ball I ever set, I would be a rich man. Thanks to the Lord's strength and help, I have spent countless hours and hours playing, coaching, teaching, and watching.

The game has rewarded me with so much: friends, teammates, travels, exercise, challenges, satisfaction, fun, enjoyment, laughter, tears, exhilaration of victory, and the disappointment of defeat. I would not trade any of it. If I had a secret wish, it would be to go back in time and play it again. I am so thankful for all of the memories.

My Goal

I have shared with you that my main goal of writing this book was to glorify God. My desire is that if you don't know Christ as your Savior or if you don't have a personal relationship with Jesus Christ, that the following words will change your life.

Throughout the years, I have never coached a player who didn't make mistakes from time to time. I, myself, have done things wrong and as a result, fallen short of God's glory. Romans 3:23 tells us that "all have sinned and come short of the glory of God." To come short means to miss the mark as an archer would miss the bull's eye or a server would miss a serve.

Because we have all sinned, we deserve to pay for that sin. Romans 6:23 states, "For the wages of sin is death; but the gift of

God is eternal life through Jesus Christ our Lord." When we work a job, we earn wages. We get paid money. The wages we earn from our sin is death or separation from God forever.

The second part of the verse says God has a gift. It is a free gift for those who will ask for it. That gift is eternal life. We will live with God forever. How does the gift come? The verse ends with "through Jesus Christ." The gift comes only through Jesus Christ. Our church cannot give us the gift. We cannot earn it or purchase it. It is free. John 14:6 says, "Jesus saith unto him, I am the way the way, the truth, and the life: no man cometh unto the Father, but by me." We cannot get to the Father some other way. It is only through Christ.

We cannot earn eternal life by working for it or doing good things. In fact, the Bible states that our own righteousness is as filthy rags before Him. Our wonderful Savior paid the debt of our sin on the cross and took our punishment for us. His blood covers our sins.

First John 5:13 declares, "These things have I written unto you that believe on the name of the Son of God that ye may know that ye have eternal life." We find in Romans 10:13 – "For whosoever shall call upon the name of the Lord shall be saved." The "whosoever" can be you.

May I ask you the most important question anyone will ever ask you? Have you been born again? Have you called upon Him to receive the gift of eternal life? Are you 100% sure? If you are not, will you pray right now? You might say, "How do I do that?" First, tell God that you are a sinner and cannot save yourself. Believe that Jesus died on the cross to pay for your sins. Ask Him to forgive you and give you the gift of eternal life. Then thank Him for saving you. Jesus said in John 10:27-30, "My sheep hear my voice, and I know them, and they follow me; and I give unto them eternal life; and they shall never perish, neither shall any man pluck them out of my hand. My father which gave them me, is greater than all; and no man is able to pluck them out of my Father's hand. I and my father are one."

If you have prayed that prayer, you are now in the Father's hand. You are a child of God. There is no safer place than that.

I hope that you have gained an understanding of the kind of outstanding sport volleyball can be, but it is my greatest prayer that you are a child of God. May God bless you as you seek to find His way and will in your life.

Endnotes

[1] Steinhaus, Arthur A, *Toward an Understanding of Health and Physical Education*, (William C. Brown Company Publishers, Dubuque, IA, 1963)

[1] volleyball.org/history.html

[2] volleyball.org/history.html

[3] volleyhall.org/FIVB.htm.

[4] Phillips John, Exploring Genesis, (Loizeaux Brothers, Neptune NJ, 1980 originally published Moody Press, 1992,)

Breinigsville, PA USA
19 August 2010
243887BV00001B/32/A